LABORATORY Manual

PHYSICS

CBSE Class XI

Author
Priyasha Gupta

Name..

Class......................... Section......................... Roll No.......................

School..

arihant
SUCCESS AND NOTHING LESS
Arihant Prakashan (School Division Series)

Arihant Prakashan (School Division Series)

Administrative & Production Offices

Regd. Office

'Ramchhaya' 4577/15, Agarwal Road, Darya Ganj, New Delhi -110002
Tele: 011- 47630600, 43518550; Fax: 011- 23280316

Head Office

Kalindi, TP Nagar, Meerut (UP) - 250002, Tel: 0121-7156203, 7156204

Sales & Support Offices

Agra, Ahmedabad, Bengaluru, Bareilly, Chennai, Delhi, Guwahati, Hyderabad, Jaipur, Jhansi, Kolkata, Lucknow, Nagpur & Pune

Price : ₹375.00

PO No. : TXT-59-T071764-7-26

Published by Arihant Publications (India) Ltd.

For further information about the books from Arihant, log on to **www.arihantbooks.com** or email to **info@arihantbooks.com**

Follow us on    

Contents

Activities

SECTION B

Experiments

Activities

Projects

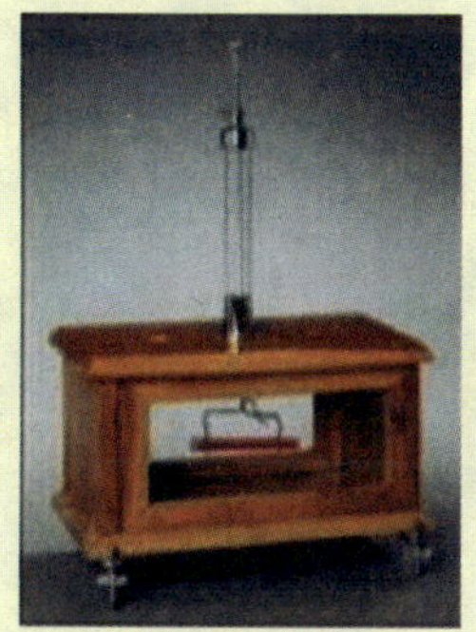

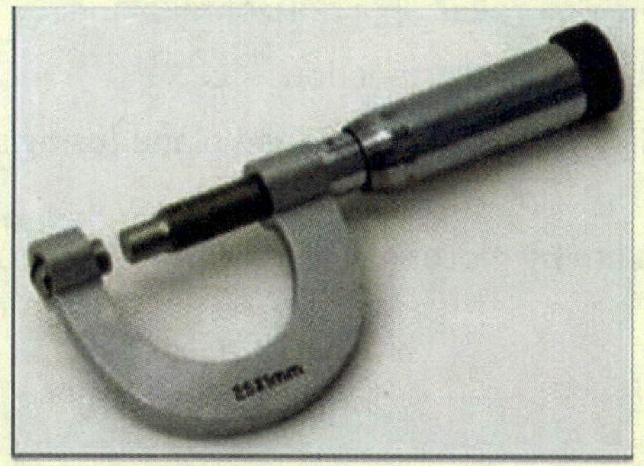

Syllabus

SECTION A

Experiments

1. To measure diameter of a small spherical/cylindrical body and to measure internal diameter and depth of a given beaker/calorimeter using Vernier Callipers and hence find its volume.
2. To measure diameter of a given wire and thickness of a given sheet using screw gauge.
3. To determine volume of an irregular lamina using screw gauge.
4. To determine radius of curvature of a given spherical surface by a spherometer.
5. To determine the mass of two different objects using a beam balance.
6. To find the weight of a given body using parallelogram law of vectors.
7. Using a simple pendulum, plot its L-T^2 graph and use it to find the effective length of second's pendulum.
8. To study variation of time period of a simple pendulum of a given length by taking bobs of same size but different masses and interpret the result.
9. To study the relationship between force of limiting friction and normal reaction and to find the coefficient of friction between a block and a horizontal surface.
10. To find the downward force, along an inclined plane, acting on a roller due to gravitational pull of the earth and study its relationship with the angle of inclination θ by plotting graph between force and sin θ.

Activities

1. To make a paper scale of given least count, e.g., 0.2cm, 0.5 cm.
2. To determine mass of a given body using a meter scale by principle of moments.
3. To plot a graph for a given set of data, with proper choice of scales and error bars.
4. To measure the force of limiting friction for rolling of a roller on a horizontal plane.
5. To study the variation in range of a projectile with angle of projection.
6. To study the conservation of energy of a ball rolling down on an inclined plane (using a double inclined plane).
7. To study dissipation of energy of a simple pendulum by plotting a graph between square of amplitude and time.

SECTION B

Experiments

1. To determine Young's modulus of elasticity of the material of a given wire.
2. To find the force constant of a helical spring by plotting a graph between load and extension.
3. To study the variation in volume with pressure for a sample of air at constant temperature by plotting graphs between p and V, and between p and $1/V$.
4. To determine the surface tension of water by capillary rise method.
5. To determine the coefficient of viscosity of a given viscous liquid by measuring terminal velocity of a given spherical body.
6. To study the relationship between the temperature of a hot body and time by plotting a cooling curve.
7. To determine specific heat capacity of a given solid by method of mixtures.
8. To study the relation between frequency and length of a given wire under constant tension using sonometer.
9. To study the relation between the length of a given wire and tension for constant frequency using sonometer.
10. To find the speed of sound in air at room temperature using a resonance tube by two resonance positions.

Activities

1. To observe change of state and plot a cooling curve for molten wax.
2. To observe and explain the effect of heating on a bi-metallic strip.
3. To note the change in level of liquid in a container on heating and interpret the observations.
4. To study the effect of detergent on surface tension of water by observing capillary rise.
5. To study the factors affecting the rate of loss of heat of a liquid.
6. To study the effect of load on depression of a suitably clamped meter scale loaded at (i) its end (ii) in the middle.
7. To observe the decrease in presure with increase in velocity of a fluid.

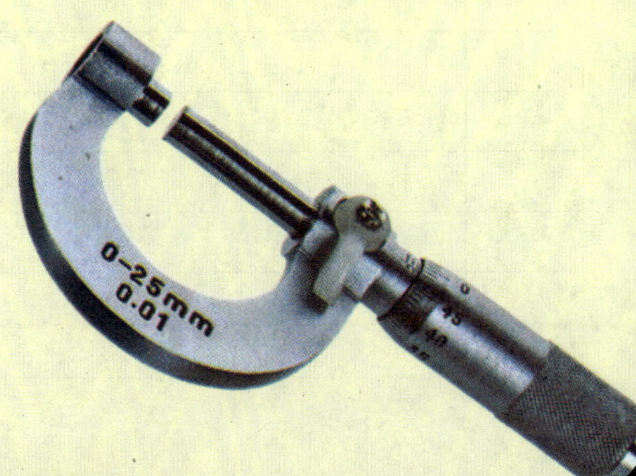

INDEX

S.No.	Name of the Experiment	Page No.	Date	Remarks

LABORATORY Manual

PHYSICS

CERTIFICATE

This is to certify that Activities & Projects recorded in this Practical Notebook have been performed by ____________________
(Student's name)

of ________ of ______________________________
(Class/Section) (School name)

during academic session ____________________

.... Examiner Signature

.... Principal Signature (with school stamp)

.... Teacher Signature

General Introduction of Practical Work

Physics, a study of the basic laws of nature and their manifestation in the different natural phenomena, raises our eagerness and helps us to utilise this understanding to make our life interesting. As we know that all branches of science needs the experimental verification. The main purpose of laboratory experiments in physics is to verify the concepts, laws, principles and hypothesis related to physical phenomena.

From the past few centuries, the inventions and the discoveries made by the great scientists have resulted in the immense growth of physics. It implies that performing experiment once by our own hands in the physics laboratory generates the feeling of direct involvement with the generation of knowledge.

Attaining the data in the form of a result or a conclusion helps in boosting up the scientific temper, logical thinking, sense of self confidence, patience and develops the spirit of inquisitiveness and analytical skills. Eventually, it can be said that **the concepts of learner are made more stronger with the help of experimental physics**.

Objectives of Practical Work

Practical work is the basic foundation for the development and growth of science. The main objective of experimentation in science is to confirm the feasibility of a process which we study theoretically. The practical work in physics involves **learning by doing**. It clarifies the concepts and hence lays the seed for enquiry. Careful and stepwise observations of sequences during an experiment or activity facilitate personal investigation as well as small group or team learning. Thus, **practical work enhances the basic learning skills**.

Some General Guidelines To Perform Experiment

1. Prepare yourself first with the experiment which you are going to perform. The principle, objective of the experiment and procedure to be followed should be clear.
2. Carefully, read all the instructions because in each and every sentence, there is some meaning which should be understood by you at the same time.
3. If at any instant, any doubt arises in your mind, then clear it from your respective physics teacher else it will create a problem in between the experiment.
4. After this, start collecting the apparatus and material required for performing the experiment.
5. Each and every item of the working apparatus should be checked initially, else if it is found with some technical defect later on, then it will result in the wastage of your time. **A minute error can create a big inaccuracy.**
6. The apparatus should be handled carefully, mainly the small weights, nuts, screws etc.

7. The table surface on which you perform the experiment should be neat, clear and free from the unnecessary articles.
8. The using apparatus should be wiped with the clean, wet cloth smeared with Vaseline.
9. Do not try to disfigure the wooden parts of the apparatus.
10. The apparatus should be arranged in proper order to avoid any damage (specially, in case of experiments). Any accidental damage or breakage of the apparatus should be immediately brought to notice of concerned teacher, otherwise, it may cause some accident.
11. While taking the observations, observe the reading two to three times correctly and note it down in your observation copy and get it checked and signed by your physics teachers. **Highly precise readings result in the accurate measurement.**
12. While recording the observations, do not forget to note down the units in which the measurements are made.
13. It is mandatory that atleast one reading should be checked and verified by the teacher in charge while performing the experiment.
14. The series of observations should always be taken and always try to record them in a tabular form as it is an effective way of representing the readings.
15. Every part of your effort should be made honestly and don't try to write the false observations in order to have an exact result. Always mention the result in proper SI unit. Wherever possible, the observations should be represented with the help of graph.
16. Before leaving the laboratory, you should get your book signed and the apparatus used are to be returned to the laboratory assistant.
17. Switch off all the power plugs, which are used in the experiment before leaving the laboratory. In case of any electric power related accident, switch off the main supply of the laboratory.

How to Record An Experiment?

A neat and systematic recording of the experiment in the laboratory notebook is very important for keeping an upto date record of the work which has been done in the laboratory. Infact, a proper record of the experimental results and conclusions is an indispensable part of scientific work. The laboratory notebook must be well maintained and protected from mechanical and chemical damage. It should be made checked regularly by the teacher.

The experiment should be recorded in the laboratory notebook under the following heads as:

Date...... Experiment No. ...... Page No. ......

Aim or Objective of the Experiment State clearly and precisely the objective of the experiment to be performed.

Apparatus and Materials Required Mention the name of the apparatus and materials to be used in the experiment clearly.

Description of Apparatus Including Measuring Devices Describe the apparatus and measuring devices used in the experiment.

Terms and Definitions State the important terms and definitions used in the experiment.

Theory or Principle Mention the concept on which the experiment is based in a very brief manner. Also, write the formula used explaining the symbols involved clearly.

Procedure Mention various steps in the experiment followed with precautions.

Diagrams Wherever required, draw the diagrams on the left hand side of the notebook.

Observations Record the observations or data in a tabular form as far as possible, neatly and without any overwriting.

Calculations and Plotting Graph (wherever desirable) For writing the calculations, substitute the observed value in the formula and do the computations systematically and neatly. Wherever is possible, use the graphical method for obtaining the result.

Result State the conclusions drawn from the experimental observations. If the result depends upon the conditions of temperature and pressure, mention these conditions also along with the result.

Precautions Mention the precautions observed during the course of setting an apparatus and the steps followed while performing the experiment.

Sources of Error Mention the possible sources of error while performing the experiment and are liable to affect the result.

Discussion Under this heading mention any special inferences or special difficulties faced during the experimentation.

These may include points for making the experiment more accurate and for better understanding of the basic principle involved.

Experimental Errors

Every measurement is done with the help of some instruments. While making the measurement, some uncertainty gets introduced in the measurement. As a result, the measured value is always some what different from the actual or true value. This is called **error** which is equal to the difference between the true value and the measured value of the quantity. It is a fact that **there is no measurement without errors**. But the errors occurred during the experiment can be minimised upto a certain extent after knowing about them.

Different Types Of Errors

1. Systematic Errors

The errors which tend to occur in one direction, either positive or negative, are called systematic errors. We can eliminate such errors once we know the rule which governs them. These errors are of following types:

(a) **Instrumental Errors** These errors occur due to inbuilt defect of the measuring instrument. This error can be detected by measuring a physical quantity with two different instruments of the same type or by measuring the same physical quantity by two different methods.

(b) **Imperfection in Experimental Technique** These errors can also be occurred due to the limitations of the experimental arrangement. Such errors cannot be eliminated altogether but necessary corrections can be applied for them.

(c) **Imperfection in Experimental Technique or Procedure** These errors can also be occurred due to the imperfection in experimental technique. e.g. to determine the temperature of a human body, a thermometer placed under armpit will always give a temperature lower than the actual value of the body temperature.

(d) **Personal Errors** These errors arise due to inexperience of the observer, such as lack of proper setting of the proper apparatus, reading an instrument without setting it properly, taking observations without observing proper precautions etc. e.g. If we keep our eye to read the scale in inclination, then an error called **parallax error** is occurred.

(e) **Errors due to External Causes** The external conditions such as changes in temperature, pressure, humidity, wind velocity etc., during the experiment may systematically affect the measurement.

2. Random Errors

The random errors are the errors which occur irregularly. They are random with respect to the sign and size. The random errors are sometimes called the **chance errors**.

They may arise due to random and unpredictable variations in experimental conditions, i.e. temperature, pressure, voltage supply, vibration, etc. These errors can be minimised by repeating the observation a large number of times and taking arithmetic mean of all the observations. The accuracy of measurement is related to the systematic errors but its precision is related to the random errors, which also include least count error.

Least Count (or Permissible) Error

The smallest value that can be measured by a measuring instrument is called least count of the instrument.

e.g. A metre scale having graduations at 1 mm division scale spacing has a least count of 1 mm or 0.1 cm. Thus, in the measurement of length using a metre scale reliability is up to 1/10 cm. By using instruments of higher resolution and by improving experimental technique, we can reduce the least count errors.

Hence, **least count error is the error associated with the resolution of the instrument.**

Note The least count of an instrument is inversely proportional to the precision of the instrument.

Absolute Error, Relative Error and Percentage Error

Consider the values obtained in the several measurements be $x_1, x_2, \ldots, x_n$. The arithmetic mean of these values will be considered as the best possible value of the quantity.

$$x_{\text{mean}} = \frac{x_1 + x_2 + \ldots + x_n}{n} \quad \text{or} \quad x_{\text{mean}} = \frac{\sum_{i=1}^{n} x_i}{n}$$

These three errors (i.e. absolute, relative and percentage) are related with arithmetic mean of the measured values and are discussed below:

Absolute Error

It is the magnitude of the difference between the true (actual) value and individually measured value of the quantity.

$\therefore$ Absolute error $|\Delta a_i|$ = True value (a_{mean}) − measured value (a_i)

The value of a physical quantity a is the arithmetic mean of all the absolute errors.

i.e. $$\Delta_{\text{mean}} = \frac{|\Delta a_1| + |\Delta a_2| + \ldots + |\Delta a_n|}{n} = \frac{\sum_{i=1}^{n} |\Delta a_i|}{n}$$

For a single measurement, the value of the physical quantity may be in a range of $a_{\text{mean}} \pm \Delta a_{\text{mean}}$.

Relative Error

It is the ratio of the mean absolute error Δa_{mean} to the mean value a_{mean} of the physical quantity measured.

i.e. $$\text{Relative error} = \frac{\Delta a_{\text{mean}}}{a_{\text{mean}}}$$

Percentage Error

If the relative error is expressed in percent, it is called percentage error. Therefore,

$$\text{Percentage error} = \frac{\Delta a_{\text{mean}}}{a_{\text{mean}}} \times 100\%$$

Significant Figures

The digits that are known reliably plus the first uncertain digit are known as significant digits or significant figures.

e.g. when a measured distance is reported to be 374.5 cm, it has four significant figures 3, 7, 4 and 5. The digits 3, 7 and 4 are certain and reliable, while the digit 5 is uncertain. When time period of a simple pendulum is reported as 1.37 second it has three significant digits 1, 3, 7. The digits 1 and 3 are certain and reliable, while digit 7 is uncertain. Clearly, the digits beyond the significant digits reported in any result are superfluous.

The significant figures of the measured value should match with that of the error.

Rules for Counting Significant Figures

- All non-zero digits are significant.
  e.g. $x = 2356$ has 4 significant figures
- All zeros occurring between two non-zero digits are significant no matter where the decimal point is, if at all.
  e.g. $x = 1098$ has 4 significant figures,
  $x = 1.0709$ has 5 significant figures.
- If the number is less than one, the zero(s) on the right of the decimal point and to the left of first non-zero digit are not significant.
  e.g. In $\underline{0}.\underline{0}\ \underline{0}5804$, the underlined zeroes are not significant. The zero between 8 and 4 is significant. The number of significant figure is 4.
- In a number without a decimal point, the terminal or trailing zeroes are not significant.
- However, in a number with decimal point, the trailing zeroes are significant.
  e.g. $x = 3.600$ has four significant figures
  Similarly, $x = 0.0079000$ has five significant figures.
- Change of units does not change the number of significant figures in a measurement.
- The digit 0 conventionally put on the left of a decimal for a number less than 1 is never significant.
  e.g. $\underline{0}.3580$ has four significant digits. The underlined zero is not significant.
- The multiplying or dividing factors, which are neither rounded numbers nor numbers representing measured values, are exact. They have infinite number of significant digits as per the situation.

  e.g. radius $(r) = \dfrac{\text{diameter } (d)}{2}$ and circumference,

  $S = 2\pi r$, the factor 2 is an exact number. It can be written as 2.0, 2.00 or 2.000 as required.

Logarithms

Logarithm of a number to a given base is the index of the power to which the base must be raised to equal that number. If we relate a, x and N such that

$$a^x = N$$

then x is called the logarithm of N to the base a and is written as

$$x = \log_a N \quad \text{[read as log } N \text{ to the base } a]$$

If $2^6 = 64$, then the log of 64 to the base 2 is equal to 6.

$$\log_2 64 = 6$$

Generally to represent a number, we use logarithm to the base 10. Here, $\log 10 = 1$, $\log 100 = 1$ and so on.

Similarly, $10^4 = 10000$, log of 10000 to base 10 is equal to 4 or

$$\log_{10} 10000 = 4$$

Note Logarithm is of two types

(i) **Naperian**, in which the base is e. This is not used in general practice.

(ii) **Common**, in which base is 10. This is generally used in practice. Logarithm to base 10 is usually represented as log.

Properties Of Logarithm

1. $\log_a mn = \log_a m + \log_a n$
2. $\log_a \dfrac{m}{n} = \log_a m - \log_a n$
3. $\log_a m^n = n \log_a m$
4. $\log_a m = 2.303 \log_{10} m$

Common Logarithm

The logarithm of a number consists of two parts

1. integral part, called **characteristics**.
2. decimal or fractional part, called **mantissa**.

Note Characteristic may be either positive or negative but mantissa is always positive.

How to Find Characteristic of a Number?

The characteristics of a number depends on its magnitude and is determined by the position of the decimal point.

We use the following rules to find the characteristics of a number:

1. If the given number is greater than 1, its characteristic is positive. Count the number of digits to the left of decimal point. Subtract 1 from this number. This is the characteristics of the log of given number.

For example, Characteristic 1795.2 is 4 – 1 = 3

Characteristic 16.78 is 2 – 1 = 1

Characteristic of 17.943 is 2 – 1 = 1

2. If the given number is less than one, its characteristic is negative. It is put under the bar. Count the number of zeros immediately after the decimal point. Add 1 to this number. It gives us the characteristic of log of given number. For example,

   Characteristics of 0.7821 = – (0 + 1) = $\bar{1}$

   Characteristics of 0.0618 = – (1 + 1) = $\bar{2}$

How to Find Mantissa of a Number?

The value of mantissa depends upon the digits and their order. It is independent of the position of the decimal point. As long as the digits and their order is same, mantissa of numbers is same, whatever be the position of the decimal point.

The logarithm tables give the mantissa of a number only. They are usually meant for numbers consisting of four digits, and if a number contains more than four figures, it is rounded off to four figures after finding out the characteristic.

To determine the mantissa, the logarithm tables are used in the following manner.

1. In the given number, omit the decimal point and zeros in the beginning and at the end. e.g. In the number 0.001184, we have to look up the mantissa of 1184.
2. Take first two digits, i.e. 11 and locate it in the first vertical column of the four figure log table.
3. Go through the horizontal row beginning with 11 and look up the value under the column, headed by the fourth digit. i.e. 8 from the log table. We find this number as 0719.
4. Continue moving in the same horizontal row and note the number in small differences column, headed by the fourth digit. i.e. 4. This number is 15.
5. Add 15 to 0719. We get 0734

   ∴ The mantissa = .0734

   Now, with the help of characteristic and mantissa, one can find the logarithm from the table.

Example 1 Find the logarithm of 132.4.

Sol. Step I ***Find the characteristic of 132.4.***

The number has 3 figures to the left of the decimal point.
Therefore, its characteristics is 3 – 1 = 2.

Step II ***Find the mantissa of 132.4.***

To determine mantissa, ignore the decimal point and look for 13 in the first vertical column in the logarithm table. For 2, look in the central topmost column. Proceed from 13 along a horizontal line towards the right and from 2 vertically downwards. The two lines meet at a point where number 1206 is written. This is the mantissa of 132.

Step III ***Looking up the figures just after the decimal point.***

Proceed further along the horizontal line in the logarithm table and look vertically below the figure 4 in different column. You will find 13 there.
Thus, the mantissa of 1324 is 1206 +13 = 0.1219

Step IV ***Finding the final logarithm of 132.4.***

∴ Logarithm of 132.4 is 2.1219 i.e. log 132.4 = 2.1219

Example 2 Find the logarithm of 132400.

Sol. The characteristics of this number is 5. The mantissa is the same as in example 1,above. We can find the mantissa of only four significant figures, therefore, we neglect last two zeros.

$\therefore$ $\log 132400 = 5.1219$

Example 3 Find the logarithm of 0.00132422.

Sol. The characteristic of this number is $\bar{3}$, as there are only two zeros after the decimal point.

We can find the mantissa of only four significant numbers, therefore, we neglect the last two figures (22) and determine the mantissa of 1324 which is 1219.

$\therefore$ $\log 0.00132422 = \bar{3}.1219$

When the last figure of a number containing more than four significant figures is equal to or more than 5, the figure next to the left of it is raised by one and so on till we have only four significant figures. However, if the last figure is less than 5, then it is neglected as in the above example.

For example, if the number is 1324.57, the last figure is 7, therefore, we shall raise the next figure to 6 and since 6 is again more than 5, therefore, we shall raise the next figure to 5 and determine the logarithm of 1325.

Antilogarithm

The number whose logarithm is x, is called antilogarithm and is denoted by antilog x.

Therefore, as log 2 = 0.3010, then antilog 0.3010 = 2

Example 4 Find the number whose logarithm is 1.7086 by using antilogarithms table.

Sol. Step I ***Identifying figures in the fractional part.***

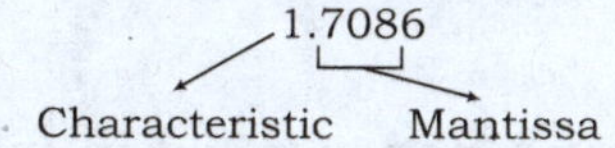

In the fractional part, the first two figures from the left are 0.70, the third figure is 8 and the fourth figure is 6.

Step II ***Finding the number of mantissa .708.***

In antilogarithms table, first look in the vertical column for 0.70. In this horizontal row under the column headed by 8, we find the number 5105 at the intersection. This implies the number for mantissa 0.708 is 5105.

Step III ***Finding the number of mantissa .7086.***

Proceeding further along the horizontal line and under the mean difference column on the right under 6, we find the number 7 at the intersection. On adding 7 to 5105, we get 5112. Therefore, 5112 is the figure of which .7086 is the mantissa.

Step IV ***Putting the decimal according to the characteristic of the given number.***

The characteristic of number is 1, which is one more than the number of digits in the integral part of the required number.

Therefore, the number of digits in the integral part of required number = 1 + 1 = 2.

Step V ***Finding the final algorithm.***

Thus, the required number is 51.12, i.e. antilog $1.7086 = 51.12$

Study of Graphs

A Graph is a pictorial way of representing relationships between various quantities, parameters, or measurable variables in nature. It basically summarizes how one variable called **dependent variable** changes if another variable called **independent variable** that is related to it also changes.

e.g. In an experiment of extension in length, if the length of the string changes due to corresponding increase in weight suspended from it, weight which is being suspended is called independent variable, whereas the length which is being changed due to weight is called dependent variable.

For a learner, graphs are useful because they can summarize a lot of information into one picture. Graphs are often the only way to represent data that has been collected. When one collects data in an experiment, he/she does not know the exact relationship and interdependence between the various quantities that are being measured. A graph can give an idea about how these variables change relative to one another.

Apart from this, graph not only gives us the relation between two variable quantities in pictorial form, but it also enables the verification of certain laws (such as Boyle's law) to determine the mean value from a large number of observations, etc.

In any graph, the independent variable is represented along *X*-axis and the dependent variable is represented along *Y*-axis.

Plotting A Graph

Graphs are generally plotted on a graph paper ruled in millimeter or centimeter squares. The following steps should be followed by a learner while plotting a graph:

1. Identify the independent variable and dependent variable and represent them along *X*-axis and *Y*-axis, respectively.
2. The horizontal line represents the **abscissa** or *X*-axis and the vertical line represents the **ordinate** or *Y*-axis, intersecting at a point *O*, called the **origin**.
3. Find out the range of each of the variables and count the number of big square available to represent each, along the respective axes.
4. To choose the scale for plotting a graph, the smallest division on the graph paper should be ideally equal to the least count of measurement or the accuracy to which the particular parameter is known.
5. Choose (0, 0) as origin when the relation between variable begins from zero or it is desired to determine the zero position of one of the variables, if its actual determination is not possible. But in all the other situations, the origin can be represented by a round number nearest to but less than the smallest value of the corresponding variable.
6. The scale marking on each of the axis should not be crowded. Write the numbers at every fifth cm of the axis. Also, write the units of the physical quantity plotted. Give the scientific representations of the numbers i.e. write the number with the decimal point following the first digit and multiply the number by appropriate power of ten. Give a suitable caption of physical quantities involved below the plotted graph.

7. For drawing a graph, take at least six to seven readings extending equally over a wide range.
8. Plot the points for various pairs of corresponding values to two quantities and draw a small circle i.e. ⊙ or put a × around each of the plotted points. Along with the circle, two bars are also drawn such as ⊙. The distance between these two bars gives the **uncertainty in measurement**.
9. If the graph appears to be a straight line, draw a straight line passing exactly through most of the points and symmetrically through the rest. However, if graph does not appear to be a straight line, then draw a free hand smooth curve so that maximum number of points lie exactly on it.
10. Give the name of the graph at the top of the graph paper i.e. write the heading **Graph showing relation between** x (independent variable) **and** y (dependent variable).

Applications of Graph

1. The shape of the graph plotted for two quantities provide us, the clear idea about the relationship between those two quantities. Let say, if the graph is a straight line and passes through the origin, it may be represented by a relation $y = mx$. If the graph is a straight line having positive or negative intercepts on Y-axis, it is represented by $y = mx + c$.
2. The slope of the graph and its intercepts on the X or Y-axis give us the value of physical quantities.
3. The graph plotted between the two quantities helps us in identifying the accuracy in the experimental data.
4. We can find out the mean value easily from a large number of observations.

Determination of the Slope of a Straight Line

The slope of a straight line is determined by pointing the two values of a variable on Y-axis due to the corresponding two values of a variable on X-axis. If the change in two values on Y-axis is Δy while on X-axis is Δx, then, the slope of a straight line can be given as

$$\text{Slope, } m = \frac{\Delta y}{\Delta x}$$

We will get the positive slope when both Δy and Δx are of same sign as shown in Fig. (a). In the contrast to this, the slope will be negative if Δy is of opposite sign than that of Δx as shown in Fig. (b).

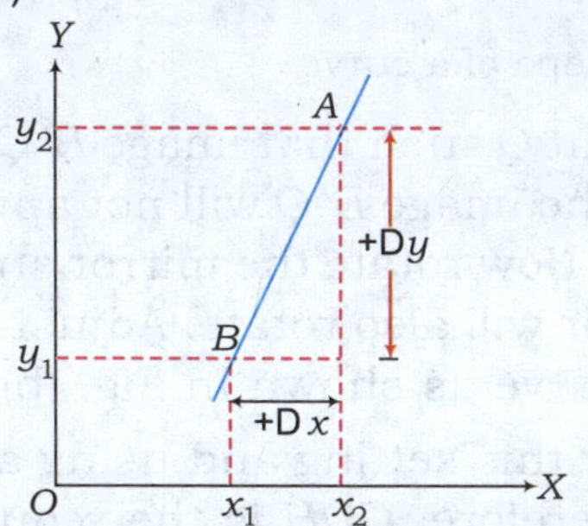

(a) Figure showing positive slope

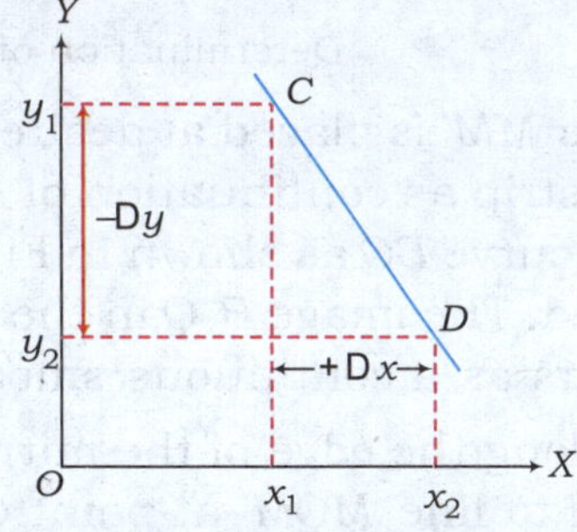

(b) Figure showing negative slope

The slope of a given straight line has the same value for all points on the line i.e. $\Delta x = \Delta y$. It means that the change in x and the corresponding change in y will be same. Thus, for a given straight line, the slope is fixed.

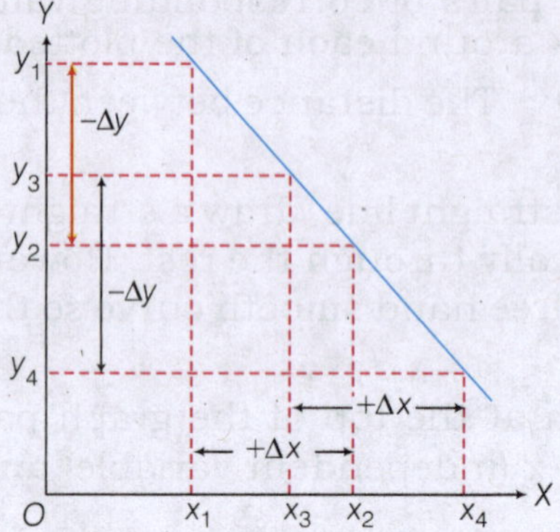

Slope is fixed for a given straight line

Determination of the Slope of a Curve

The slope of the curve may have different values of slope at different points on the curve. Therefore, in case of curve, slope at a particular point is taken i.e. point Q.

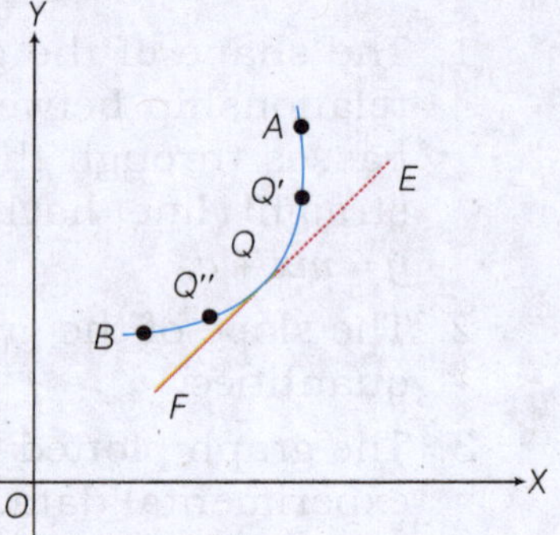

Tangent at point Q

To find the slope of a curve at a given point, one must draw a tangent to the curve at the desired point with the help of a plane mirror strip attached to a wooden block, so that it stands perpendicular to the paper on which the curve is to be drawn. This is shown in figures (a) and (b).

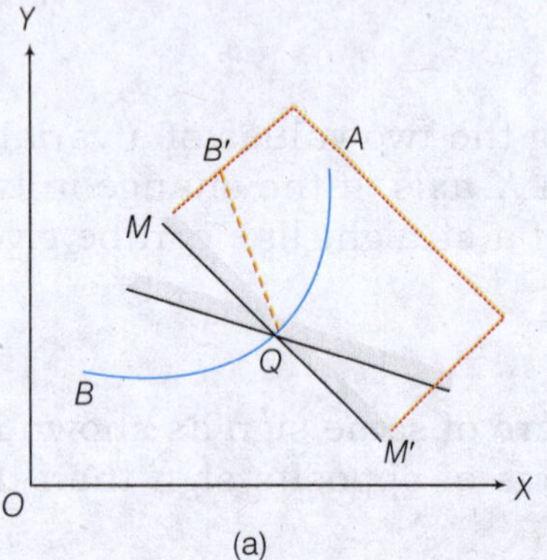

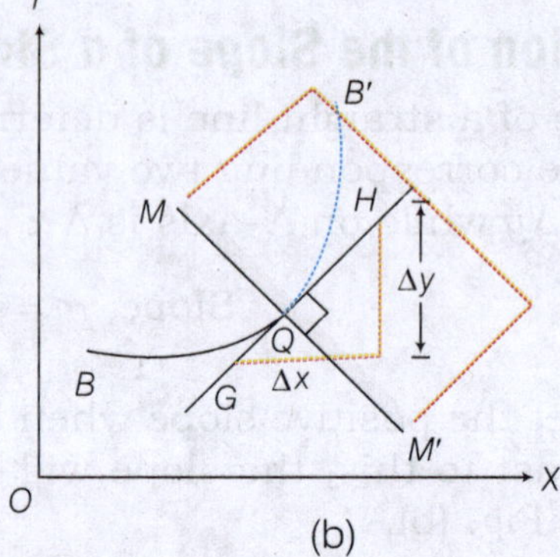

Determination of the slope of a curve

The plane mirror strips MM' is placed at desired point Q such that image $B'Q$ of part BQ of curve appears in the mirror strip as continuation of BQ. The image $B'Q$ will not appear to be smoothly joined with the part of curve BQ as shown in Fig. (a). Now rotate the mirror strip MM', keeping its position at point Q fixed. The image $B'Q$ in the mirror will also rotate. Adjust the position of MM' such that BQB' appears as a continuous smooth curve as shown in Fig. (b).

Draw the line MQM' along the edge of the mirror for this setting and using a protractor, draw a perpendicular line GH to line MQM' at point Q. Therefore, GQH is the required tangent to the curve BQA at point Q. The slope of tangent GQH i.e. $\frac{\Delta y}{\Delta x}$, is the slope of curve AQB at point Q.

Section A

Experiment 1

AIM

To measure the diameter of a small spherical/cylindrical body using a vernier calliper.

Apparatus and Materials Required

A magnifying glass, a spherical body and a vernier calliper.

Description of Apparatus

Vernier Calliper

Vernier calliper was designed by French mathematician Pierre Vernier. The name Vernier calliper, after the name of the inventor. It can accurately measure upto $\left(\frac{1}{100}\right)$th of a centimetre.

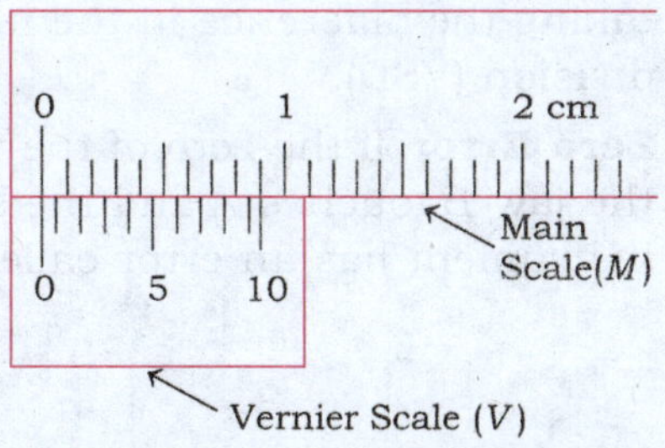

Principle of vernier callipers

Vernier calliper consists of vernier scale V and main scale. Both the scales are divided into division of different magnitude. The main scale M is fixed, while vernier scale V slides along the main scale M as shown in figure. It is also known as auxiliary scale.

Construction of Vernier Calliper

The main parts of the vernier calliper are

1. **Main Scale** The main scale M is graduated in mm and cm on one side. It is made of steel bar.

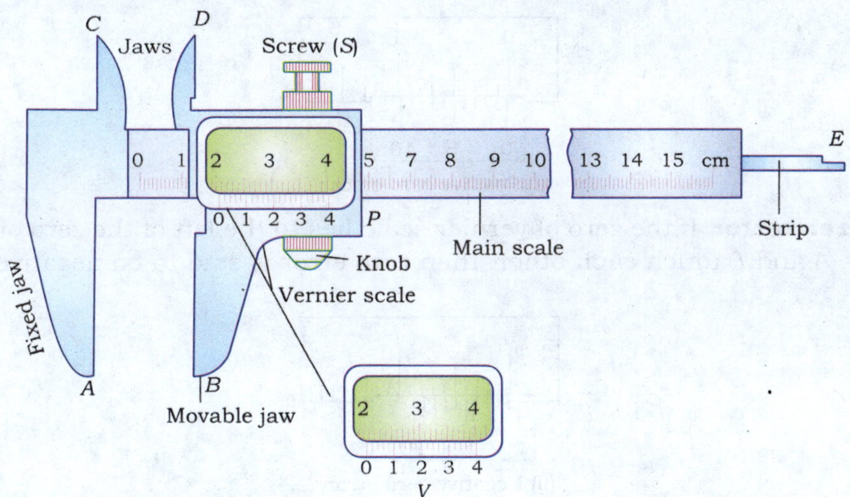

2. **Vernier Scale** It is sliding scale. The side of vernier scale lying towards the mm side of the main scale has ten equal parts. The ten divisions of the vernier scale are equal to nine divisions of the main scale shown in the figure.
3. **Jaws** It has two jaws *AC* and *BD*. The jaw *AC* lies on the zero end of the main scale and *BD* is attached to vernier. Jaw *AC* is fixed while *BD* moves with vernier.

   The upper jaws *C* and *D* are used to measure the internal diameter of a hollow objects, while lowers jaws *A* and *B* are used to measure the length or diameter of objects that are gripped between them.
4. **Metallic Strips** The strip *N* is attached to the vernier scale. This strip is used to measure the depths of the hollow objects.

Terms Related to Experiment

Vernier Constant The difference between the values of one main scale division and one vernier scale division is known as vernier constant.

Least Count The smallest division which can be accurately measured with the particular scale is known as its least count value. Mathematically, the least count is calculated by taking the difference in the magnitude of one main scale division (MSD) and one vernier scale division (VSD).

Zero Error If the zero of the vernier scale does not coincide with the zero of main scale when the jaw *B* touches *A* and the straight edge of *D* touches the straight edge of *C*, then the instrument has an error called zero error.

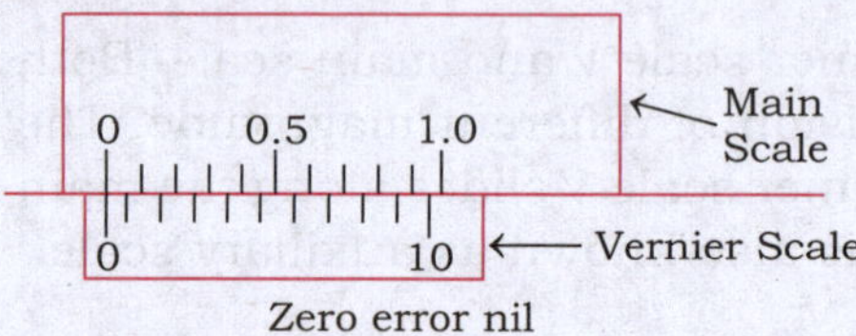

Zero error nil

It is of two types :

(i) **Positive zero error** If the zero of vernier scale lies to the right of the zero of the main scale when jaws *A* and *B* touch each other, then zero error is said to be positive.

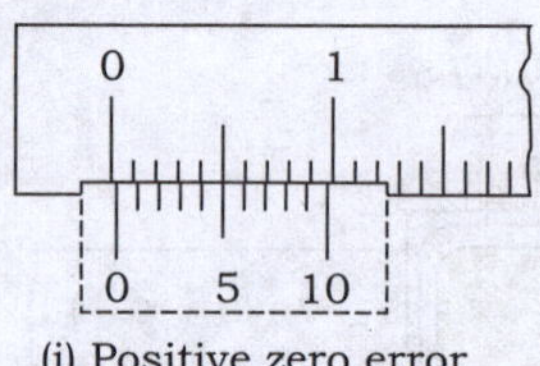

(i) Positive zero error

(ii) **Negative zero error** If the zero of vernier scale lies to the left of the zero of the main scale when jaws *A* and *B* touch each other, then zero error is said to be negative.

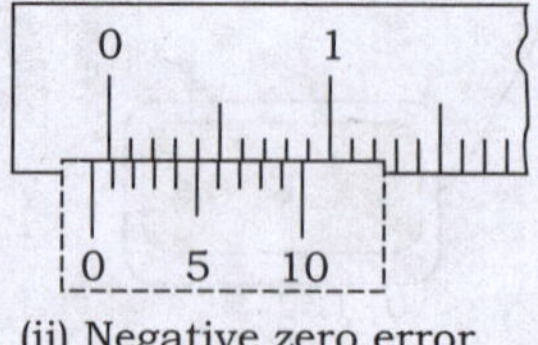

(ii) Negative zero error

Theory/Principle

Let the value of one of the smallest division on the main scale be x and y be that on the vernier scale. So, when the fixed and the movable jaws get joined, then

$$(n-1)\text{ MSD} = n\text{VSD}$$

$$(n-1)\times \text{ divisions on main scale} = n\times \text{ divisions on the vernier scale}$$

$$\Rightarrow \quad (n-1)\,x = ny$$

$$\Rightarrow \quad (x-y)\,n = x \;\Rightarrow\; (x-y) = \frac{x}{n}$$

Therefore,

$$\text{Least Count (LC)} = \frac{\text{Value of one of the smallest division on main scale}}{\text{Total number of small divisions on the vernier scale}}$$

Diameter of an Object

Now, consider ath and bth be the readings of the main scale and the vernier scale respectively, which coincide with any main scale division, then observed diameter (D) is given by

$$\text{Diameter } (D) = \text{Main scale reading} + \text{Vernier scale reading} = a + (b \times \text{LC})$$

Procedure

Measurement of Least Count and Zero Error

1. Find out the Vernier Constant (VC) or Least Count (LC) of the vernier calliper.
2. Now, take the movable jaw BD close towards the fixed jaw AC, so that they both touch each other. Observe the zero mark of the main scale. It must perfectly coincide with that of the vernier scale. If not so, note down the zero error of the vernier calliper by using the magnifying glass.

   One can determine the zero error by using the following relation

   $$\text{Zero error} = x \times \text{Least count}$$

   where, x is that value of the vernier scale division which is exactly coinciding with the main scale division when both the jaws (i.e. movable and fixed) touch each other.
3. Repeat the step (2) and record the zero error for three times.

Place a Spherical Body between the Jaws

4. Gently loosen the screw (S) to release the movable jaw and fix the spherical or cylindrical body between the two jaws A and B and make the jaw BD get adjusted, so that, they (jaws A and B) hold the body without any external pressure on it. Now, tighten the screw (S) attached to the vernier scale.
5. The jaws should be perfectly perpendicular to the diameter of the body. Now, gently tighten the screw, so as to clamp the instrument in this position.

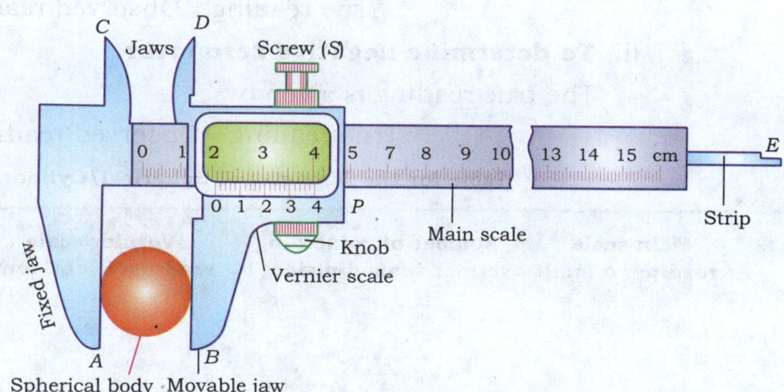

To measure the diameter of small spherical body using vernier calliper

Measurement of Diameter of the Spherical Body

6. After tightening the screw attached to the vernier scale, note down the position of zero mark of the vernier scale. Usually, it will not perfectly coincide with any of the small divisions on the main scale.
7. Take the main scale reading just before the zero mark of vernier scale, it is called **Main Scale Reading** (MSR)
8. Now, note the number of vernier scale divisions coinciding with the divisions of main scale. The number of divisions (say *n*) should be counted from left to the right end.
9. Repeat the observations for the diameter at least three times, for three different positions of the sphere or cylinder. Now, record the observations on the table.

Observations

1. Determination of Least Count of Vernier Calliper

Since, 1 main scale division = 1 mm

Also, 10 vernier scale divisions = 9 main scale divisions

Therefore, 1 vernier scale division = $\frac{9}{10}$ main scale division

Thus, least count = 1 main scale division – 1 vernier scale division = (1 – 0.9) mm

= 0.1 mm main scale division

= (0.1×10^{-1}) cm

Vernier Constant (VC) = 0.01 cm

2. For the Determination of Zero Error

Zero error (e_1) = ... cm

Zero error (e_2) = ... cm

Zero error (e_3) = ... cm

Mean zero error (e) = $\frac{e_1 + e_2 + e_3}{3}$ = ... cm

(i) **To determine positive zero error**

The true reading is given by

True reading = Observed reading – (+ Zero error)

(ii) **To determine negative zero error**

The true reading is given by

True reading = Observed reading – (– Zero error)

Table for the Diameter of Spherical/Cylindrical Body

S.N.	Main scale reading, a (cm)	Number of coinciding vernier scale division, b	Vernier scale reading, $b \times$ LC (cm)	Observed diameter, $D_1 = a + (b \times LC)$ (cm)	Corrected diameter, $D_2 = D_1 - (\pm e)$ (cm)
1.					$D_2(1)$ =
2.					$D_2(2)$ =
3.					$D_2(3)$ =

Calculation

Mean corrected diameter,

$$D = \frac{D_2(1) + D_2(2) + D_2(3)}{3} \text{ cm}$$

$$D = \text{.........} \text{ cm} = \text{.........} \times 10^{-2} \text{ m}$$

Result

The diameter of given spherical/cylindrical body is ...... m.

PRECAUTIONS

1. *Undue pressure on the body of vernier calliper should be avoided.*
2. *Tighten the screw of the vernier scale without exerting excess pressure to avoid any damage.*
3. *The necessary lubricant should be used in order to obtain the smooth movement of vernier scale on the main scale.*
4. *The zero error in the experiment should always be taken into account while measuring the diameter of any spherical body.*
5. *The least count and zero error should be carefully recorded.*
6. *Record each observation with correct significant figures and units.*

Sources of Error

1. Main scale and jaws may not be perpendicular to each other.
2. There may not be any overlapping of vernier scale with the main scale.
3. Incorrect record of readings can be a cause of wrong observation.
4. Zero error may not be considered at the time of observation.
5. Parallax error may be there while taking observations.
6. Vernier scale may be loosely fitted with the movable jaw.
7. Body may not be perfectly spherical or cylindrical.

Viva-Voce

Q. 1 What is the least count formula of vernier calliper?

Ans Least count formula of vernier calliper is given by

$$\text{Least Count (LC)} = \frac{\text{Value of smallest main scale division}}{\text{Total number of divisions on the vernier scale}}$$

Q. 2 Differentiate between zero correction and zero error.

Ans The zero correction is equal to the negative of the zero error with its proper sign.

Q. 3 Why do we usually calculate the least count of an instrument?

Ans From the calculation point of view, by knowing the least count, we can easily find out the accuracy in the measurements with an instrument.

Q. 4 What is the utilisation of the thin sliding jaw of vernier calliper?

Ans The thin sliding strip attached to the sliding jaw of vernier calliper is used to determine the depth of vessel like calorimeter, beaker, etc.

Q. 5 How would the precision of measurement by vernier calliper be affected by increasing the number of divisions on its vernier scale?

Ans Since, Least Count (LC) of vernier calliper

$$= \frac{\text{The magnitude of smallest division on main scale}}{\text{Total number of divisions on the vernier scale}}$$

So, as per the question, if the total number of divisions on vernier scale gets increased, then value of least count of vernier calliper scale gets reduced which increases the precision of measurement by vernier calliper.

Q. 6 How can you find the value of π using a cylinder and a pair of vernier calliper?

Ans Using the vernier calliper, measure the diameter D and find the circumference of a cylinder using a thread. Therefore, ratio of the circumference to the diameter gives the value of π.

Q. 7 Can you tell the function of upper jaws of vernier calliper?

Ans Upper jaws of vernier calliper are used to determine the internal diameter of a beaker or calorimeter.

Experiment 2

AIM

To measure the internal diameter and depth of a given beaker/calorimeter by using vernier calliper and hence, find its internal volume.

Apparatus and Materials Required

Vernier callipers, a beaker or calorimeter, magnifying glass.

Description of Apparatus

See Experiment 1.

Theory/Principle

Difference in the magnitude of one Main Scale Division (MSD) and one Vernier Scale Division (VSD) is called least count of vernier calliper,

i.e. $n\,(\text{VSD}) = (n-1)\,\text{MSD}$

Least count can also be defined as

$$\text{Least Count (LC)} = \frac{\text{Magnitude of the smallest division on main scale}}{\text{Total number of small divisions on the vernier scale}}$$

It should be noted that the upper jaws of the vernier calliper are used for measuring internal diameter of a hollow cylindrical vessel and thin strip is used for measuring the depth of the vessel.

Therefore, Volume of a given beaker or calorimeter = Internal area of cross-section × Depth

$$\Rightarrow \qquad V = \pi\left(\frac{D}{2}\right)^2 \cdot E$$

where, D = Internal diameter of beaker or calorimeter and

E = Depth of the beaker or calorimeter

Procedure

Measurement of Least Count and Zero Error

1. To observe the least count and zero error of the vernier calliper, follow the same procedure given in steps (1) to (3) of Experiment 1.

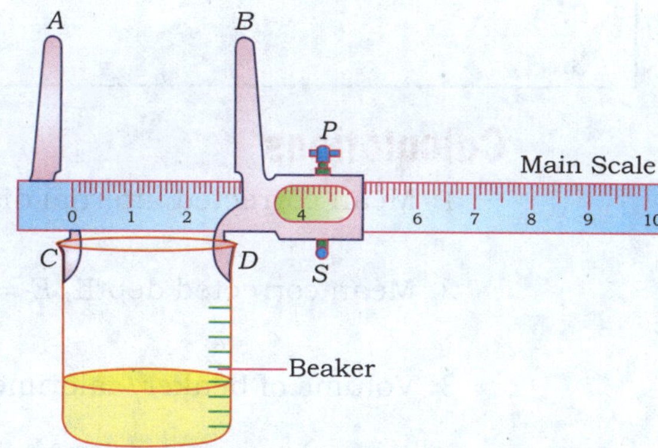

Measuring internal diameter of beaker

Measurement of Internal Diameter

2. Put the beaker/calorimeter on the two jaws C and D of vernier calliper in such a way that the jaws just touch the beaker or calorimeter from inside without any undue pressure on the walls and tighten the screw attached to the vernier scale gently .
3. Now, follow the same procedure given in steps (6) to (9) of Experiment 1 and measure the internal diameter of the beaker.

Measurement of Depth

4. To measure the depth of beaker or calorimeter, we have to keep the right edge of the main scale on the upper edge of the beaker or calorimeter.
5. Keep sliding the movable jaw D downwards till the outer edge of strip E touches the bottom of the beaker or calorimeter.
6. Repeat the above steps for different positions along the circumference of the upper edge of the beaker.
7. Now, find the total reading and apply zero correction.
8. Take four different values of the depth at four different positions. Calculate the volume by using proper formula.

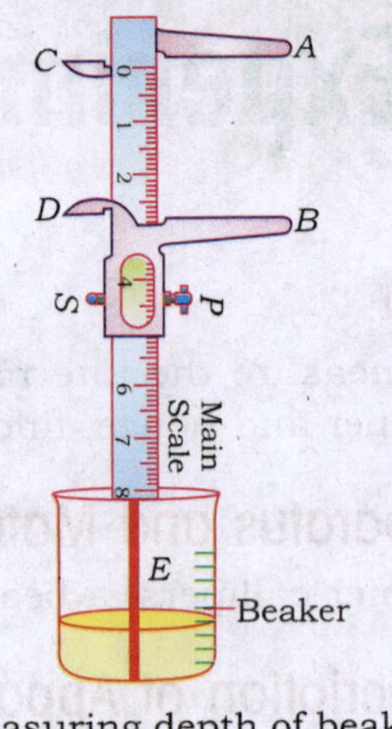

Measuring depth of beaker

Observations

1. Determination of Least Count of Vernier Calliper

Same as in Experiment 1.

2. For the Determination of Zero Error

Same as in Experiment 1.

Table for the Internal Diameter of Beaker

S. N.	Main scale, a (cm)	Vernier scale division, b	Vernier scale reading, $b \times LC$ (cm)	Observed diameter, $D_1 = a + (b \times LC)$ (cm)	Corrected diameter, $D_2 = D_1 - (\pm e)$ (cm)
1					$D_2(1) =$
2					$D_2(2) =$
3					$D_2(3) =$

Table for the Depth of Beaker

S. N.	Main scale reading, F (cm)	Vernier scale division, G	Vernier scale reading $G \times LC$ (cm)	Observed depth, $E_2 = [F + G \times LC]$ (cm)	Corrected depth, $E_1 = E_2 - (\pm e)$ (cm)
1.					$E_1(1) =$
2.					$E_1(2) =$
3.					$E_1(3) =$

Calculations

1. Mean corrected internal diameter of beaker/calorimeter, $D = \dfrac{D_2(1) + D_2(2) + D_2(3)}{3} = \ldots \text{cm}$
2. Mean corrected depth, $E = \dfrac{E_1(1) + E_1(2) + E_1(3)}{3} = \ldots \text{cm}$
3. Volume of beaker/calorimeter $= \pi \left(\dfrac{D}{2}\right)^2 E = \ldots \text{cm}^3$

Result

The volume of the beaker/calorimeter is ...... cm^3.

PRECAUTIONS

1. *While measuring the depth, the strip should be perpendicular to the bottom surface.*
2. *While measuring the depth, the edge of the main scale should not get out of contact from the edge of the circumference of the calorimeter when the end of strip E touches the bottom.*

Sources of Error

Same as in Experiment 1.

Viva-Voce

Q.1 What is the definition of angular vernier?

Ans. It is an instrument which is used for measuring fraction of a degree of an angle. It is usually provided in sextants and spectrometers, which measures angular displacement.

Q.2 When the zero error in the instrument is said to be positive or negative?

Ans. The zero error is said to be positive if the zero mark of the vernier scale lies towards the right side of the zero of the main scale, when the jaws are brought in contact with each other. If the zero mark of the vernier scale lies towards the left side of zero of the main scale, then the zero error is said to be negative.

Q.3 How can you find the thickness of the sheet used for making a steel tumbler using vernier callipers?

Ans. Measure the internal diameter (D_i) and external or outer diameter (D_o) of the tumbler. Then, the thickness of the sheet, $D_f = \left(\frac{D_0 - D_i}{2}\right)$.

Q.4 Distinguish between the vernier scale and main scale divisions?

Ans. n vernier scale divisions are normally equal to the $(n - 1)$ main scale divisions.

Q.5 One can undertake an exercise to know the level of skills developed in making measurements using vernier calliper. Objects such as bangles/kangans, marbles whose dimensions can be measured by using a thread indirectly. So, in order to judge the skills acquired through comparison of results, obtain the conclusion by both the methods? [NCERT]

Ans. The measurements taken by vernier calliper is more precise. While, in the case of bangles, kangans or marbles, use of thread can measure their dimensions but not as accurate as vernier calliper. So, while using a thread, there will always be a point of approximation in the answer.

Q.6 How does a vernier decrease the least count of a scale? [NCERT]

Ans Vernier calliper divides the least count of main scale into number of divisions present on the vernier scale.

Experiment 3

AIM

To measure the diameter of a given wire using screw gauge.

Apparatus and Materials Required

Screw gauge, a piece of wire, magnifying lens.

Description of Apparatus

Screw Gauge

A screw gauge is a measuring instrument used for measuring very small distances of the order $\frac{1}{100}$ th part of a mm (say thickness of a needle, a wire, etc).

A screw gauge works on the principle of a screw i.e., a screw moves forward or backward linearly when its head is rotated forward or backward.

Pitch of Screw

Pitch of a screw is defined as the distance moved forward by the screw when its head is given a complete rotation.

Construction of Screw Gauge

A screw gauge consists of the following main parts as shown in the figure

(i) Linear scale (ii) Circular scale (iii) Studs (iv) U-frame

The screw gauge has a screw *S* which advances forward or backward as one rotates the head *C* through ratchet (*R*) in clockwise or anti-clockwise direction. It also consists of a Linear Scale (LS) attached to limb (*D*) of the U-frame.

The smallest division on the linear scale is 1 mm.

There is a Circular Scale (CS) on the head, which can be rotated. A line parallel to the axis of screw is inscribed on the body of the screw, this line is called **reference line**. There are 100 divisions on the circular scale.

There are two studs *A* and *B* in the screw gauge. They serve as two jaws of the screw gauge. The stud *A* is fixed with the U-frame while stud *B* as the flat end of the screw is movable which can move forward and backward.

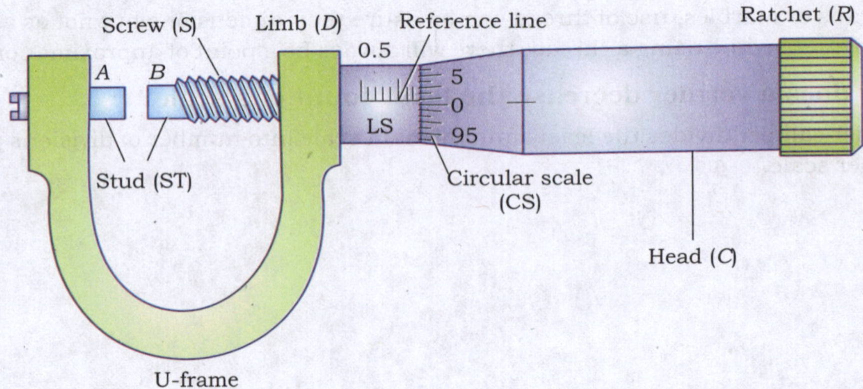

When the end B of the screw touches the surface A of the Stud (ST), the zero marks on the main scale and the circular scale should coincide with each other. When both the studs touch each other or they come in contact, the ratchet itself turns on to loose the control over the screw. This in turn helps to avoid the undue pressure over the object placed between the studs.

Errors in Measured Thickness by Screw Gauge

Zero Error of Screw Gauge

When the end of screw B and the surface of the stud A come in contact, then the zero marks of the linear scale and the main scale should coincide with each other. If it is not so, then the screw gauge is said to have zero error.

To measure the correct thickness of an object held between the studs A and B, the zero error is always subtracted algebraically from the measured value of thickness.

∴ Correct thickness of an object = Measured thickness − Zero error (whether positive or negative)

There are two types of zero error, which are as follows

1. **Positive Zero Error** If the reading of the circular scale across the linear scale is more than zero (or positive), then the screw gauge is said to have positive zero error.

   If the main scale reading is x and the number of circular scale divisions which coincides with the reference line is n, then

   Positive zero error $= +(x + n \times \text{least count})$

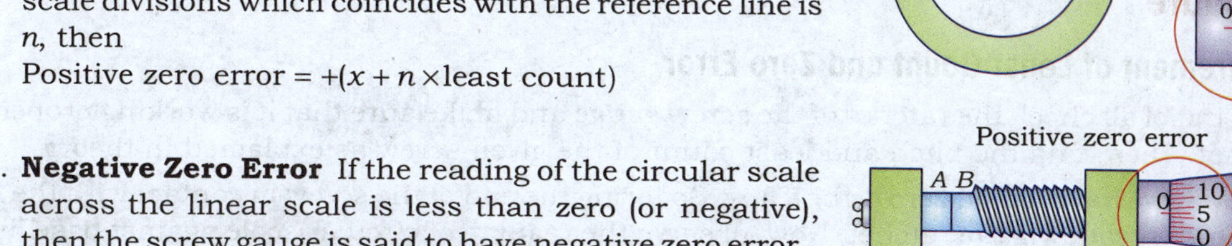

Positive zero error

2. **Negative Zero Error** If the reading of the circular scale across the linear scale is less than zero (or negative), then the screw gauge is said to have negative zero error.

   If N is the total number of the divisions of circular scale and m is the number of divisions of circular scale which coincide with reference line, then

   Negative zero error $= -[(N - m) \times \text{least count}]$

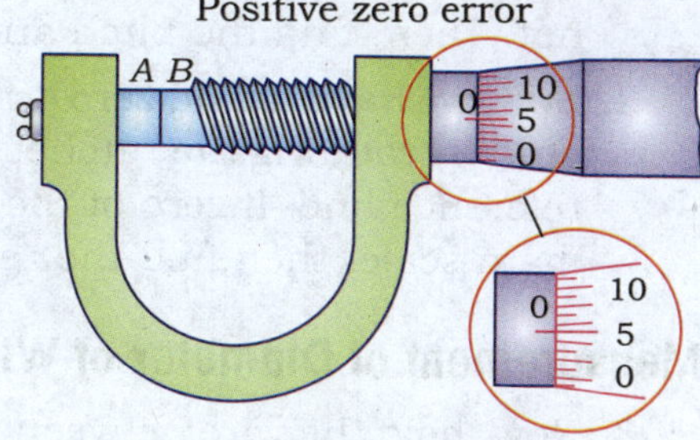

Negative zero error

Reading a Screw Gauge

Linear Scale Reading and Circular Scale Reading When a wire is held between the stud (ST) surface A and screw surface B then, the mark on the linear scale which lies close to the left edge of the circular scale is the linear scale reading and the circular scale division which coincides with the main scale is the circular scale reading as shown in figure given below.

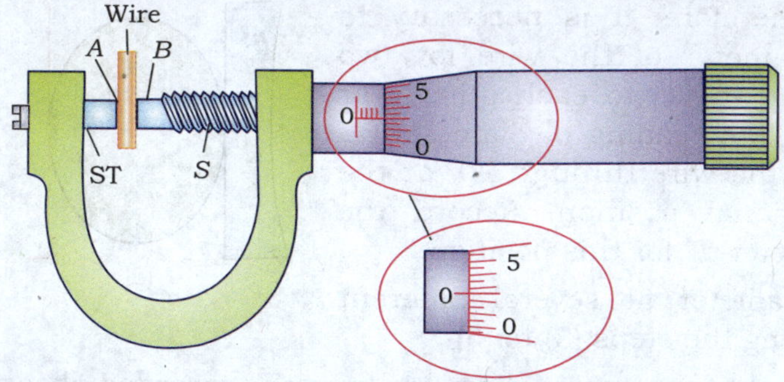

Magnified view of measurement of thickness of wire

Total Reading To know how the total reading is calculated, let us take an example of screw gauge given above in the figure.

$$\text{Total reading} = \text{Linear scale reading} + \text{Circular scale reading} \times \text{Least count}$$
$$= 0.5 + 2 \times 0.001 = 0.502 \text{ cm}$$

Theory/Principle

The principle of the screw gauge is based on the least count. Since, pitch is the linear distance travelled by screw in one complete rotation of its head and least count of screw gauge is the ratio of pitch to the total number of divisions on the circular scale.

Therefore,
$$\text{Pitch} = \frac{\text{Distance moved by the screw}}{\text{Number of rotations given to the screw}}$$

and
$$\text{Least count} = \frac{\text{Pitch of the screw}}{\text{Number of divisions on circular scale}}$$

e.g. For a screw gauge with a pitch of 1 mm and 100 divisions on the circular scale,

$$\text{Least count} = \frac{1 \text{ mm}}{100} = 0.01 \text{ mm}$$

This is the smallest length one can measure with this screw gauge.

Note The screw gauge have a least count of 0.001 mm or 10^{-6} m is called micrometer screw.

Procedure

Measurement of Least Count and Zero Error

1. First of all check the ratchet of the screw gauge and make sure that it is working properly or not. Then, find the pitch and least count of the given screw as explained in theory.
2. Now, we have to find zero error if any. So, bring the end of the screw in contact with the fixed stud by rotating the ratchet. Now, observe the reading of circular scale against base line or reference line. If zero of the circular scale does not coincide with the reference line of the main scale, then find the zero error from the concept given earlier.

Measurement of Diameter of Wire

3. Now, hold the wire between screw *B* and stud *A* of the screw gauge. Move the screw forward by rotating the ratchet till the wire is gently gripped between the screw and the stud. Stop rotating the ratchet the moment you hear a click sound.
4. Now, calculate the diameter of the wire by multiplying circular scale division with least count and by adding main scale reading with it.
   Diameter of the wire = Main scale reading + Circular scale reading × Least count
5. The wire may not have an exactly circular cross-section. Therefore, it is necessary to measure the diameter of the wire for two positions at right angles to each other. For this, first record the reading of diameter d_a and then rotate the wire through 90° at the same cross-sectional position. Record the reading for diameter d_b for this position.

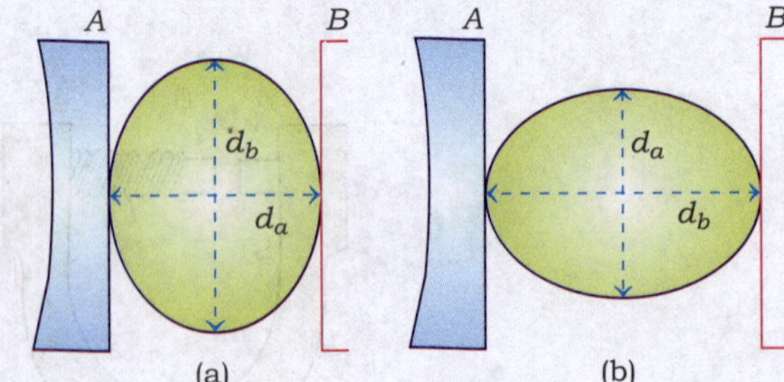

6. Measure the diameter at several different places by repeating the steps (3) to (5).
7. Find the mean and the corrected diameter from the recorded observations.

Observations

Measurement of Least Count and Zero Error

1. Value of smallest division on main scale = ...mm.
2. The distance moved by the screw when it is rotated through x complete rotations, y = ...mm
3. Pitch of the screw = y/x = ... mm.
4. Total number of divisions on the circular scale, n = ...
5. Least count of the screw gauge = $\frac{\text{Pitch}}{n} = \frac{y/x}{n}$ = ... mm.
6. Zero error with sign (e)
   = Number of division of circular scale division coinciding with reference line × LC = ... mm.

Table for the Diameter of a Given Wire

S.N.	Reading along one direction, (d_a)			Reading along perpendicular direction, (d_b)			Measured diameter, $d_i = \frac{d_a + d_b}{2}$ (mm)
	Main scale reading, x (mm)	Circular scale divisions, y	Diameter, $d_a = x + y \times LC$ (mm)	Main scale reading, x' (mm)	Circular scale divisions, y'	Diameter, $d_b = x' + y' + LC$ (mm)	
1.							
2.							
3.							
4.							
5.							

Measurement of Diameter of Wire

Mean observed diameter $= d_0 = \frac{d_1 + d_2 + d_3 + d_4 + d_5}{5}$ = ... mm

Mean corrected diameter = $d` = d_0 - (e)$ = ... mm

Result

From the above calculation and observations, the diameter of the given wire measured by the screw gauge is = ... mm

PRECAUTIONS

1. *Zero error should always be taken into consideration while measuring the diameter.*
2. *In order to avoid backlash error, rotate the screw only in one direction.*
3. *Diameter should be measured at four different places along the length of the wire.*
4. *At each place, diameter should be measured in two mutually perpendicular directions.*
5. *Take all readings carefully by keeping the eye perpendicular to the scale. This helps to keep away from the parallax error.*
6. *Avoid undue pressure on the wire as this may change the diameter.*
7. *Screw should move freely without friction.*

Sources of Error

1. The threads of the screw may not be of equal pitch.
2. The wire taken may not have uniform cross-section.
3. There may be some difference in size of circular scale division.
4. The divisions on linear scale and circular scale may not be evenly spaced.
5. The screw gauge may have backlash error.

Viva-Voce

Q. 1 What is a 'micrometer screw gauge'?

Ans. The device which is used to measure the linear dimensions of small objects, e.g. diameter of a wire. This instrument has a least count of 0.001 m (i.e. 10^{-6} m) and therefore, is called micrometer screw gauge.

Q. 2 State the principle used in this experiment.

Ans. Screw gauge works on the principle that linear distance travelled by an accurately cut screw which is rotating in closely fitting fixed nut, is directly proportional to the number of rotations given to it.

Q. 3 How the zero error can be corrected?

Ans. Zero error can be corrected by subtracting zero error from the observed reading with suitable sign.

Q. 4 How can you define the term 'least count'?

Ans. Least count is the ratio of pitch to the total number of divisions on the circular scale.

Q. 5 The zero error in a screw gauge is –0.05 mm and observed diameter is 1.67mm. What is the correct diameter?

Ans. 1.67 mm + 0.05 mm = 1.72 mm

Q. 6 How can the backlash error be avoided?

Ans. It can be avoided by turning the screw always in one direction while taking observations.

Q. 7 Mention the name of the metal of which the screw is made of?

Ans. The metal of which the screw is made up of is gun-metal or stainless steel.

Q. 8 What is the reasons for zero error?

Ans. Wear and tear of the screw and also the defect in manufacturing can be the reasons for zero error.

Q. 9 Which is more accurate - a screw gauge or vernier calliper?

Ans. A screw gauge is more accurate because its least count is less than vernier calliper.

Q.10 What can be a reason of measuring the diameter of the wire in two mutually perpendicular directions?

Ans. In order to eliminate error due to non-uniformity of thickness, the diameter of the wire is measured in two perpendicular directions.

Q.11 Why does a screw gauge develop backlash error with use? [NCERT]

Ans When the thread on the screw and that on nut gets tightly fit with each other, then with the repeated use of the threads of both the screw and the nut may get worn out. So, as a result, a gap gets developed between these two threads, which is called play and this introduces an error in measurement of screw gauge and this error is called backlash error due to which the screw slips a small linear distance without rotation.

Q.12 Is the screw gauge with the smaller least count always better? So, if you are given two screw gauges, one with 100 divisions on circular scale and another with 200 divisions, which one would you prefer and why? [NCERT]

Ans Yes, the screw gauge with the smaller least count is always better.

Since, we know that

$$\text{Least Count} = \frac{\text{Pitch}}{\text{Number of divisions on circular scale}}$$

So, if we are given a screw gauge with 100 circular scale divisions and another with 200 circular scale divisions, then we would prefer the screw gauge with 200 circular scale divisions because as per the formula, if number of circular scale divisions is more, then the least count will be less and lesser is the least count, more accurate will be the reading and ultimately an accurate desired value is obtained.

Q.13 For measurement of small lengths, why do we prefer screw gauge over vernier calliper? [NCERT]

Ans Since, a screw gauge is mainly preferred for the small measurements, due to which it can record the measurements in micrometers as well, which results in an accurate desired value. So, this is a reason of preferring screw gauge over vernier calliper.

Experiment 4

AIM

To measure thickness of a given sheet using screw gauge.

Apparatus and Materials Required

A screw gauge, some sheets of paper and magnifying glass.

Description of Apparatus

See Experiment 3.

Theory/Principle

Same as Experiment 3.

Formula used If d is the thickness of n pieces of sheet of paper, then thickness of the given sheet of paper, $t = d/n$

Procedure

Measurement of Least Count and Zero Error

1. First of all, we have to determine the pitch, least count and zero error as calculated in Experiment 3 in steps (1) to (3).

Measurement of Thickness of Given Sheets

2. A single sheet is quite thin. Therefore, it is difficult to measure the thickness of single sheet accurately. Hence, cut the sheet into various small pieces (consider n such pieces) and then find the thickness of these pieces.
3. Hold the pieces of sheet of paper whose thickness is to be measured in between screw and the stud and move the screw with the help of ratchet till the click sound is heared and ratchet becomes free.
4. Now, record the main scale reading (in mm) and the number of divisions of the circular scale coinciding with the reference line.
5. Multiply circular scale division with least count and then add it to main scale reading and observe the thickness of number of sheets.
6. Now, follow the steps (3) to (5) in repetitive manner to determine the thickness at four different places.
7. Find the mean observed thickness of pieces of sheet of paper.
8. Now, in order to get the correct thickness, subtract the zero error with proper sign from the observed thickness of total number of sheets.
9. At last calculate the thickness of the sheet.

Observations and Calculations

Measurement of Least Count and Zero Error

Same as Experiment 3.

Measurement of Thickness

Table for the Thickness of Given Sheets

S. N.	Main scale reading, a (mm)	Circular scale reading		Total reading	
		Number of circular scale division on reference line, b	Fraction to be added, $b \times LC$ (mm)	Observed thickness, $Z_0 = a + (b \times LC)$ (mm)	Corrected thickness, $Z = Z_o \pm e$ (mm)
1					$Z_1 =$ ....
2					$Z_2 =$ ....
3					$Z_3 =$ ....
4					$Z_4 =$ ....
5					$Z_5 =$ ....

Mean corrected value of thickness of given sheets,

$$d = \frac{Z_1 + Z_2 + Z_3 + Z_4 + Z_5}{5} = \text{......} \text{ mm}$$

Therefore, thickness of the given sheet = $\dfrac{\text{Thickness of n sheets}}{\text{Number of sheets}} = \dfrac{d}{n}$

= .... mm = ... cm

Result

Thickness of the given sheet of paper = ... cm.

PRECAUTIONS

Same as Experiment 3.

Sources of Error

1. Some of instrumental and human errors may persist.
2. The sheets of paper may not be uniform.
3. The screw gauge may have backlash error.
4. The divisions on linear scale and circular scale may not be evenly spaced.

Viva-Voce

Q. 1 Is it possible to find the thickness of a thin paper by screw gauge?

Ans. Yes, it is possible to find the thickness of a thin paper by screw gauge. In order to find the thickness of paper, firstly we will find the thickness of 30 sheets of paper, then divide this value by 30 to get the thickness of a paper.

Q. 2 How can we correct the screw gauge itself for the zero error?

Ans. To correct the screw gauge itself for the zero error, the fixed stud is adjusted by screwing it, in or out.

Q. 3 How can you define the term pitch of the screw gauge?

Ans. The distance moved by the screw in one complete rotation is known as the 'pitch' of the screw gauge. It is equal to the distance measured between the consecutive threads of the screw.

Q. 4 What is the most important precaution that should be followed while performing this experiment?

Ans. It is very necessary to check the instrument for zero error and along with this, the spindle should be wiped clean as dust particles cause the false readings.

Q. 5 Mention the formula for the least count of a screw gauge?

Ans. The least count of a screw gauge is the distance moved by the screw when it is rotated by one circular scale division.

$$\therefore \quad \text{Least count} = \frac{\text{Pitch}}{\text{Total number of divisions on circular scale}}$$

Q. 6 What do you mean by ratchet?

Ans. The arrangement inside the milled head connected at the end of the screw through a weak spring is known as ratchet. It helps in preventing the screw from getting under pressure.

Q. 7 In which way, you can attain a screw gauge with smaller least count? [NCERT]

Ans. As we know that, least count of a screw gauge can be given as

$$\text{Least count} = \frac{\text{Pitch}}{\text{Total number of divisions on the circular scale}}$$

So, by decreasing the pitch of the screw and increasing the number of divisions on the circular scale, we can attain a screw gauge with smaller least count.

Q. 8 What are the limitations of the screw gauge. If it is used to measure the thickness of a thick cardboard sheet? [NCERT]

Ans. If a screw gauge is used to measure the thickness of a thick cardboard sheet, then the screw gets slipped by a small linear distance without any rotation which in turn leads to a backlash error.

Experiment 5

AIM

To determine volume of an irregular lamina using screw gauge.

Apparatus and Materials Required

A millimeter graph paper, an irregular lamina, pencil and screw gauge.

Description of Apparatus

See Experiment 3.

Theory/Principle

To find the thickness, refer to theory/principle of Experiment 3.

The volume of irregular lamina can be given by

Volume of irregular lamina (V) = Area of lamina (A) × Mean thickness of lamina (t)

Procedure

Measurement of Least Count and Zero Error

1. First of all, calculate the pitch, least count and zero error same as in Experiment 3.

Measurement of Thickness of Lamina

2. Measure the thickness of lamina by following the same steps as in Experiment 4 and then determine the mean corrected thickness.

Determination of Area of Irregular Lamina

3. Place the given irregular lamina on the sheet of paper with millimeter graph and draw an outline of the lamina on the millimetre graph paper with a sharp pencil.

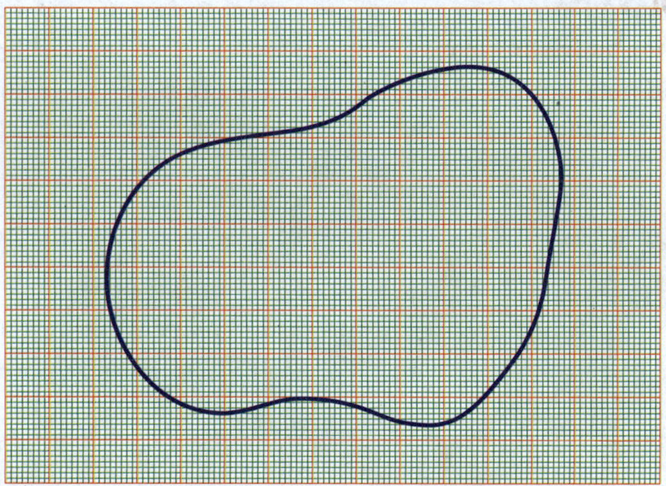

Surface area of an irregular lamina

4. Count the number of complete squares and also more than the half squares within the boundary of the lamina.
5. At last, calculate total area (A) in mm^2.

   Area = $x \times$ area of a square + $y \times$ area of more than half squares.

   where, x and y represent the number of complete squares and the number of squares more than half respectively.

Observations

Measurement of Least Count and Zero Error

Same as Experiment 3.

Measurement of Thickness

Same as Experiment 4.

Measurement of Area and Volume

From the outline drawn on the graph paper,

Total number of complete squares (x) = ... mm^2 = ... cm^2

Total numbers of more than the half squares (y)......... mm^2 = ... cm^2

Total area ($x + y$) = ... cm^2

Volume of lamina = Area × Mean corrected thickness of lamina =........ mm^3 = ... cm^2

Result

The volume of given lamina = area × thickness = ... cm^3

PRECAUTIONS

Same as in Experiment 3.

Sources of Error

1. The screw may not be frictionless.
2. The lamina taken may not be of uniform cross-section.

Viva-Voce

Q. 1 Mention the conditions, when the zero error is said to be positive and negative?

Ans. If the zero of the circular scale advances beyond the reference line, then zero error is said to be negative and if it is left behind the reference line, then the zero error is said to be positive.

Q. 2 Give the direct formula for calculating the volume of given irregular lamina.

Ans. Volume of given irregular lamina = Area of irregular lamina (A) × Thickness of lamina (t)

Q. 3 Is it possible to measure the backlash error?

Ans. No, it is not possible to measure the backlash error because it is not same over the entire length of the screw.

Q. 4 Mention the function of ratchet in screw gauge.

Ans. When the object is fixed between the stud and the screw then ratchet is provided in order to avoid excess pressure.

Q. 5 What are the types of motions possessed by a screw?

Ans. There are two types of motions possessed by a screw,

(i) its axis has a linear motion and

(ii) its surface has a circular motion.

Q. 6 Can you tell me the least count of the screw gauge?

Ans. The least count of the screw gauge is 0.001 cm.

Q. 7 Is there a situation in which the linear distance moved by the screw is not proportional to the rotation given to it? [NCERT]

Ans. Yes, the linear distance moved by the screw is not proportional to the rotation if the screw threads are damaged or worn out.

This can cause irregularities in the movement, leading to inaccurate measurements.

Q. 8 Is it possible that the zero of circular scale lies above the zero line of main scale, yet the error is positive zero error? [NCERT]

Ans. Yes, it is possible, if the zero mark on circular scale lies above the zero mark on the main scale. It means the micrometer shows a reading even when it should be zero, leading to positive zero error.

Experiment 6

AIM

To determine radius of curvature of a given spherical surface by a spherometer.

Apparatus and Materials Required

Spherometer, a convex mirror, a plane glass strip.

Description of Apparatus

Spherometer

A spherometer is an instrument for the precise measurement of the radius of a sphere and thickness. This instrument is primarily used by opticians to measure the radius of curvature of the spherical surface of lens.

Construction of Spherometer

A spherometer consists of a triangular metallic frame *F*.

It has three legs *A*, *B* and *C* of equal length which form three corners of an equilateral triangle *ABC* and it lies on the periphery of a base circle of known radius *r*. The plane which contains the pointed end of the three legs is called reference plane or ground plane.

The circumference of the disc *D* is divided into 100 or 50 equal parts. This forms the head scale or the circular scale.

A small vertical linear scale *P* graduated in millimeters is fixed vertically to the frame *F* such that it is parallel to the axis of screw and it just touches the rim of the circular scale. This vertical scale is called **pitch scale** or **linear scale.**

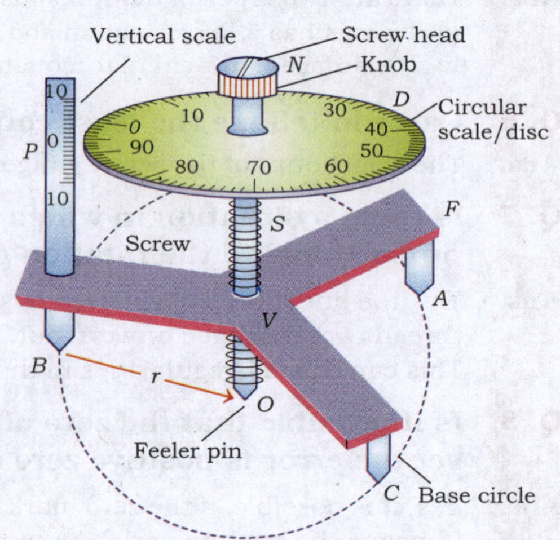

Terms Related to Experiment

Pitch The linear distance travelled by the screw in one complete rotation of its head, is called pitch.

$$\text{Pitch } (P) = \frac{\text{Distance moved by the plane of the disc along the vertical scale}}{\text{Number of complete rotations of the circular scale}}$$

Least Count The least measurement that is done by the spherometer accurately is called least count.

$$\text{Least Count (LC)} = \frac{\text{Pitch } (P)}{\text{Total number of divisions on circular scale } (n)}$$

Zero Error If the three fixed legs and the central screw are touching the plane surface and the zero mark on the disc is in line with the zero mark on main scale, then the spherometer possess no zero error, otherwise the spherometer has zero error. The zero error can occurre in any of the two manners discussed as follows

Positive Zero Error If on the circular scale, zero mark lies little above the zero mark of main scale, it is called positive zero error.

$$\text{Positive zero error} = n \times \text{LC}$$

where, n = number of divisions of circular scale coinciding with vertical scale

and LC = Least Count.

Negative Zero Error If on the circular scale, zero mark lies little below the zero mark of main scale or vertical scale, it is called negative zero error.

$$\text{Negative zero error} = -(n - n') \times \text{LC}$$

where, n = number of divisions on the circular scale

and n' = number of divisions coinciding with the vertical scale.

Theory/Principle

Radius of Curvature of a Spherical Surface

Let us consider that the radius of curvature of a lens is to be measured. The spherometer is placed on the convex surface of this lens in such a way that all three legs and screws of the spherometer touch the convex surface. The two legs touch the surface at points A and B and the third leg cannot be shown in the figure. The tip of the screw on the spherical surface at point O lies above the plane of the three legs at height h.

Suppose that (a) convex surface whose radius of curvature is to be measured in XY as shown in figure. Here, it must be noted that point M as shown in the figure, is not only the mid-point of the line AB but also the centre of the equilateral triangle ABC.

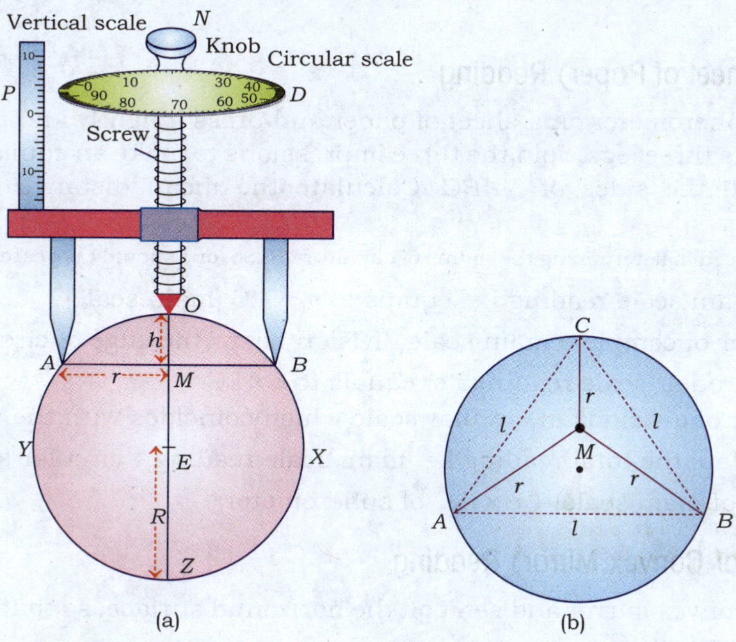

Measuring the radius of curvature with the help of a spherometer

The distance OM is called **Sagitta.** From the property of the circle, we know that if the two chords of the circle intersect at a point, inside the circle, then the product of the lengths of the segments of one chord equals the product of the lengths of the segments of the other chord.

$\therefore$ $$AM \cdot MB = OM \cdot MZ \quad \ldots(i)$$

$\Rightarrow$ $$(AM)^2 = OM\,(OZ - OM) \quad (\because MB = AM)$$

or $$r^2 = h(2R - h)$$

Thus, $$R = \frac{r^2}{2h} + \frac{h}{2}$$

If l is the distance between any two legs of a spherometer, then from fig. (b)

$$r = \frac{l}{\sqrt{3}}$$

$\therefore$ Radius of curvature, $$R = \frac{l^2}{6h} + \frac{h}{2}$$

Procedure

Initial Observations

1. First of all, take a spherometer and examine it properly, so that its legs and vertical scale are not shaky and screw at the centre is not loose.
2. Note the value of one division on pitch scale of the given spherometer.
3. Note the number of divisions on circular scale.
4. After that, calculate the least count and pitch of the spherometer.

Setting Up the Three Legs and Screw of the Spherometer

5. Place the spherometer on a glass slab and move the central screw till its tip just touches the surface of glass slab.
6. During the motion of central screw, count the total number of rotations till it touches the glass slab.

Plane Surface (Sheet of Paper) Reading

7. Place the spherometer on a sheet of paper and press it lightly and take the impressions of the tips of its three legs. Join the three impressions to make an equilateral triangle ABC and measure all the sides of ΔABC. Calculate the mean distance l between two legs of spherometer.

Note The term l is used in determining the radius of curvature R. So, one should take care of measuring the length l.

8. Read the main scale reading i.e. equals to $m \times$ LC (main scale)
   (m = number of complete main scale division below the edge of circular scale)
9. Read the circular scale reading i.e. equals to $c \times$ LC
   (c = number of divisions in circular scale which coincides with the edge of main scale)
10. Now, calculate the total reading i.e. main scale reading + circular scale reading
    $\Rightarrow m \times$ (LC of main scale) + $c \times$ (LC of spherometer)

Curved Surface (or Convex Mirror) Reading

11. Now, take convex mirror and set it on the horizontal surface, so that its convex surface is in upward direction.
12. Put the spherometer on the convex surface, so its legs rest on it.
13. Now, move the central screw till it touches the surface of the convex part. It is to be ensured that the screw touches the given spherical surface gently. One can observe its image formed due to reflection from the surface beneath it.

14. Again, note the reading of the circular scale, main scale and note whether the zero of the circular scale has moved down or up the zero of main scale.
15. The difference between two sets of observations with a proper sign, i.e. (curved surface – plane surface) gives the value of h called Sagitta.
16. Repeat the steps (7) to (15) and calculate the mean value of h.

Observations

Pitch of the Spherometer Screw

1. Value of smallest division on the vertical scale =……… mm
2. Distance (q) moved by the screw for complete rotations (p) of the circular disc =……… mm
3. Pitch of the screw (q / p) =……… mm

Least Count of Spherometer

4. Total number of divisions on the circular scale (N) =……… mm
5. Least count (LC) of the spherometer $= \dfrac{\text{Pitch of the spherometer screw}}{\text{Number of divisions on the circular scale}}$

$$= \frac{\text{Pitch of the screw}}{N} = \text{………}\ \text{cm}$$

Table for Measurement of Sagitta (h)

S.N.	Curved surface reading				Plane surface reading				Mean corrected reading, $H = h_1 - h_2$
	MSR x (cm)	CSD y (cm)	CSR $z = y \times$ LC (cm)	Curved surface total reading, $h_1 = x + z$ (cm)	MSR x' (cm)	CSD y' (cm)	CSR $z' = y' \times$ LC (cm)	Plane surface total reading, $h_2 = x' + z'$ (cm)	
1									H_1 = … cm
2									H_2 = … cm
3									H_3 = … cm
4									H_4 = … cm

Calculations

1. Mean distance (l) between two legs of spherometer, $\dfrac{AB + BC + CA}{3}$ =……… cm

   where, AB, BC and CA are measured distances of equilateral triangle ABC.
2. Mean corrected value of Sagitta, (H) $= \dfrac{H_1 + H_2 + H_3 + H_4}{4}$ =……… cm
3. Radius of curvature, (R) $= \dfrac{l^2}{6h} + \dfrac{h}{2}$ =……… cm

Result

The radius of curvature of given mirror = ……… cm.

PRECAUTIONS

1. *Before starting the experiment, you must examine the spherometer properly.*
2. *The screw of the spherometer should move freely without friction.*
3. *The screw should be moved only in one direction to avoid the backlash error.*
4. *Legs of spherometer must touch the spherical surface.*
5. *Screw present at centre must touch the curved or plane surface.*
6. *You must note the curved surface and plane surface readings carefully with proper sign.*

Sources of Error

1. The screw may have friction.
2. Graduations may not be uniform on scale.
3. Circular scale division may not be equal in size.
4. The main scale may not be exactly vertical.
5. Spherometer may have backlash error.

Viva-Voce

Q.1 Mention the purpose of using the spherometer.

Ans The purpose of using the spherometer is to measure the reading of curvature of spherical surface.

Q. 2 Define the term pitch of the spherometer.

Ans. Pitch of the spherometer can be defined as the distance between the consecutive strings of the screw taken parallel to the distance moved by the screw in one complete rotation of the circular scale.

Q. 3 Mention the formula through which you can calculate the least count of the spherometer.

Ans. The formula through which the least count of the spherometer can be calculated is given as

$$\text{Least count of the spherometer, (LC)} = \frac{\text{Pitch } (P)}{\text{Total number of divisions on the circular scale}}.$$

Q. 4 State the conditions to decrease the least count of a spherometer.

Ans. The followings are the conditions to decrease the least count of a spherometer

(i) By decreasing the pitch.

(ii) By increasing the number of divisions on the circular scale.

Q. 5 What do you think, what can be a reason of using the good spherometer made of gun metal?

Ans. In order to reduce the wearing and tearing, the good spherometers are made up of gun metals.

Q. 6 What is the formula for the determination of radius of curvature with the help of a spherometer?

Ans. The formula for the determination of radius of curvature is

$$R = \frac{l^2}{6h} + \frac{h}{2}$$

where, h is Sagitta and l is the length of the sides of an equilateral triangle formed by the tips of the legs of spherometer.

Note The term $h/2$ may safely be dropped in case of surfaces of large radii of curvature.

Q. 7 In which way, the accuracy of a spherometer can be increased?

Ans. As we know that, the least count of an instrument is always inversely proportional to its accuracy. So, lesser the least count of spherometer, greater will be its accuracy. Besides this, accuracy of the spherometer can be increased by increasing the number of divisions on circular scale and also by decreasing the pitch.

Q. 8 Which is the most necessary precaution that is to be followed while performing this experiment?

***Or* How the backlash error can be avoided?**

Ans. While performing this experiment, we should rotate the circular scale in one direction in one go only, in order to avoid backlash error.

Q. 9 Explain the reason, why does the spherometer consist of three legs?

Ans. A spherometer has three legs, so that it forms an equilateral triangle. The three legs of the spherometer are used for measuring both positively and negatively curved surfaces.

Q.10 Is it possible to measure the focal length of a lens by using radius of curvature? [NCERT]

Ans. Yes it is possible. As we know that focal length of a lens is given by

$$\frac{1}{f} = \left(\frac{n_2}{n_1} - 1\right)\left(\frac{1}{R_1} - \frac{1}{R_2}\right)$$

Measuring R_1 and R_2 by spherometer ($n_1 = 1$, n_2 = known index of material of a lens) the focal length of a lens can be known.

Q.11 Why do you require a small sized plate for measurements of thickness with spherometer? [NCERT]

Ans. The size of the plate has to be small, so that the three outer legs can rest on a bigger horizontal plate on which the experimental small sized plate can be placed and the central screw tip can rest on the experimental plate.

Q.12 Two surfaces A and B have radii of curvature of 80 cm and 150 cm, respectively. Which surface is more curved? [NCERT]

Ans. Surface A will be more curved.

Experiment 7

AIM

To determine the mass of two different objects using a beam balance.

Apparatus and Materials Required

A physical balance, weight box with a set of milligram masses, forceps, two objects whose masses are to be determined and spirit level.

Description of Apparatus

Physical Balance

A physical balance is a device that measures the weight (or gravitational mass) of an object by comparing it with a standard weight (or standard gravitational mass). The most common form of physical balance is two-pans beam. It is based on the application of **lever**. It is the first order in which the fulcrum is in middle, when the beam is horizontal.

$$\text{Force} \times \text{Force arm} = \text{Weight} \times \text{Weight arm}$$

In this balance, force arm = weight arm

$$\therefore \quad \text{Force } (P) = \text{Weight } (w)$$

The setup of a physical balance in laboratories is shown below

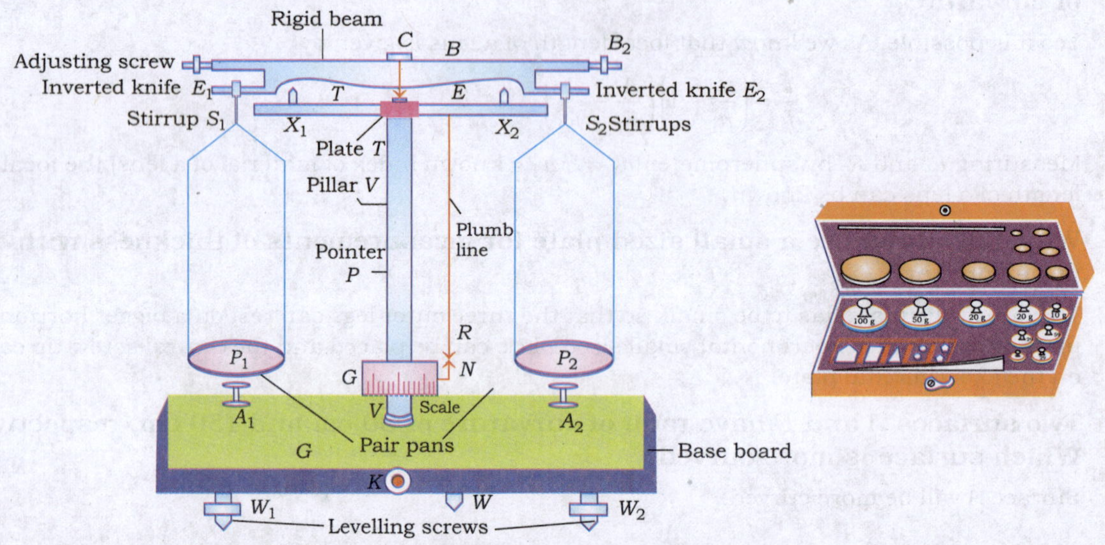

A physical balance and a weight box

Theory/Principle

The physical balance works on the **principle of moments**. In a physical balance, the two arms are of equal length and the mass of two pans are also equal. On keeping the knob at ON position and if the pans are empty, then the beam remains at horizontal position. When we place a mass on left pan, the beam moves in anti-clockwise direction that means the left pan moves downward. Now, by putting suitable standard known mass on right pan so that, the equilibrium is maintained between the two pans, we will be able to calculate the mass present at the left pan.

Thus, if an object whose mass m is to be determined is placed on the left pan and a standard mass mg is placed on the right pan, then

If both the arms are of equal length, then the weight of the body in one pan = weight of the body in other pan

i.e. $m_1 g = m_2 g$ (m_2 = standard known mass)

$\Rightarrow$ $m_1 = m_2$ (g = acceleration due to gravity = 9.8 m/s^2)

Thus, the mass in one pan is equal to the standard known mass of the other pan.

Procedure

To Measure the Mass of an Object

1. Open the shutter of the glass case of the balance. Put the object whose mass (*m*) is to be measured on the left hand pan. Add a suitable standard mass say m_1, on the right hand pan of the balance in **its rest (or arrested) position**, i.e. when the beam *B* is lowered and allowed to rest on stoppers X_1 and X_2. Always use forceps for taking out the standard mass from the weight box and for putting them back.

Note The placement of standard masses on right pan and the object whose weight is to be measured on left pan is an arbitrary choice. It has been chosen due to the ease in handling the standard masses. The person who is left handed can choose the left pan for standard masses and right pan for an object whose mass is to be measured.

2. Using the knob *K*, gently raise the beam (now the beam's knife edge *E* will rest on plate *T* fixed on the top of the pillar *V*) and observe the motion of the pointer *P*. It might rest on one side of the scale or might oscillate more in one direction with reference to the central zero mark on the scale *G*.
3. Check whether m_1 is more than *m* or less. For this purpose, the beam needs to be raised to the full extent.
4. Arrest the physical balance. Using forceps, replace the standard masses kept in the right pan by another mass (say m_2). It should be lighter if m_1 is more than the mass *m* and *vice-versa*.
5. Raise the beam and observe the motion of the pointer *P* and check whether the standard mass m_2 kept on the right-hand pan is still heavier (or lighter) than the mass *m*, so that the pointer oscillates more in one direction. If so, repeat step (11) using some other standard mass (say m_3 this time) in gram till the pointer swings nearly equal on both sides of the central zero mark on scale *G*.
   Make the standard masses kept on right-hand pan to be slightly lesser than the mass of the object. This would result in the measurement of mass *m* of the object with a precision of 1 g. Lower the beam *B*.

Observations

Observation for First Object

S.N.	Standard mass		Mass of the object, $m = a + b$ (g)
	Gram weight, a (G)	Milligram weight, b (mg)	
1			m_1 = ...
2			m_2 = ...
3			m_3 = ...

Observation for Second Object

S.N.	Standard mass		Mass of the object, $m = a + b$ (g)
	Gram weight, a (g)	Milligram weight, b (mg)	
1			m_1 = ………
2			m_2 = ………
3			m_3 = ………

Calculations

Mass of the object in gram = ... g, Mass of the object in milligram = ... mg

Total mass of the object = Mass of the object in gram + Mass of the object in milligram × 10^{-3}

Mean mass of the object $= \dfrac{m_1 + m_2 + m_3}{3}$ = ... g

Result

1. The mass of the first object by physical balance is ... g.
2. The mass of the second object by physical balance = ... g.

PRECAUTIONS

1. *All the parts of physical balance should be clean and dry, so that the friction between the parts of the beam balance can be minimised.*
2. *The error in the measurement can also be occurred due to the friction between the knife edge E and plate T. The friction can be minimised by making the knife-edge sharp and plate T smooth.*
3. *Pan must stay at rest position while taking the observations. If they swing, then the swinging may be stopped by touching the pan with the finger carefully.*
4. *The physical balance should not be used to measure masses more than 250 g.*
5. *Weighing of hot and cold bodies using a physical balance should be avoided. Similarly, active substances like chemicals, liquids and powders should not be kept directly on the pan.*
6. *The forceps used to load/unload the weights should be free from dust particles.*

Sources of Error

1. The balance may have lower accuracy.
2. The weights used may not be standard.
3. Some errors may be introduced due to the friction at the various parts of the balance.
4. The accuracy of the physical balance is 1 mg. This limits the possible instrumental error (± 0.005 g) in the measurement of mass.

Viva-Voce

Q. 1 Differentiate between mass and weight of the body.

Ans. Mass is the measure of the amount of matter in an object while weight is the force with which the earth attracts a mass towards its centre.

Q. 2 State some characteristics of a true balance.

Ans. Some characteristics of a true balance are:

(i) In order to attain stable equilibrium, the centre of gravity of the beam should be just below the fulcrum.

(ii) Both the arms must be of equal lengths. (iii) Both the pans must be of equal masses.

Q. 3 How can you define the sensitivity of a physical balance?

Ans. The sensitivity of a physical balance means that it can detect a change of 1 mg in the masses kept in the pan or it is possible to determine the mass with a precision of 1 mg.

Q. 4 State the variation of density with temperature.

Ans. Since, for the same mass, volume of a body increases due to thermal expansion. So, due to this reason, the density of a substance decreases with rise in temperature.

Q. 5 What is the working principle of a beam balance?

Ans. According to the working principle of a beam balance, in equilibrium, the clockwise moment due to standard masses is equal to the anti-clockwise moment due to unknown mass.

Q. 6 Mention the reason of not handling the weights using forceps by bare hands.

Ans. If some grease or dirt gets transferred on the weights from our hands then it might result into the change in its mass. So, the object will not be weighed accurately. So, that's why, the weights should be handled carefully with forceps.

Q. 7 What is the usage of balancing screws of the beam at its extreme two ends?

Ans. The balancing screws at the two ends of the beam are adjusted only if the swing of the pointer on the either side of the zero mark is not equal.

Q. 8 State the principle of moments.

Ans. According to this principle, the bodies of equal weight suspended at the equal distances from the fulcrum on the two sides of the beam keep the beam horizontal.

Q. 9 What is difference between a physical balance and an ordinary Grocer's balance?

Ans. Grocer's balance is used to measure large quantities of masses but a physical balance can measure small masses of the order of milligram accurately.

Q. 10 What is the stability of a balance?

Ans. A balance is said to be stable if its beam returns quickly to its original position after it gets slightly displaced.

Q. 11 What are the requisities of a good balance?

Ans. Truth, sensitivity and stability are the three requisities of a good balance.

Q. 12 What is the mass of a body that weighs 10 N at a place, where $g = 10\ \text{ms}^{-2}$?

Ans. We know, $w = mg$ or $m = \frac{w}{g} = \frac{10\ \text{N}}{10\ \text{ms}^{-2}} = 1\ \text{kg}$

Q. 13 How will you find the true mass of a body with such a balance?

Ans. The body is first weighed in one pan and then in the other. If w_1 and w_2 are observed weights and w the true weight of the body. Then $w = \sqrt{w_1 w_2}$.

Q. 14 There are two physical balances : (a) one with equal arms and other with unequal arms. Which one should be preferred? (b) What additional steps do you need to take to use a physical balance with unequal arms? [NCERT]

Ans. (a) The balance with equal arms is preferred.

(b) In the case of balance with unequal arms, length of the two arms should also be measured for appliying the principle of moments to get the mass of a body.

Q. 15 Instead of placing the mass (say a steel block) on the pan, suppose it is hanged from the same hook S_1 on which the pan P_1 is hanging. Will the value of the measured mass be same or different? [NCERT]

Ans. No, the value of the measured mass will be different and also be inaccurate because hanging the mass on the beam balance can disrupt the equilibrium by changing the moment of force or torque on both the sides.

Q. 16 Why it is necessary to close the shutters of the glass case for an accurate measurement? [NCERT]

Ans. For an accurate measurement, it is necessary to close the shutters of the glass case because air may enter in the weighing box which may affect the accurate measurement of the substance.

Experiment 8

AIM

To find the weight of the given body using parallelogram law of vectors.

Apparatus and Materials Required

Sheets of white paper, a meter scale, protractor, a spring balance, Gravesand's apparatus (parallelogram law of vector apparatus), a string or a strong thread, a body of unknown weight, slotted weights with hangers, set squares, a strip of plane mirror and plumbline.

Description of Apparatus

Gravesand's Apparatus

In the laboratory, the Gravesand's apparatus is used to determine the unknown weight of the body by verifying the **parallelogram law of vactors.** This apparatus can also be used to verify the **triangle law** and **Lami's theorem.** The Gravesand's apparatus is shown below

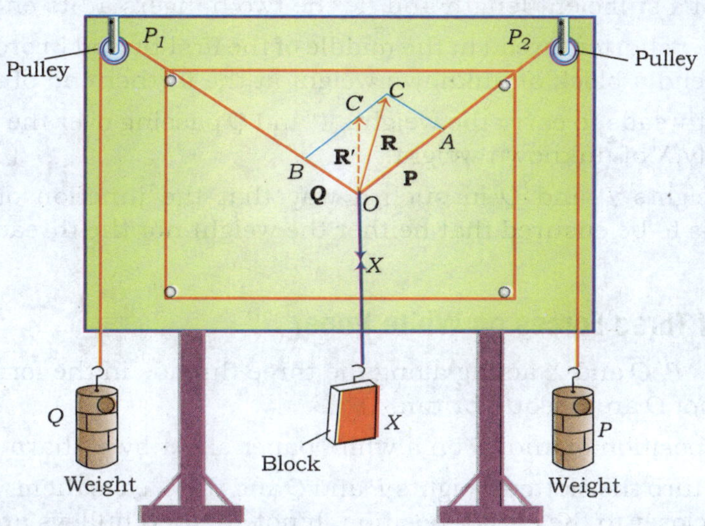

Theory/Principle

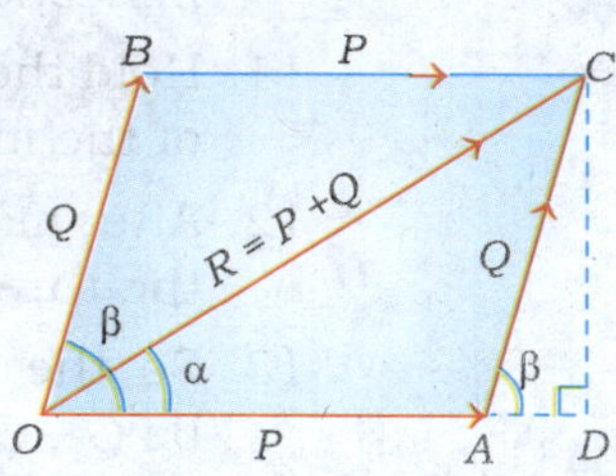

The working principle of Gravesand's apparatus is based on the **parallelogram law of vector addition**. According to this law,

"When two forces act simultaneously at a point and are represented in magnitude and direction by the two adjacent sides of a parallelogram, then the resultant of forces can be represented both in magnitude and direction by the diagonal of the parallelogram passing through the point of application of the two forces"

If **P** and **Q** are two vectors acting simultaneously on a particle placed at a point *O* at an angle β as shown in figure, then these two vectors will be represented by the two sides of the triangle *OAC*, i.e. *OA* represents **P** and *AC* represents **Q** and the third side will represent the resultant vector **R** of these two vectors **P** and **Q**, i.e. *OC* represents the resultant vector **R** in the figure. Thus, the resultant vector **R** is given by

$$\mathbf{R} = \mathbf{P} + \mathbf{Q} \qquad \text{...(i)}$$

The magnitude of the resultant **R** can be calculated as

$$R = \sqrt{P^2 + Q^2 + 2PQ \cos \beta} \qquad \text{...(ii)}$$

Procedure

Setting Up the Apparatus

1. Firstly check whether the pulleys are fixed or not. If not, then fix them gently and ensure that they are moving smoothly.
2. Now, set up the Gravesand's apparatus along with its board in a vertical position with the help of plumbline.
3. After fixing the board, fix a white sheet paper on the wooden board with the help of drawing pins.
4. Take a thread of a sufficient length and tie the two hangers at its ends.
5. Again, tie another shorter thread in the middle of the first thread in order to make knot at *O*. After this, suspend a block of unknown weight at the farther end of thread.
6. Now, make the threads to carry the weights *P* and *Q* passing over the pulleys and the third thread with body *X* of unknown weight.
7. Arrange the weights *P* and *Q* in such a way that the junction or knot *O* remains in equilibrium. It is to be ensured that neither the weight nor the threads touch the board or the table.

Taking Impression of Three Forces on White Paper

8. Now the weights *P*, *Q* and *X* acting along the three threads in the form of three forces **P, Q** and **X** at the knot *O* are in equilibrium.
9. Now, mark the position of knot *O* on a white paper sheet by a sharp pencil.
10. Now slightly disturb the slotted weights *P* and *Q* and then leave them. Note the position of *O* that should be closer to the earlier position. If not so, then pulleys are not frictionless and hence, they are to be lubricated with oil.
11. Hold the mirror strip lengthwise under each thread and then mark the position of the ends of the image of thread formed in the mirror.
12. After marking the position of the ends of the thread image in the mirror, cover the image by the thread. This helps to keep away from parallax error.
13. So, the respective positions for thread of weight *P* would be P_1, P_2 and for thread of weight *Q* be Q_1, Q_2 and for thread of weight *X* be X_1, X_2 .

14. Now, remove the hangers and note the weight of each hanger and slotted weights on them with the help of spring balance.

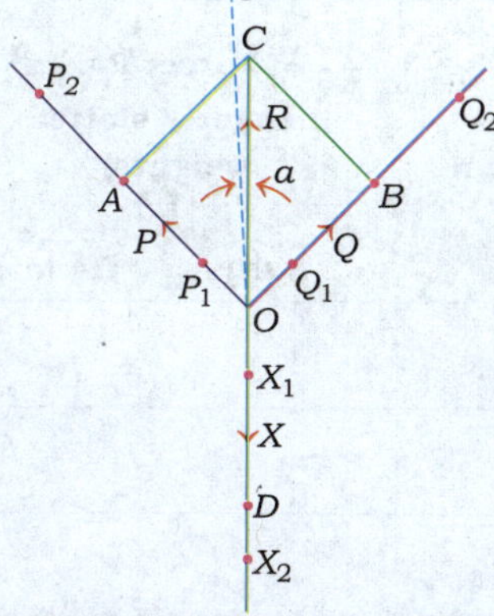

Determination of weight of

Drawing of Parallelogram

15. Detach the white paper sheet from board. Join the three pairs of points marked on the paper to meet at *O*, as shown in the figure.
16. With the help of set squares, complete the parallelogram *OACB* and join the points *O* and *C* to get the line *OC*.

Note Check whether the line *OC* is exactly along the straight line *XO* or not. If not, then let it meet with *BC* at some point *C'* and measure the angle *COC'* with the help of protractor. Choose a suitable scale say 0.5 N (50 g-wt) = 1 cm and cut off length *OA* and *OB* to represent the forces *P* and *Q* respectively acting at point *O*. It should be ensured that the parallelogram, we have drawn covers the maximum area of sheet.

17. After joining the line *OC*, we will get the resultant **R** of all three forces.

Measurement of the Weight of the Body

18. Now measure the dimensions of *OC* (in cm) and then find the value of weight of the body (w_1) by multiplying the dimensions of *OC* with the selected scale as given below.

    Geometrically, weight, $w_1 = OC \times 50\,\text{gwt}$ [$\because$ 1 cm = 50 g-wt = 0.5 N]
19. If the condition of angle β is occurred, then measure the weight (w_2) by using parallelogram law of vector addition as

$$w_2 = \sqrt{P^2 + Q^2 + 2PQ\cos\beta}$$

20. Take different sets of observations by changing the weights *P* and *Q* and then perform the above steps again.
21. Now find the mean weight of the various weights that were calculated geometrically, and then mean of those weights which has been determined by the parallelogram law of vector addition. Hence, the weight of the body is given by

$$w = \frac{w_1 + w_2}{2}$$

    where, w_1 = mean of those weights which were calculated geometrically and

    w_2 =mean of those weights which were calculated by parallelogram law of vector addition.
22. Next, measure the weight of the body (say *w'*) with the help of a spring balance. This is essential to determine thereby the percentage error can be found.

Note Zero error of the spring balance should be taken into account while measuring the weight of the body.

Observations and Calculations

Scale 1 cm = ... N.

Zero error of the spring balance = ... g-wt.

Zero error correction = ... g-wt.

Weight of each hanger = ... N.

Table for the Weight of the Given Body

S. N.	Force, P (hanger + slotted weights)		Force, Q (hanger + slotted weights)		Dimensions of $OC = R$ (cm)	Unknown weight of given body, (N) = $OC \times 50$ gwt	Angle COC' (β)	Unknown weight, $w_2 = \sqrt{P^2 + Q^2 + 2PQ\cos\beta}$
	P (N)	OA (cm)	Q (N)	OB (cm)				

Measurement of the Weight of the Body

Dimensions of OC = ... cm.

Mean weight as determined geometrically, w_1 = ... N.

Mean weight as determined by the parallelogram law, w_2 = ... N.

Hence, the weight of the body, $w = \frac{w_1 + w_2}{2}$ = ... N.

Determination of the Percentage Error

To find the percentage error, measure the weight (w') of the body with the help of spring balance and then put the values in the formula given below.

$$\text{Percentage error} = \frac{\text{Actual value} - \text{Experimental value}}{\text{Actual value}} \times 100$$

$$= \frac{w' - w}{w} \times 100 = \text{.........} \ \%$$

Result

The determined (or unknown) weight of the body, w = ... N.

PRECAUTIONS

1. *The Gravesand's apparatus should be stable and set vertically with the help of plumbline.*
2. *Frictionless pulley should be used.*
3. *Neither weights nor threads should touch the board.*
4. *The knot (or junction) should be in the middle of the paper in order to achieve exact dimensions of parallelogram so as to reduce the error in the measurement.*
5. *Marking of the points on the white sheet of paper should be done with the sharp pencil and this marking should be done when threads and the weight come to rest.*
6. *The threads should exactly cover their image formed in the mirror strips placed under them.*
7. *The zero error of the spring balance should be taken into account while measuring the weights.*

Sources of Error

1. The knot may not be in the middle of the paper, which leads to incorrect dimensions and ultimately to the error in the measurement.
2. There may be an inaccuracy while marking the points on the white sheet of paper.
3. The pulleys may not be free to rotate.
4. The measurement of weight may not be accurate.
5. Error due to parallax.

Q 1 What can be the reason for keeping the suspended weights free from board or table?

Ans. The suspended weights are kept free from the board or table because of their effective weight which may not become different due to reaction of the board or table.

Q. 2 Define polygonal law of vector addition.

Ans. It is defined as the number of vectors represented in the magnitude and the direction by the sides of the polygon taken in cyclic order. So, the side (closed one) of the polygon in the reverse order will represent the magnitude and the direction of resultant vector.

Q. 3 What do you understand by resolution of vectors?

Ans. The reverse of the composition of vectors or the breaking of a single vector into its components is called resolution of vectors.

Q. 4 "Gravesand's apparatus, a proper device for measuring weights". Do you agree with this statement? Give the reason.

Ans. No, because it is an indirect method. Moreover, the pulleys are not completely frictionless and the threads are not massless, which is impossible to achieve.

Q. 5 Define the equilibrant vector.

Ans. A single vector which balances the other vectors is called the equilibrant of other vectors. Also, it must be equal and opposite of the resultant of other vectors.

Q.6 What is the other method to add two vectors except the parallelogram law of vector addition?

Ans. Except the parallelogram law of vector addition, there is one more method to add two vectors i.e. triangular law of vector addition.

Q. 7 What can be the necessary condition to attain the equilibrium?

Ans. When a body is said to be in translational equilibrium, then there would not be any resultant force acting on the body, i.e. the body will have no acceleration. In the same way, the body will be in rotational equilibrium, when the resultant torque on it, is zero.

Q. 8 What is the way to verify parallelogram law of vector addition from Gravesand's apparatus?

Ans. In this case, the hanger weight system will be used due to which the resultant obtained by the parallelogram law of vectors will be equivalent to the considered hanger weight system.

Q. 9 What does the point of intersection of strings in the setup represent?

Ans. The equilibrium point of all forces acting on the body.

Q.10 Can the resultant of the two forces of 7 N and 5 N be 1 N?

Ans. No, the resultant of 7 N and 5 N will be between 7 + 5 = 12 N and 7 – 5 = 2 N. Since, 1 N does not come in this range, therefore, the resultant of 7 N and 5 N cannot be 1 N.

Q.11 What is Lami's theorem?

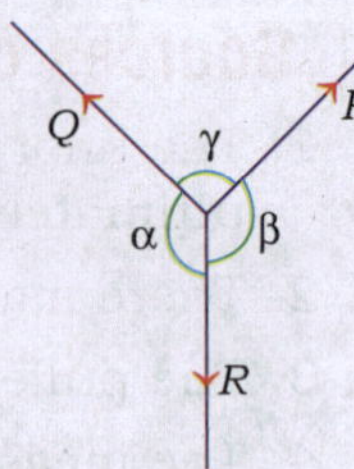

Ans. It states that, if three forces acting simultaneously on a body are in equilibrium, then each is proportional to the sine of the angle between the other two.

Stated mathematically, as

$$\frac{P}{\sin\alpha} = \frac{Q}{\sin\beta} = \frac{R}{\sin\gamma}$$

Q.12 Do you mean that a body in equilibrium has to be necessarily at rest?

Ans. No, a body in uniform motion can also be in equilibrium. The condition for equilibrium is that there is no net force acting on the body, i.e. there is no acceleration produced in the body.

Q.13 How will you check whether there is friction at the pulleys or not?

Ans. Give a slight disturbance by pulling down the middle hanger. If the common junction, occupies the same position of rest on the paper, then the pulleys are almost frictionless.

Q.14 What are the main sources of error in the experiments using Gravesand's apparatus?

Ans. (i) Friction at the pulleys. (ii) Thread cannot be weightless.

Q.15 Why is the force due to the weight of the body resolved into two components?

Ans. To apply vector addition using the parallelogram law.

Q.16 State the parallelogram law of vector addition? [NCERT]

Ans. According to this law "when two forces act simultaneously at a point and are represented in magnitude and direction by the two adjacent sides of a parallelogram, then the resultant of forces can be represented both in magnitude and direction by the diagonal of the parallelogram passing through the point of application of the two forces".

Q.17 In which situation, the parallelogram can be a rhombus? [NCERT]

Ans. A parallelogram can be a rhombus if and only if both the forces acting on it is equal.

Q.18 If all three forces are equal in magnitude, how will the parallelogram modify? [NCERT]

Ans. If all the three forces are equal in magnitude, then the direction of diagonal of parallelogram (which gives the resultant force) gets reversed in opposite direction. Consider the figure.

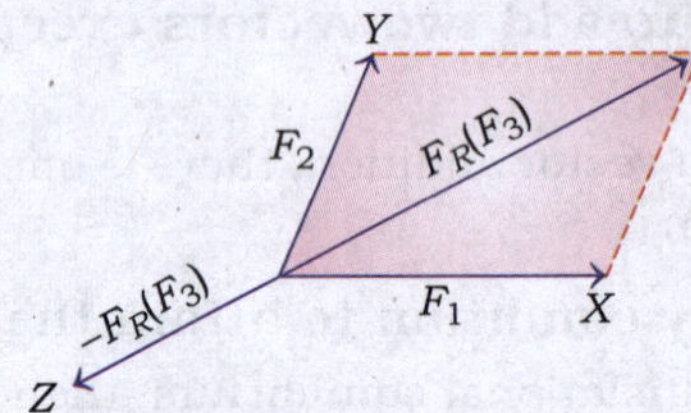

So, we can see, if $\mathbf{F_1}$, $\mathbf{F_2}$ and $\mathbf{F_3}$ or $\mathbf{F}_R$ are acting in same direction, the reversed direction of diagonal of parallelogram is given by $-\mathbf{F}_R$.

Q.19 When the knot is in equilibrium position, is any force acting on the pulleys? [NCERT]

Ans. When the knot is in equilibrium position, then there will be a force (normal reaction) which will be acting on the pulleys but the resultant force on the knot in the equilibrium position will be zero.

Experiment 9

AIM

Using a simple pendulum, plot L-T^2 graph and use it to find the effective length of second's pendulum.

Apparatus and Materials Required

Clamp stand, a heavy metallic bob (brass/iron), strong cotton thread/string of about 2.0 m, stopwatch / stop clock, meter scale, vernier calliper, graph paper.

Note Since, the least count of stopwatch is much less than that of stop clock, therefore in laboratory, stop watch is usually preferred.

Terms Related to Experiment

Simple Pendulum

A simple pendulum is one which can be considered to be a point mass (bob) suspended from an inextensible string or rod of negligible mass. Simple pendulum (if practically defined) has a heavy mass bob of brass and of radius r much smaller than the length of suspension. This bob is suspended with the help of thin, strong cotton thread from a rigid support.

Amplitude of Simple Pendulum Amplitude of the simple pendulum can be defined as the maximum displacement from its mean position to the extreme position.

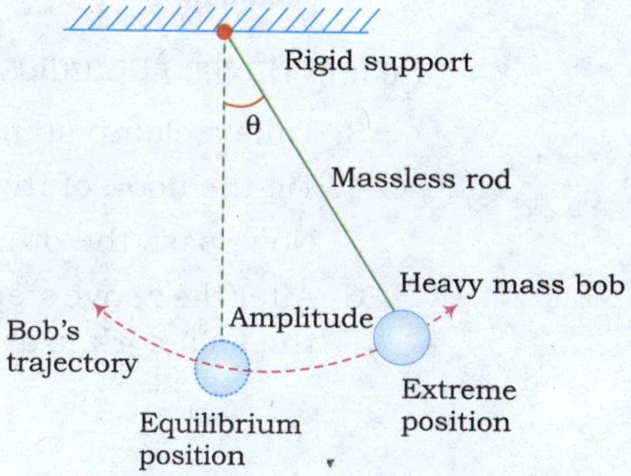

Oscillation The movement of bob from one extreme position to another and again return back at the first extreme position is called one complete oscillation.

Frequency of Simple Pendulum It can be defined as the number of complete oscillations performed by the bob in 1 s. Its SI unit is s^{-1} or Hz.

Effective Length of Simple Pendulum Effective length of simple pendulum is the total length (L) from the point of suspension of pendulum to the centre of gravity of metallic bob.

Rigid support
θ
Massless rod
Heavy mass bob
Bob's trajectory
Amplitude
Extreme position
Equilibrium position

Simple pendulum

i.e. Total length (L) = Length of thread (l) + radius of metallic bob (r) + length of the hook (e).

$$\Rightarrow \qquad L = l + r + e$$

Second's Pendulum

The pendulum having time period of two seconds is called second's pendulum. It means that it takes precisely one second to move from one extreme position to other.

Theory/Principle

Simple pendulum executes **Simple Harmonic Motion** (SHM) as the acceleration of the bob at any instant is directly proportional to its displacement from the mean position at that instant and directed towards the mean position. The time taken by it to complete one full oscillation is called the **time period of simple pendulum**.

It is denoted by T and can be given by the relation

$$T = 2\pi\sqrt{\frac{L}{g}} \qquad \ldots(i)$$

where, L = effective length of simple pendulum and g = acceleration due to gravity.

Since, we know that if the simple pendulum has the time period of 2 s, then it becomes second's pendulum. For second's pendulum, $T = 2$ s. So, after considering the above equation, it can be written as

$$L = \frac{gT^2}{4\pi^2} = \frac{980 \times (2)^2}{4 \times (3.14)^2} = 99.39 \text{ cm}$$

Thus, the length of the second's pendulum is 99.39 cm.

From the result, $L = \frac{gT^2}{4\pi^2}$, it is also clear that **graph between L and T^2 will be a straight line.**

Procedure

Initial Observations Before Setting Up the Apparatus

1. Find out the vernier constant and zero error of the vernier callipers and determine the mean diameter and hence, mean radius of the spherical bob as discussed in Experiment 1.
2. Find the length (e) of the hook with the help of meter scale and record this observation.

Note The radius of the bob and the length of hook are essential to determine to know the effective length of simple pendulum.

Setting Up the Apparatus and Measurement of Effective Length

3. Take a clamp stand and place it on the table at its edge.
4. Tie the hook of the bob to one end of the string of about 150 cm in length.
5. Now, pass the other end of string through two half-pieces of a split cork.
6. After the above step, firmly fix the cork in the clamp stand, such that the line of separation of the split cork is at right angle to the line OA along which the pendulum oscillates.

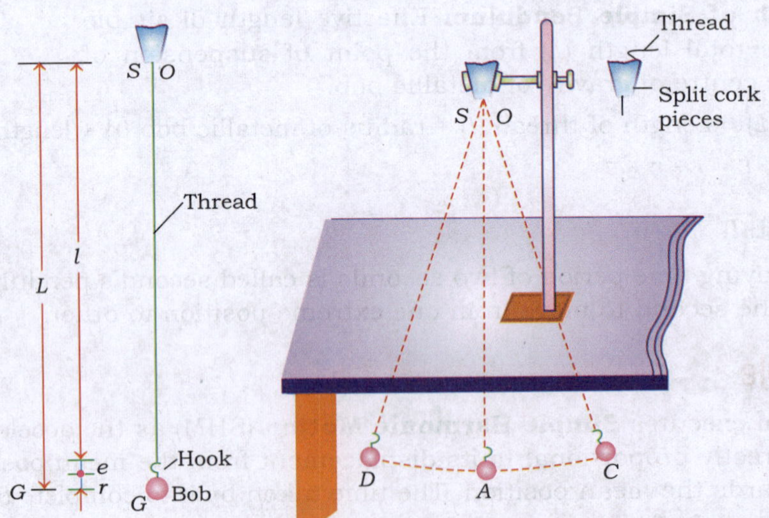

Effective length, $L = l + r + e$

In this figure, points D and C are showing the extreme positions

7. Fix the cork in such a way that the thread hangs in front of the edge of the table vertically about 2 cm above the floor. Here, it is to be ensured that the bob and the thread hang freely (or without touching the table) beyond the edge of the table so that the bob can oscillate without any obstruction.
8. Now, measure the effective length of simple pendulum. i.e. $L = l + r + e$.

Measurement of Number and Time of Oscillations

9. Mark a vertical line with a piece of chalk or ink on the edge of the table along the vertical thread *OA*. This line should be marked just behind the thread. This line is marked to know the mean or rest position of the bob.
10. Find the least count and zero error of the stopwatch/clock and then achieve the zero position of its hands.
11. Now, displace the bob to one side, not more than 15° of angular displacement from the vertical position *OA* marked on the table and release it gently.
12. Keep the pendulum oscillating for sometime. After completion of few oscillations, start the stopwatch when the thread attached to the pendulum bob just crosses the mean position *OA*.
13. On starting the stopwatch or stop clock, keep on counting the number of oscillations every time, it crosses the mean position *OA* in the same direction as we had started the stopwatch. It means that if we move the bob from right extreme position *C* towards *A*, then count one oscillation when the bob again crosses the position *A* towards *C* after coming from the left extreme position *D*.
14. Read the total time taken by the bob for n oscillations.
15. Repeat it few times (the above step) by noting the time for same number of oscillations and take its mean value.
16. Now, calculate the time taken for one complete oscillation,
17. Again, differ the length of pendulum by 10 cm and repeat the above steps to calculate its time period for one oscillation.

Note In this case, the effective length will also be changed, so it has to be calculated again.

18. At last, plot the graph by taking L along X-axis and T^2 along Y-axis, by using observed values.

Observations and Calculations

Least Count and Zero Error of the Vernier Calliper

Vernier constant or least count of the vernier calliper = ... cm.

Zero error (if any) of the vernier calliper = ... cm.

Zero error correction of the vernier calliper (Z) = ... cm.

Finding the Mean Radius of the Pendulum

Mean observed diameter of the bob, d = ... cm.

Mean observed corrected diameter of the bob, $d_0 = d + Z$ = ... cm.

Mean radius (r) of the pendulum bob = $\frac{d_0}{2}$ = ... cm.

Effective Length of the Pendulum

Least count of the meter scale = ... mm = ... cm.

Length of the hook (e) .... cm.

Length of the thread, l = ... cm.

Effective length of the simple pendulum, $L = l + e + r$ = ... cm.

Time Period of Oscillation

Least count of the stopwatch/clock = ... s. Number of oscillations, n = ... cm.

Time taken to complete n oscillations, t = ... s.

Time taken for one complete oscillation (time period), $T = t/n$ = ... s.

Table to Measure Time Period T and Effective Length L of the Simple Pendulum

S. N.	Length of the thread from the top of bob to the point of suspension, l	Effective length (L), $L = l + r + e$		Number of oscillations, n	Time for n oscillations, t (s)				Time period, $T = (t / n)$
	(cm)	(cm)	(m)		(i)	(ii)	(iii)	Mean t(s)	s
1									
2									
3									
4									

Plotting Graph

Draw a graph L versus T^2 with the help of readings in the observation table. Take length of simple pendulum L along X-axis and time period along Y-axis. As a result, you will get a straight line passing through the origin.

From the L *versus* T^2 graph, locate the effective length of second's pendulum for

$$T^2 = 4\,\text{s}^2$$

[$\because$ For second pendulum, $T = 2$ s]

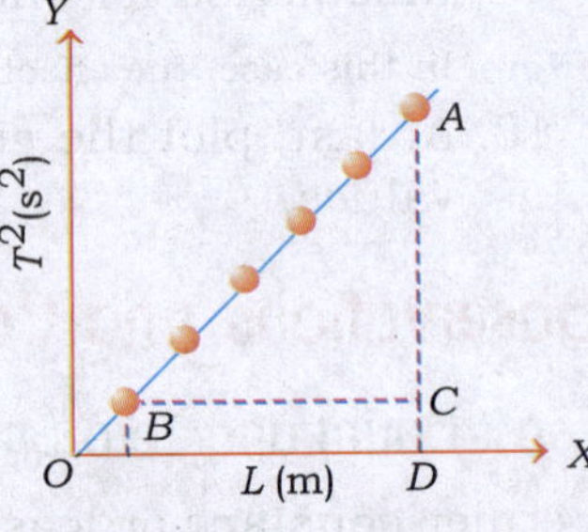

Graph of L *versus* T^2

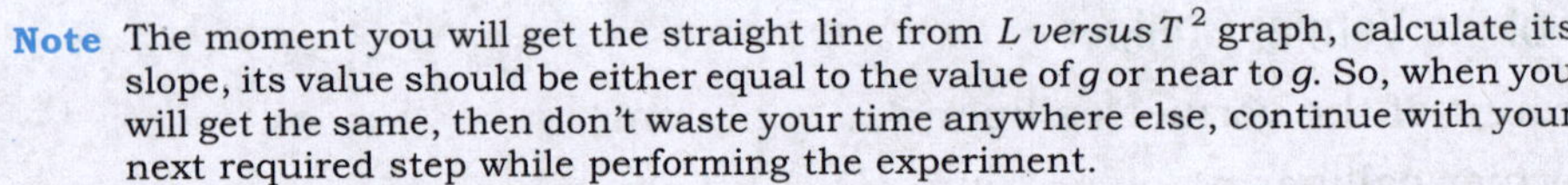

Note The moment you will get the straight line from L *versus* T^2 graph, calculate its slope, its value should be either equal to the value of g or near to g. So, when you will get the same, then don't waste your time anywhere else, continue with your next required step while performing the experiment.

Result

1. The graph L *versus* T^2 is a straight line.
2. The effective length of second's pendulum from L *versus* T^2 graph is ...... cm.

PRECAUTIONS

1. The zero error and least count of vernier calliper must be taken into account while measuring the mean radius of the pendulum bob.
2. The thread used should have negligible mass and it should be strong and inextensible.
3. The point where the thread is to be suspended, i.e. the point of suspension should be fixed in a rigid support.
4. The pendulum bob should move along a reference line without any jerky motion.
5. The place of the experiment should be free from any vibration even disturbance of air current can affect the readings.
6. The counting of oscillations should be from zero and the number of oscillations of pendulum bob should be of small amplitude.
7. The position of slot should be at the right angle to the plane of oscillations.
8. Test the stopwatch, it should be accurate and after the fly back action, the hands should achieve the zero mark accurately.
9. The point of suspension should be fixed in a rigid support.

Sources of Error

1. The observations taken from vernier calliper may be inaccurate.
2. Laboratory fan may be switched ON while performing the experiment which can produce air disturbances.
3. Stopwatch may be inaccurate.
4. Thread may be extensible.
5. Point of suspension may not be rigid.
6. The base of the stand may not be heavy.
7. Error may occur due to delay in starting and stopping the stopwatch.

Viva-Voce

Q 1 Which pendulum is independent of change in value of acceleration due to gravity (g) ?

Ans. A spring pendulum which works on inertia and elasticity, has no effect on its time period due to the change in value of g.

Q 2 What do you think, what can be the reason of decreasing amplitude of an oscillating pendulum?

Ans. When the pendulum oscillates, then it is only the air resistance due to which a part of energy is lost in every oscillation. As a result the amplitude of the pendulum gradually decreases and the oscillations die out slowly.

Q 3 What is ticker-tape timer?

Ans. It is a time measuring device which can measure the time intervals of the order of $\frac{1}{50}$ th or $\frac{1}{100}$ th of a second.

Q 4 **Define the effective length of simple pendulum.**

Ans. The distance between the point of suspension of pendulum and its centre of gravity is called effective length of simple pendulum.

Q 5 **What is the reason of keeping the small amplitude of oscillation?**

Ans. While deriving the expression for the time period of simple pendulum, we always consider $\sin\theta \simeq \theta$. So, it is possible only when θ is small. So, this is the reason of keeping the amplitude of oscillation small.

Q 6 **What effect can be observed if the same experiment is performed on the moon?**

Ans. The increase in time period will be observed. As we know that, the value of acceleration due to gravity on the moon is less than that on earth. Moreover, the value of g on the moon is 1/6 th of that on earth. i.e., $g_m = g_e/6$

Also, time period of a simple pendulum, $T = 2\pi\sqrt{L/g}$, which shows that the time period is inversely proportional to the acceleration due to gravity.

Q 7 **Why an inextensible string with negligible mass is usually preferred while performing the experiment?**

Ans. It is very difficult to obtain an ideal simple pendulum or perfect experimental set up. So, in order to achieve this, a massless and inextensible string is preferred.

Q 8 **How can you define simple pendulum?**

Ans. An ideal pendulum which consists of a heavy point mass (can be a bob) tied to one end of a perfectly inextensible, weightless thread suspended from a solid support is called simple pendulum.

Q 9 **Define the term damping.**

Ans. It is the opposition offered to the free vibrations of the bob of a simple pendulum due to the presence of air around it.

Q 10 **How can you define the second's pendulum?**

Ans. A pendulum whose time period is 2 s is called a second's pendulum.

Q.11. **Why does the time period of the pendulum become infinite in case of freely falling lift?**

Ans. Because in a freely falling lift, value of g is zero. According to the formula,

$$T = 2\pi\sqrt{\frac{L}{g}}$$

$T \to \infty$, when $g \to 0$

Q.12. **Why should the amplitude be small for a simple pendulum experiment?**

Ans. Because $T = 2\pi\sqrt{\frac{L}{g}}$ and this relation is based on the assumption that $\sin\theta \cong \theta$, which is truly only for small amplitude, such that value of θ lies between 0° to about 80°.

Q.13. **It is always advisable to start taking time period after a few variations, why do you not start with the very first vibration?**

Ans. During the first few vibrations, the bob is under the influence of external force used to set it into motion.

Accordingly, it is not vibrating with its natural time period. Hence, first few vibrations are not considered.

Q14. **What is the weight of a body at the centre of the earth?**

Ans. Zero, since weight = mg. At the centre of the earth, $g = 0$.

Q.15 What will happen, if the bob is made to vibrate in liquid? [NCERT]

Ans. Due to the upthrust of liquid, the effective weight and hence g will decrease and hence time period $\left(T = 2\pi\sqrt{\frac{l}{g}}\right)$ will increase

Q.16 Interpret the graphs between L and T^2 and also between L and T that you have drawn for simple pendulum. [NCERT]

Ans. Consider L *versus* T graph, it can be drawn as

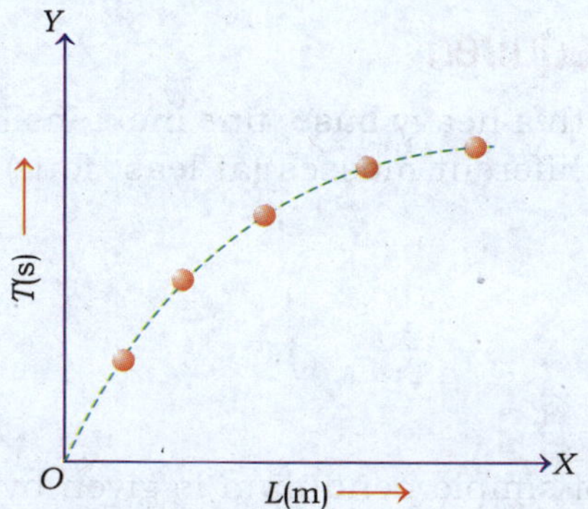

So, after taking length of the simple pendulum along X-axis and time period along Y-axis, we get the curve (or a part of parabola). It means that T is parabolically increased with respect to L.

Now, consider L *versus* T^2 graph,

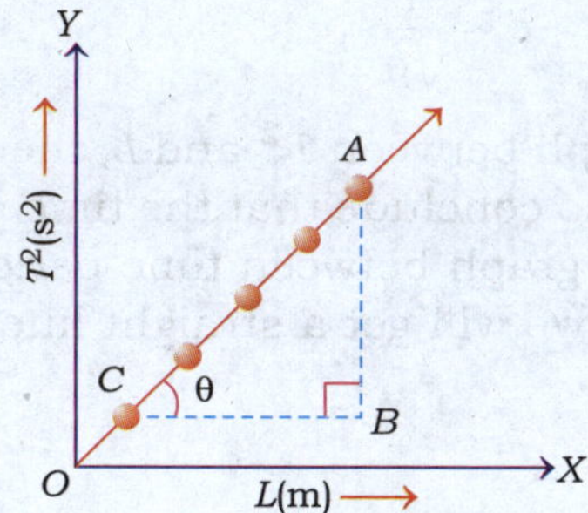

So, after taking length of simple pendulum along X-axis and time period along Y-axis, we get the straight line. It means that the time is linearly increased with respect to the length of simple pendulum.

Experiment 10

AIM

To study the variation of time period of a simple pendulum of a given length by taking bobs of same size but different masses and interpret the result.

Apparatus and Materials Required

A clamp and a long iron stand with a heavy base, fine inextensible thread, stopwatch/stopclock, meter scale, pendulum bobs of different masses (at least four) vernier calliper a split cork and spring balance.

Theory/Principle

Simple Pendulum

We know that, the time period of simple pendulum is given by, $T = 2\pi\sqrt{\frac{L}{g}}$

Here, the above formula shows that the time period of simple pendulum is independent of the amplitude of oscillation of pendulum.

So, it clearly indicates that $T \propto \sqrt{L} \Rightarrow T^2 \propto L$ ...(i)

and $T \propto \frac{1}{\sqrt{g}}$

Eq. (i) shows that, if we plot the graph between T^2 and L, then we will get a straight line passing through the origin. Here, we can also conclude that the time period of pendulum is independent of mass of the bob. So, if we plot a graph between time period (T) by taking it along Y-axis and mass (m) by taking it along X-axis, we will get a straight line parallel to X-axis.

Procedure

To Study the Measurement of Effective Length on the Time Period

1. Follow the steps (3) to (7) of Experiment 9 for determining the effect of change in effective length on the time period of the simple pendulum. Refer Fig. of Experiment 9 (Page 50).

To Study the Effect of Bobs of Different Masses on the Time Period

2. Firstly determine the least count and zero error of the spring balance. The zero error of spring balance is found by suspending it freely.
3. Now, find out the masses of different metallic bobs with the help of spring balance.
4. Now, repeat the above steps (1) to (18) of Experiment 9 with a constant length of pendulum while using the bobs of different masses.
5. After measuring, note down the time period of oscillation of the pendulum.

Observations and calculations

Calculations will be done in same way as Experiment (9).

Table to Measure the Time Period when Bobs of Different Masses are Used

S. N.	Length of the thread from the top of bob to the point of suspension, l	Effective length (L) $L = l + r + e$		Mass of the bob, m	Number of oscillations, n	Time for n oscillations, t (s)				Time period, $T = (t/n)$
	(cm)	(cm)	(m)			(i)	(ii)	(iii)	Mean t (s)	
Bob 1										
Bob 2										
Bob 3										
Bob 4										

r = Mean radius of the pendulum.

e = Length of the hook.

Note The effective length of the simple pendulum will be kept same in each case.

Plotting graph

From the observation table, if we plot a graph between L and T^2 by taking L along X-axis and T^2 along Y-axis, we will get a straight line graph passing through the origin. Refer Experiment 9 for graph L and T^2.

If we plot a graph between m and T by taking mass along X-axis and the time period along Y-axis, we will get a straight line parallel to X-axis.

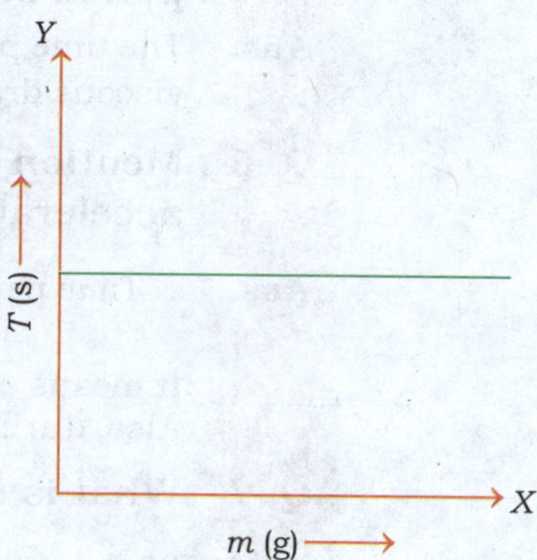

Graph between m and T

Result

1. From the graph between L and T^2, we notice that as the length of the pendulum increases, then the value of square of time period increases in a linear form with it.

   It means $T^2 \propto L$

   i.e. $T \propto \sqrt{L}$

2. From the graph between m and T, we notice that the time period for simple pendulum having bobs of different masses almost remains the same.

   So, we can say that the time period of a simple pendulum is independent of mass of the bob used.

PRECAUTIONS

Same as Experiment (9).

Sources of Error

Same as Experiment (9).

Viva-Voce

Q. 1 Whether a wall clock gain or lose time during summer.

Ans. A wall clock runs fast in winter and it loses its time during summer because its time period increases due to increase of length of the pendulum.

Q. 2 How can you define damping?

Ans. The opposition to the free vibrations of bob of a simple pendulum due to air presence around it, is known as damping.

Q. 3 State the working principle of simple pendulum.

Ans. A pendulum repeats its motion after regular interval of time. This constitutes the working principle of simple pendulum.

Q. 4 On which factors, does the time period of a simple pendulum depend?

Ans. The time period of a simple pendulum depends upon the following factors

(i) Length of the pendulum (ii) Acceleration due to gravity at that place.

Q. 5 Mention the effect of buoyancy of air and viscous drag due to air on the time period of the simple pendulum.

Ans. The time period of simple pendulum always increases due to the effect of buoyancy of air and viscous drag due to air.

Q. 6 Mention the relation between the time period of simple pendulum and the acceleration due to gravity.

Ans. $\because$ Time period of simple pendulum is given by $T = 2\pi\sqrt{\frac{L}{g}} \Rightarrow T \propto \frac{1}{\sqrt{g}}$

It means, as acceleration due to gravity g decreases at height and depth, time period T increases. Also, during free fall, when $g = 0$, then T becomes infinite.

Q. 7 What is the length of a second pendulum in terms of acceleration due to gravity?

Ans. We know that, $T = 2\pi\sqrt{\frac{L}{g}}$ $\quad \therefore \quad 2 = 2\pi\sqrt{\frac{L}{g}}$ [for a second's pendulum, $T = 2s$]

$$1 = \pi\sqrt{\frac{L}{g}},\ \frac{1}{\pi^2} = \frac{L}{g},\ L = \frac{g}{\pi^2}$$

Q. 8 Does the relation $T = 2\pi\sqrt{\frac{L}{g}}$ hold good for large amplitude?

Ans. No, it is applicable only if $\sin\theta = \theta$, i.e. its amplitude is small.

Q. 9 How is the effect due to buoyancy and viscous drag reduced?

Ans. This effect can be reduced to a large extent by taking a small heavy bob of a material of high density.

Q.10 How can you determine the value of g (acceleration due to gravity)? [NCERT]

Ans. To determine the value of g (acceleration due to gravity) from a T^2 *versus* l graph.

1. **Plot the graph** Plot T^2 (square of time period) on the Y-axis and l (length of the pendulum) on the X- axis.
2. **Find the slope** Calculate the slope of the straight line from the graph.
3. **Calculate** g using the formula, $g = \frac{4\pi^2}{\text{slope}}$.

Experiment 11

AIM

To study the relationship between force of limiting friction and normal reaction and to find the coefficient of friction between a block and a horizontal surface.

Apparatus and Materials Required

A frictionless pulley which can be fixed at the edge of the horizontal table, a wooden block with a hook, spirit level, a meter scale, a spring balance, weight box, a horizontal plane with a glass or a laminated table top, a fine thread.

Terms Related to Experiment

Friction

Whenever an object moves or tends to move over the surface of another object, then a force comes into play which acts parallel to the surface of the contact and opposes the relative motion. This tendency to oppose the relative motion between two surfaces is called friction.

Types of Friction

1. **Static friction** It is the friction between the two surfaces of bodies at rest due to impending motion.
2. **Limiting friction** It is the maximum value of static friction when one body is at the verge of moving over the surface of another body in contact with it.
3. **Dynamic (or kinetic) friction** It is the friction between the two surfaces of bodies when they are in relative motion. It is always less than the static friction.

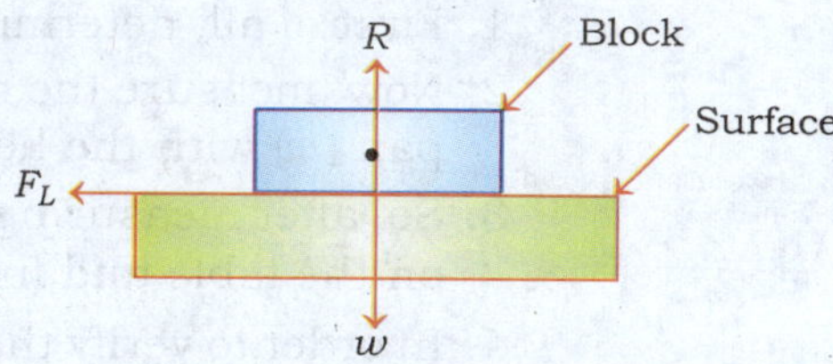

Body at rest due to static friction

Relationship between Force of Limiting Friction and Normal Reaction

The ratio of limiting friction (F_L) to the magnitude of normal reaction (R) is a constant known as **coefficient of limiting friction** (μ_L).

$$\mu_L = \frac{F_L}{R}$$

Thus, **the limiting friction is directly proportional to the normal reaction.** Hence, if we plot a graph between limiting friction F_L and the normal reaction R by taking them along Y and X-axes respectively, then we will get a straight line.

Theory/Principle

Consider a wooden block of suitable weight having hook at its one end, placed on the horizontal surface of the table. A thread is tied with the hook of block from the one end and at the other end of the thread passing through a frictionless pulley, a pan is tied.

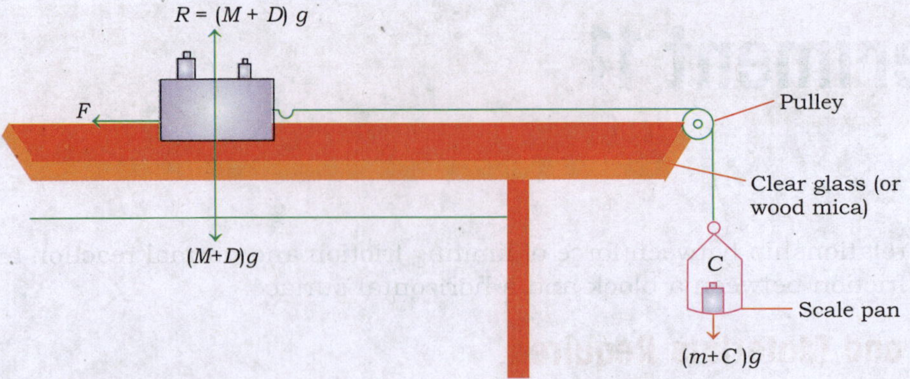

Experimental apparatus to study limiting friction

When the force is applied on the block in order to displace it (a little bit) from its rest position, then force of limiting friction comes into existence which is directly proportional to the normal reaction.

$$F_L \propto R \quad \text{or} \quad F_L = \mu_L R \Rightarrow \mu_L = \frac{F_L}{R} \qquad \ldots\text{(i)}$$

where, μ_L= coefficient of limiting friction between the two surfaces in contact.

From Eq. (i), it is clear that if we plot a graph between F and R, it should be a straight line.

Procedure

Setting up the Apparatus

1. First of all, determine the least count of the spring balance.
2. Now, measure the mass (M) of the given wooden block with hook on its sides and the scale pan (m) with the help of a spring balance.
3. So, after measuring the respective masses of wooden block and the scale pan, put the glass on the table and fix it horizontally by inserting a cardboard below it.
4. In order to verify that the top surface of the table is horizontal, use the spirit level. It is to be ensured that the top surface must be clean and dry.
5. Now, fix a frictionless pulley at the edge of table top and tie one extreme end of thread to a scale pan. Lubricate the pulley if required.
6. After this, tie the another extreme end of the thread to the hook of the wooden block.
7. Now, put the wooden block on the horizontal plane and pass the thread over the pulley.
8. It should be ensured that, there should be a horizontal portion of the thread between the pulley and the wooden block. This can be done by adjusting the height of the pulley to the level of hook of the block.

Relation between Force of Friction and Normal Reaction

9. Now, put some mass (C) on the scale pan. Also, tap the top of the table gently with your finger and check whether the wooden block starts moving or not.
10. Now, step by step, increase the mass (C) on the scale pan until the block starts sliding on tapping the table top. Record the total mass kept on the scale pan.
11. Put some known mass (D) on the top of the wooden block and arrange the mass (C) on the scale pan in such a way that mass D just tends to slide on tapping the table top.
12. Record the values of C and D.
13. Repeat the steps (10) to (12) for more values of C and record them for the corresponding values of D. A minimum of five observations may be required for plotting a graph between F_L and R.

Observations and Calculations

1. Least count of spring balance = ... gf
2. Zero error of the spring balance = ... gf
3. Zero correction......... gf
4. Range of spring balance = ... gf to .... gf
5. Weight of the wooden block, M = ... gf
6. Weight of the scale pan, m = ... gf

Acceleration due to gravity where the experiment is being performed = ... ms^{-2}

Table for Observing the Variation of Limiting Friction with Normal Reaction

S. N.	Mass on the wooden block (D) (g)		Normal force R due to mass, $R = (M + D)\,g$		Mass on the scale pan, (C) (g)	Force of limiting friction, $F_L = (m + C)\,g$	Coefficient of friction, $\mu_L = \frac{F_L}{R}$
	(g)	(kg)	(N)	(gf)	(kg)	(N)	
1							
2							
3							
4							
5							

Plotting Graph

On plotting a graph between limiting friction (F_L) and normal reaction (R) by taking them along Y and X-axes respectively, we get a straight line. Extend this straight line backwards to check whether the line passes through the origin.

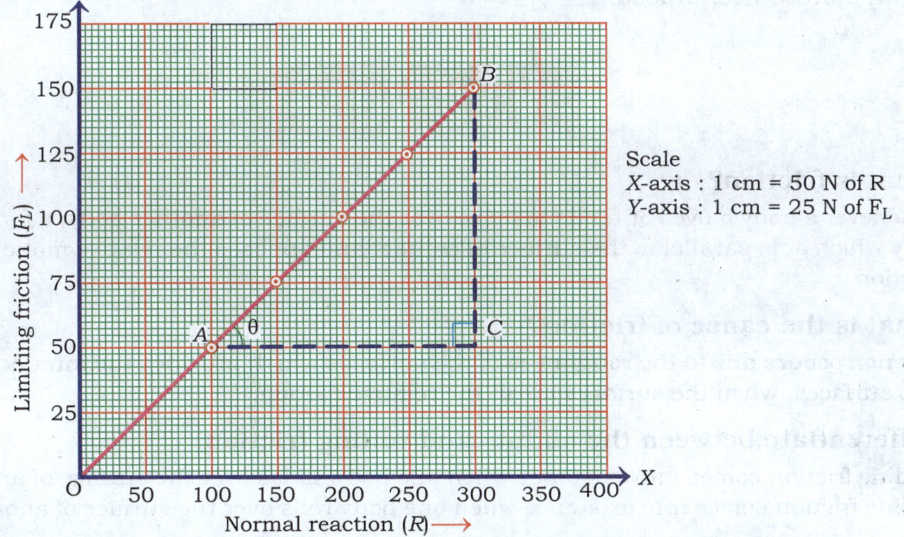

Graph between limiting friction (F_L) and normal reaction (R)

The slope of this straight line graph AB gives the value of coefficient of limiting friction, i.e.

$$\mu_L = \tan\theta = \frac{F_L}{R} = \frac{BC}{AC}$$

where, the point C is the point of intersection of the lines which were drawn from the chosen points A and B that are far apart from each other.

Result

1. From the graph, we can conclude that the force of limiting friction between the two surfaces in contact is directly proportional to the normal reaction.
2. The value of coefficient of limiting friction μ_L between the surface of wooden block and the table top is
   (i) From observation table, μ_L= ....
   (ii) From graph, μ_L= ....

PRECAUTIONS

1. *The surface of the table should be horizontal, clean and dry.*
2. *Frictionless pulley should be used. If it is not, so then it should be lubricated with oil.*
3. *Adjustment of the thread between the block and pulley should be done properly and it should be horizontal.*
4. *There should not be the oscillation or rotation of scale pan.*
5. *Gently, tap the table top each time while performing the experiment.*
6. *The scale pan should not touch any part of the table.*

Sources of Error

1. The table may not be horizontal
2. Pulley may not be frictionless.

Q. 1 What is friction?

Ans. Whenever a body moves or tends to move over the surface of another body, a force comes into play which acts parallel to the surface of contact and opposes the relative motion. This is called friction.

Q. 2 What is the cause of friction?

Ans. Friction occurs due to the roughness of the surfaces which provides the interlocking between the two surfaces, when the surfaces are in the relative motion.

Q. 3 Differentiate between the sliding and rolling friction.

Ans. Sliding friction comes into existence when one body slides over the surface of another body, while rolling friction comes into existence when one body rolls over the surface of another body.

Q. 4 What do you think, whether the normal reaction always equal to the weight of the body or not?

Ans. The normal force is not always equal to the objects, if there are other forces acting on the object, or if the object is accelerating, so that the net force is not zero.

Q. 5 What is the reason of using the frictionless pulley?

Ans. It is usually done to keep the weight of the pan and weights inside it to be totally or completely effective. So, if friction exists, then it will reduce its effective value.

Q. 6 Define angle of friction.

Ans. Angle of friction between the two surfaces is the angle that the resultant of limiting friction and the normal reaction make with the direction of normal reaction.

Q. 7 State the relation between angle of friction and angle of repose.

Ans. Angle of repose is equal to the angle of friction.

Q. 8 What are the factors upon which limiting friction depend?

Ans. It depends upon the normal reaction and the nature of the two surfaces in contact.

Q. 9 Does μ depend upon the area of two surfaces in contact?

Ans. No, it is independent of the area of two surfaces in contact.

Q.10 How does a body start moving over the surface of another body when the force of friction is always there to oppose it?

Ans. The force of friction has the maximum value called limiting friction. When the applied force acting on the body is greater than the limiting friction, the motion starts.

Q.11 Why friction is necessary?

Ans. It is very necessary because without friction, a moving body cannot be stopped. For example, without friction, matchstick will not ignite. There are many other reasons due to which friction is necessary.

Q.12 On the basis of your observations, find the relation between the limiting friction and the mass of sliding body. [NCERT]

Ans. According to the law of limiting friction, frictional force can be given by

$$F_L = \mu_L R \quad \text{...(i)}$$

where, μ_L = coefficient of limiting friction and R = normal reaction acting on the body.

Since, $R = mg$

Therefore, Eq. (i) becomes, $F_L = mg\mu_L$

This is a required relation.

Q.13 Why do we not choose a spherical body to study the limiting friction between the two surfaces? [NCERT]

Ans. We avoid spherical bodies in limiting studies because a spherical body rolls rather than sliding and we want to study limiting friction which is related to sliding, not rolling. Rolling friction is not the same as limiting friction.

Q.14 Why should the horizontal surfaces be clean and dry? [NCERT]

Ans. The presence of dust particles between the wooden block and horizontal plane surface can affect the friction, which in turn leads to error in the observations. That's why, the horizontal surfaces should be dry and clean.

Q.15 Why should the portion of thread between the moving body and pulley be horizontal? [NCERT]

Ans. The portion of the thread between the moving body and pulley should be horizontal, because if it would not be so, then only a component of tension in the thread would act as the force to move the block.

Q.16 Why is it essential in this experiment to ensure that the surface on which the block moves should be horizontal? [NCERT]

Ans. It is essential to ensure that the surface on which the block moves should be horizontal because in order to get maximum normal reaction, a horizontal surface is required for the movement of block.

Q.17 Comment on the statement "the friction between two surfaces can never be zero." [NCERT]

Ans. Yes, the friction between the two surfaces cannot be zero. It is because the surface contains many microscopic grooves and irregularities, so even if we use a lot of lubricants, then the friction will be reduced but can never be completely eliminated because every surface will still have some minor irregularities which cause resistance when they come in contact.

Q.18 In this experiment, usually unpolished surfaces are preferred, why? [NCERT]

Ans. As we know that, according to laws of limiting friction, friction depends upon the nature and the material of the surfaces in contact. So, if the surface is unpolished, then it shall provide a greater amount of friction which is useful for this particular study. That's why, unpolished surfaces are preferred.

Q.19 What do you understand by the self-adjusting nature of force of friction? [NCERT]

Ans. Friction is self adjusting force. This means it automatically adjust its magnitude and direction to remain equal and opposite to the applied force that attepts to move a body at rest. As long as the body does not move, the rictional force exactly balance the applied force, preventing motion.

Q.20 In an experiment to study the relation between force of limiting friction and normal reaction, a body starts sliding on applying a force of 3 N. So, what will be the magnitude of force of friction acting on the body when the applied forces on it are 0.5 N, 1 N, 2.5 N and 3.5 N, respectively? [NCERT]

Ans. According to the question, the body starts sliding when a force of 3 N is applied. So the limiting friction is 3 N for the applied force of 0.5 N, 1 N and 2.5 N, the body does not move. In these cases, the frictional force is equal to the applied force i.e. 0.5 N, 1 N and 2.5 N respectively. When the applied force is 3.5 N, it exceeds the limiting friction so the body slides and the frictional force becomes less than 3 N.

Experiment 12

AIM

To find the downward force, along an inclined plane, acting on a roller due to gravitational pull of the earth and study its relationship with the angle of inclination θ by plotting graph between force and $\sin\theta$.

Apparatus and Materials Required

Weight box, inclined plane with protractor, spring balance, spirit level, thread, pan, pulley, roller, half meter scale.

Theory/Principle

Let us consider a roller of mass m (or weight = mg) has been placed over an inclined plane having angle of inclination θ with the horizontal. The weight mg acts normally downwards and can be resolved into two components as given here.

(i) $mg\cos\theta$, which acts normally downwards on the inclined plane and is balanced by the reaction R that acts upwards on the inclined plane.

(ii) $mg\sin\theta$, which acts downwards parallel to the inclined plane and produces motion in the roller.

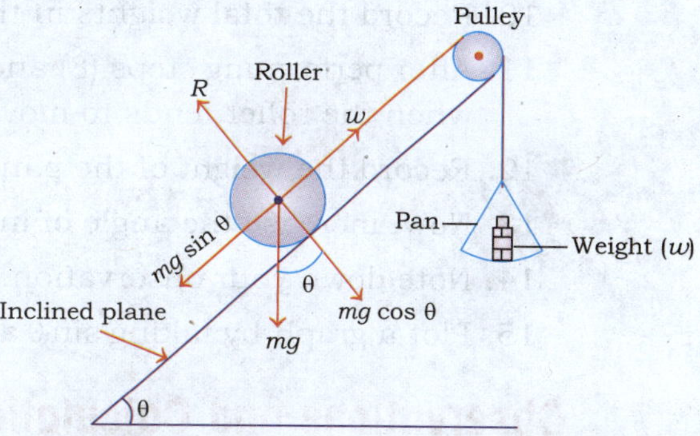

Motion of roller down an inclined plane

In real practice, a friction is always present between the roller and the inclined plane. This friction acts opposite to the motion of the roller which means, if roller moves downward, the friction acts upward and if the roller moves upward, the friction acts downward.

If the total weight $w_1 = M_1 g$ moves the roller in upward direction, we have

$$w_1 = M_1 g = mg\sin\theta + f \quad \text{...(i)}$$

(If force of friction f is present)

If the total weight $w_2 = M_2 g$ moves the roller downward, we have

$$w_2 = M_2 g = mg\sin\theta - f \quad \text{...(ii)}$$

On adding Eqs. (i) and (ii), we get

$$mg\sin\theta = \frac{(M_1 + M_2)}{2} g$$

Procedure

Setting Up the Apparatus

1. First of all, check the pulley of the inclined plane and notice that whether it is free from friction or not. If there is friction then, the pulley should be lubricated with oil.
2. After checking the pulley, make the inclined plane horizontal and stable. It should be checked with the help of spirit level.

3. Now, make the inclined plane in such a position that it should touch the base and due to which, the angle of inclination becomes zero.
4. After performing step (3), determine the weight of the roller by a spring balance and put it on the inclined plane in the middle.
5. Tie one end of the thread with the roller placed on the inclined plane.
6. After tying one end of thread to the roller, make it pass over the pulley.

Measurement of Downward and Upward Forces

7. Determine the weight of the pan with the help of a spring balance and then tie it to the other end of the thread. It is to be ensured that the thread should be kept away from the board on which inclined plane is placed.
8. Now, fix the inclined plane at an angle of 35° after raising it. Notice that the roller should start rolling down with acceleration.
9. Increase the weights on the pan in steps and increase it till the roller tends to start moving upward with uniform velocity.
10. Record the total weights in the pan (w) and also the angle θ.
11. After performing steps (8) and (9), start removing the weight from the pan till the moment, when the roller tends to move downwards with uniform speed.
12. Record the weight of the pan when roller starts to move downwards.
13. Now, increase the angle of inclination with 5° and repeat the steps (9) to (12).
14. Note down your observation.
15. Plot a graph by taking $\sin\theta$ along X-axis and w along Y-axis.

Observations and Calculations

Observations of Spring Balance

1. Least count = ... g wt
2. Zero error (e) = ... g wt
3. Zero error correction ($-e$) = ... g wt

Observations of Weight

4. Weight of the roller (w) = ... g wt
5. Corrected weight (or weight after zero correction) = $w - e$ = ...g wt
6. Weight of the pan alongwith weight placed in it (w_P) = ... g wt
7. Weight of the pan after zero correction ($w_P - e$) = ... g wt

Table to Study the Relationship between the Angle of Inclination and Downward Force

S. N.	Angle of inclination, $\theta°$	$\sin\theta$	Total weight when roller moves		Downward force acting on roller
			Upward, w_1 (g - wt)	Downward, w_2 (g - wt)	$w = \frac{w_1 + w_2}{2}$ (g - wt)
1					
2					
3					
4					

Plotting graph

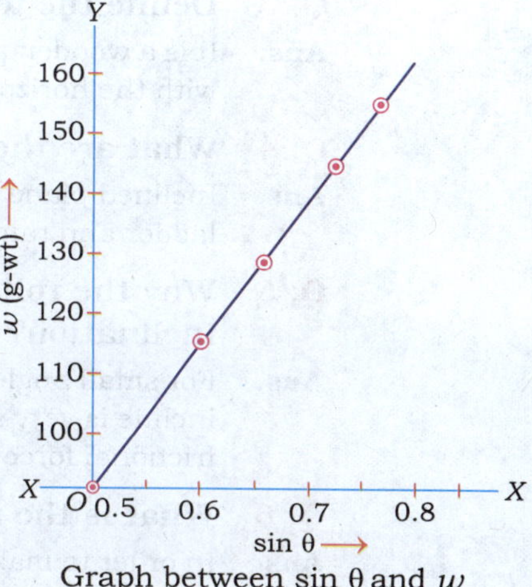

Graph between sin θ and w

When we plot the graph by taking $\sin\theta$ along X-axis and w along Y-axis, then we will get a straight line. Hence, **there is a linear relationship between the downward force along an inclined plane and the angle of inclination.**

Note While performing the experiment, increase the weight in the pan in the direct proportion with the way you increase the angle of inclination in steps in the observation table. This will help you to achieve the straight line graph between w and $\sin\theta$.

Result

1. From the graph, the variation of gravitational pull on the roller (w) along the inclined plane *versus* $\sin\theta$ is straight line. Hence, $w \propto \sin\theta$.
2. Downward force acting on the body of weight $w = mg$, can be written as $mg\sin\theta$.

PRECAUTIONS

1. *Frictionless pulleys should be used. If they are not so, then lubricate them in order to make them frictionless.*
2. *Noting down of the weights should be started when the roller is about to or tends to move up or move down.*
3. *The roller surface should be free from dust.*
4. *Weights should be increased in small steps in the pan.*
5. *The base of the inclined plane should be stable and horizontal.*
6. *Zero error correction of spring balance should be taken into consideration while measuring the weight.*

Sources of Error

1. Inclined surface may not be clean, dry and smooth.
2. Frictionless pulley may not be used.
3. The base of the inclined plane may not be horizontal.
4. Spring balance may not be accurate.

Viva-Voce

Q. 1 Why do we use a roller and not a block in this experiment?

Ans. To minimize friction and ensure smooth motion.

Q. 2 Why the pulleys used in this experiment need some lubrication, if they are not frictionless?

Ans. If the pulleys used in this experiment are not frictionless, then they definitely need some lubrication in the form of oil, greasing, etc., else these pulleys would produce errors in the observation.

Q. 3 Define the term inclined plane.

Ans. It is a wooden plane made smooth by placing a glass sheet over it and it makes an acute angle with the horizontal ground.

Q. 4 What are the applications of an inclined plane?

Ans. Inclined plane can be used as a plank which can be put at the back of truck. It can be used as a ladder and ramp of house as well.

Q. 5 Why the roller placed on inclined plane does not roll down for small angle of inclination?

Ans. For small angle of inclination, the component of gravitational pull which acts on it down the incline is very small as compared to the static friction and rolling resistance. Due to this, the frictional force can easily balance the downward force and keep the roller in equilibrium.

Q. 6 What is the reason of fixing the glass plate at the top of the inclined plane?

Ans. In order to make the surface of inclined plane smooth, the glass plate is usually fixed at the top of the inclined plane.

Q. 7 What is the normal reaction on the inclined plane?

Ans. The normal reaction is $mg\cos\theta$. There is no movement in this direction.

Q. 8 If θ is increased, how is the component of force along the incline affected?

Ans. It increases as $\sin\theta$ increases with θ.

Q. 9 What is a relation between downward force and angle of inclination of the plane? [NCERT]

Ans. The relation can be given as $w = mg\sin\theta$

where, $\sin\theta$ is the component of the weight of the body down the inclined plane.

Q.10 Give an example, where the force of friction is in the same direction as the direction of motion. [NCERT]

Ans. Consider a case, when a runner accelerates forward, the shoe pushes the ground backwards, the friction pushes him forward and the runner moves forward. So, in this case, friction and motion are acting in same direction.

Q.11 How will you ensure that the roller moves upward/downward with constant velocity? [NCERT]

Ans. To ensure that the roller moves upward or downward with constant velocity during the experiment, you must balance all the forces acting on it so that there is no net acceleration. This means the component of the roller's weight acting along the incline (mg sin) must be exactly balanced by the opposing forces, such as friction and any applied pulling force (if used). To achieve this, a smooth inclined plane and a well-balanced roller (to minimize resistance) can be used, and if the roller is being pulled, then the applied force must be carefully adjusted (e.g., using hanging weights) until the roller moves at a uniform speed. Constant velocity can be confirmed by checking that the roller covers equal distances in equal intervals of time.

Activity 1

AIM

To make a paper scale of given least count, e.g., 0.2 cm, 0.5 cm.

Apparatus and Materials Required

A paper cutter, thick ivory/drawing sheet, a thick white paper sheet, a meter scale, gum or fevicol, a sharp pencil, eraser and black ink or gel pen.

Theory/Principle

Least Count

The minimum measurement that can be measured by an instrument accurately is called its least count. e.g. A meter scale has graduation at 1 mm or 0.1 cm spacing as the smallest division on its scale, hence it has a least count of 1 mm or 0.1 cm.

Range of an Instrument

The difference between maximum and minimum readings taken by the instrument is called the range of an instrument.

Procedure

(i) Making of Paper Scale of Least Count 0.2 cm

1. First of all, fold a white paper sheet in the middle along lengthwise.
2. After folding a white paper sheet, with the help of sharp pencil, draw a line *EF* of 15 cm in the upper half along the length of paper.
3. Now, take the point *E* as zero mark point on *EF* and start marking the very small dots after every distance of 1 cm and start writing as 0, 1, 2, ... upto 15.
4. By using a sharp pencil, draw thin sharp straight line of 5 cm perpendicular to *EF* at first dot mark. Draw the same perpendicular line at each dot mark. In this way, we will get 15 straight lines perpendicular to the line *EF*.

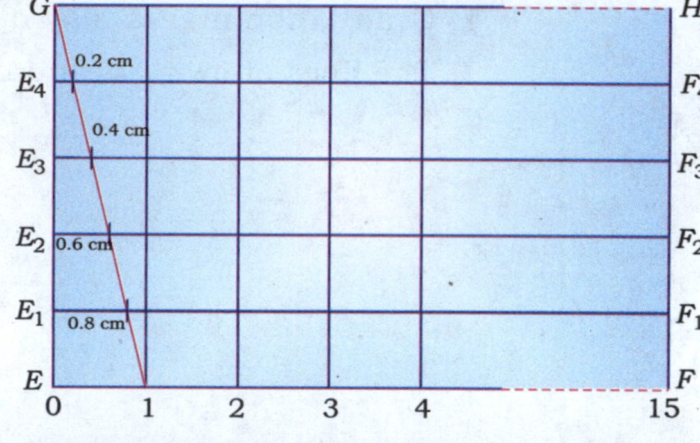

Making of paper scale of least count 0.2 cm

5. Now draw 5 thin straight lines E_1F_1, E_2F_2, E_3F_3, E_4F_4 and *GH* parallel to line *EF* at a distance of 1.0 cm, 2.0 cm, 3.0 cm, 4.0 cm and 5.0 cm, respectively.
6. From the point *G* of line *GH* at 5.0 cm from the line *EF*, draw a line joining the point *G* and first dot mark at 1 cm on line *EF*. Eventually, we will get the intersection of this line with lines parallel to *EF* at 0.2 cm, 0.4 cm, 0.6 cm and 0.8 cm from points E_4, E_3, E_2 and E_1 respectively.
7. You will find that your paper scale of least count of 0.2 cm is ready for use.

(ii) Making of Paper Scale of Least Count 0.5 cm

1. First of all, fold a white paper sheet in the middle along lengthwise.
2. After folding a white paper sheet, with the help of sharp pencil, draw a line EF of 15 cm long in the upper half along the length of paper.
3. Now, repeat the steps (3) to (6) of above activity 1 (i) but here draw only two lines E_1F_1 and GH at distances 1.0 cm and 2.0 cm respectively parallel to the line EF.
4. Now, join the point G of line GH drawn at 2.0 cm from the line EF and first dot mark at 1.0 cm on line EF by using a black ink pen. Thus, a diagonal is formed.
5. You will find that your paper scale of least count 0.5 cm is ready for use.

Making of paper scale of least count 0.5 cm

PRECAUTIONS

1. *A very sharp pencil should be used for the marking of the divisions.*
2. *There should be an overlapping of one end of the object (whose length is to be determined) with a full centimetre mark.*
3. *The scale boundaries should be made by using sharp paper cutter.*
4. *The paper scale should be pasted on thick ivory paper or drawing sheet to make it usable.*

Sources of Error

1. Graduation marks may not have equal separation.
2. The lines showing graduations may not be sharp as required.

Viva-Voce

Q 1 Define the least count of an instrument.

Ans. The minimum measurement that can be measured by the instrument accurately is called the least count of an instrument.

Q 2 Which is the most mandatory and important information that has to be kept in mind while performing this activity?

Ans. While performing this activity, the most mandatory and important information is the marking of graduations which should be done accurately.

Q 3 In this experiment, you have two scales X and Y with their least counts 0.2 cm and 0.5 cm respectively. So, which one of them will measure the length of the given pencil more accurately?

Ans. The paper scale (X) with the least count 0.2 cm will measure the length of the given pencil more accurately.

Q 4 What difference you have concluded in procedure of this experiment, in making the paper scale (X) with least count 0.2 cm and the paper scale (Y) with least count 0.5 cm?

Ans. It is very important to know that in the case of paper scale (X), on dividing each gap of 1 cm into five equal parts, each individual part of 1 cm must have length 0.2 cm.

While in the case of paper scale (Y), on dividing each gap of 1 cm into two equal parts, each individual part of 1 cm gap will be of length 0.5 cm.

Q 5 What do you mean by the range of a device?

Ans. Range of a device is defined as the difference between the maximum and minimum values that can be measured by device.

Q 6 What does accuracy mean?

Ans. It is a very crucial term in the experimental physics. Accuracy means that how close the measured value is to the true value of the quantity.

Q 7 What is the range of this paper scale which you have prepared in this activity?

Ans. The range of paper scale prepared in this activity is 15.

Activity 2

AIM

To determine mass of a given body using a meter scale by principle of moments.

Apparatus and Materials Required

A sharp edged metal, a body of unknown weight, thread, a meter scale, spirit level and a raised platform of about 20 cm height and two weight hangers.

Theory/Principle

According to the **principle of moments,**

"If a body is free to rotate about a fixed axis, then in equilibrium, the sum of the clockwise moments is equal to the sum of anti-clockwise moments".

Consider a beam from which an unknown mass m_1 is suspended at a distance x_1 on one side of the centre of gravity and a known mass m_2 is suspended at a distance x_2 on the other side of the centre of gravity. If the beam is in equilibrium, then

$$m_1 x_1 = m_2 x_2 \Rightarrow m_1 = \frac{m_2 x_2}{x_1}$$

So, by knowing m_2, x_2 and x_1, the value of m_1 can be known. Thus, **mass of a body can be determined by principle of moments.**

Procedure

1. Place the meter scale with thread loops on the wedge and adjust it till it gets balanced. Mark two points on the scale above the wedge, where the scale is balanced.
2. Take the unknown mass in one hand. Select a weight from the weight box which feels nearly equal to the unknown mass when it is kept on the other hand.

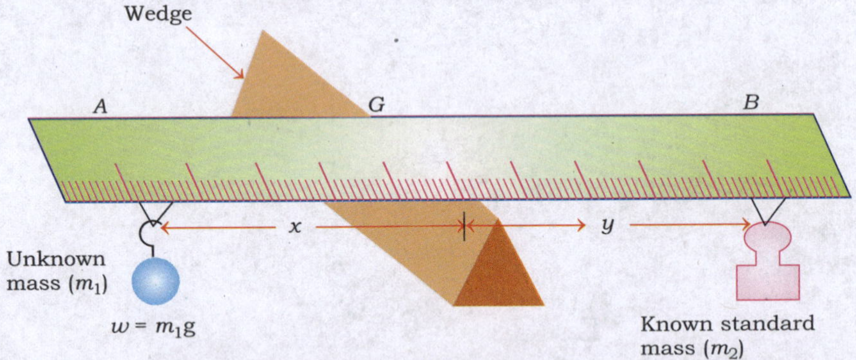

Experimental setup for determination of mass of a given body

3. With the help of hangers, suspend the unknown mass from either of the two loops of thread attached to the meter scale and also suspend the known weight from the other loop.
4. Adjust the position of the known weight by moving the loop till the meter scale gets balanced on the sharp wedge. Make sure that in balanced position, the line drawn in step 1 is exactly above the wedge and also that the thread of two loops passing over the scale is parallel to this line.

5. Measure the distance of the position of the loops from the line drawn in step 1. Record your observations.
6. Repeat the activity atleast two times with a slightly lighter and a heavier weight. Note the distances of unknown mass and weight from line drawn in step 1 in each case.

Observations

Position of centre of gravity on the scale .... cm.

Table for the Determination of Unknown Mass

S.N.	Distance of body of unknown mass, from the wedge, x (cm)	Mass of body suspended to balance the meter scale, m_2 (g) (known mass)	Distance of body of known mass, y (cm)	Unknown mass of body, $m_1 = \frac{m_2 y}{x}$ (g)
1				$m_1' =$ .... g
2				$m_1'' =$ .... g
3				$m_1''' =$ .... g

Calculations

According to the principle of moments, in balanced position of the meter scale, moments of the force on both the sides of wedge will be equal.

Moment of force due to unknown weight $= m_1 x$, Moment of force due to known weight $= m_2 y$

In equilibrium position (the position when the meter scale gets balanced on the wedge)

$$m_1 x = m_2 y$$

Unknown mass, $$m_1 = \frac{m_2 y}{x}$$

The mean (or average) value of unknown mass, $m_1 = \frac{m_1' + m_1'' + m_1'''}{3}$, $m_1 =$ .... g.

Result

The unknown mass of the body, $m_1 =$.............. g.

PRECAUTIONS

1. The meter scale should be held horizontal in the equilibrium position.
2. A broad sharp wedge should be used and it should be always perpendicular to the length of the scale.
3. The thread used to make the loops should be thin, light and strong.
4. For each reading, the thread loop should be parallel to the marking on the meter scale.
5. The centre of gravity should be determined accurately.
6. Air currents should be minimised.

Sources of Error

1. The edge may not be sharp.
2. Meter scale may have faulty calibration.
3. The thread used may be thick and heavy.
4. The thread of the loop may not be parallel to the wedge when the weight are balanced.

Viva-Voce

Q. 1 What is the most important and mandatory information (or precaution) that should be followed while performing this experiment?

Ans. The most important and mandatory information that should be followed while performing this experiment is the determination of centre of gravity of the scale accurately and it should be checked before and after every reading, so that the edge of the wedge remains under this position only.

Q. 2 What do you mean by the term weight of the body? Give its SI unit.

Ans. The gravitational pull exerted by the earth on the body towards its centre is called the weight of the body. SI unit of weight is newton (N).

Q. 3 Define couple.

Ans. Couple can be defined as a pair of equal and opposite forces whose lines of action do not coincide and which tend to produce rotational only.

Q. 4 Does spring balance make use of the principal of moments?

Ans. No, it makes use of the fact that extension produced in a spring is proportional to the weight.

Q. 5 For what angle torque will be maximum?

Ans. $\tau = \mathbf{r} \times \mathbf{F}$

$\tau = r\,F \sin\theta$, τ will be maximum when $\theta = 90°$

Q. 6 What is the name given to the point on the scale at which it is balanced horizontally on the wedge? [NCERT]

Ans. Centre of gravity is a point on the meter scale at which it is balanced horizontally on the wedge.

Q. 7 How does the least count of the meter scale limit the accuracy in the measurement of mass? [NCERT]

Ans. Since, a meter scale can measure accurately upto one length part of 1 cm, its least measurement 0.1 cm is called least count of the scale. There is a limitation of meter scale that it cannot measure the value less than 0.1 cm, so due to this reason, the least count of the meter scale limits the accuracy in the measurement of mass.

Q. 8 What is the resultant torque on the meter scale, due to the gravitational force, when the scale is perfectly horizontal? [NCERT]

Ans. When the scale is perfectly horizontal, then due to the gravitational force, the torque on the meter scale will be zero.

Q. 9 Explain how a physical balance works on the principle of moments? [NCERT]

Ans. A physical balance is a device that is used to measure mass. The physical balance consists of two pans of equal weights balanced by a beam and the known weight is added on one side, while the unknown weight to be measured is added on the other.

Q.10 What problems would air currents cause in this activity? [NCERT]

Ans. Since, air currents can be caused by differences in temperature, pressure or impurity concentration. So, the temperature differences can cause air currents because the warmer air is less dense than cooler air, causing the warmer air to appear lighter. So, ultimately, it results into an error in the measurement.

Activity 3

AIM

To plot a graph for a given set of data, with proper choice of scales and error bars.

Apparatus and Materials Required

A ruler, an eraser, a sharp pencil, millimetre square graph paper and given data.

Set of Data

Load (gf)	100	200	300	400	500	600
Extension (cm)	0.16	0.32	0.48	0.64	0.80	0.96

Theory/Principle

Graph is a curve or a straight line which shows the variation of two variable quantities of which one changes as a result of change in the other. It helps us in

1. the calibration of certain instruments and to find out their exact readings.
2. determining the value of quantity which is usually not observed while performing the experiment.

So, the graph provides clear picture of the interdependent relationship between the two quantities due to which, a general idea of relationship can be known.

Error Bar When the value of variable is not represented on the graph by a point only, so it can be represented by a bar called **error bar** around the point. The width of the bar is equal to the least count of the measuring instrument.

Steps Involved in Plotting a Graph

Steps involved in plotting a graph are given below

Step 1 Selecting the Dependent and Independent Variables

First of all in the given problem, the dependent and independent variables should be selected. e.g. Consider an experiment in which the change in length of a string occurs due to the corresponding increase in weight. So here, length is a dependent variable and weight is an independent variable.

The independent variable is selected to plot along X-axis and the dependent variable along Y-axis.

Y
Dependent variable →
X
Independent variable →

Axes showing dependent and independent variables

Step 2 Finding the Range of Each Physical Variable

To find the range of the two variables (i.e. dependent and independent), one should know the minimum and maximum values of these two variables. The difference between these two values gives the range of a physical variable.

After obtaining the range of two variables, the physical variable of large range should be plotted on the longer side of the graph paper.

Step 3 Selecting the Scale

The scales should be selected in such a way that the graph will cover about 80% of the space of the graph paper.

The scale should be selected in such a way that it should neither be too small nor too big and attempt should be made to present one big squares by 1,2 or 5 units of the variable. Thus, the available 10 small boxes in a big square can represent 1, 2 or 5 units of the variable by taking 1, 5 or 2 equal segments respectively in the big square.

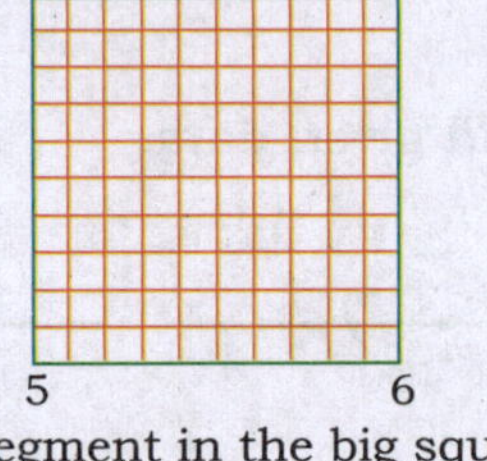

1 segment in the big square after the origin

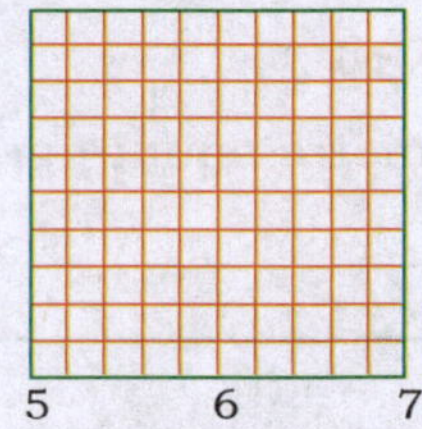

2 segments in the big square after the origin

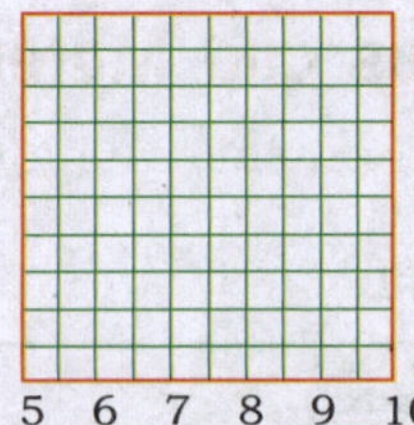

5 segments in the big square after the origin

Step 4 The Number of Readings

For plotting a graph, at least six to seven observations should be taken.

Step 5 Joining the Points

After pointing the various observations as points in the graph, one should mark the crosses or enclose them in a small circle as shown in figure.

Thereafter join all these points by a straight line or a smooth and a free hand curve.

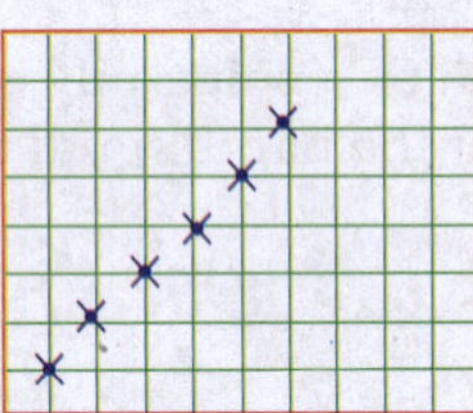
Crosses on the points

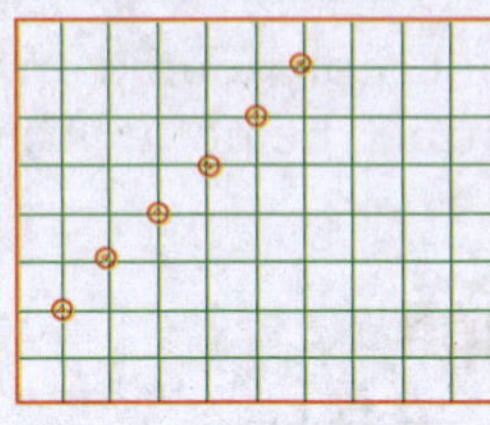
Small circle enclosing the points

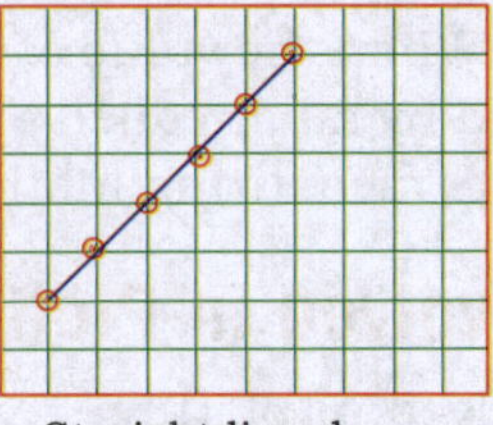
Straight line drawn in the graph

Step 6 Portion of a Graph for Special Purpose

Sometimes from plotted graph, a particular segment of the line drawn is selected to determine the result. e.g. In case of a second's pendulum having time period of 2 s and length of 99.3 cm or about 100 cm, the observations should be taken in such a manner that the 100 cm marks falls in the middle portion of the graph. It means for the given time periods, the corresponding lengths of the pendulum should be 75 cm, 85 cm, 95 cm, 105 cm, 115 cm and 125 cm. This type of graph helps to keep away from the error occurred in the results.

Step 7 Giving Name (or Title) of the Graph

Give the name of the graph at the top of the graph paper, i.e. write the heading "Graph showing relation between X (independent variable) and Y (dependent variable)".

Procedure

Identification of Dependent and Independent Variables

1. From the given data, it is well understood that the length is increasing due to the corresponding increase in weight or load. So here, consider the load to be as an independent variable and it should be taken along *X*-axis and the extension to be as dependent variable and it should be taken along *Y*-axis.

Determination of Range

2. Determine the range of load and of extension as well.

   Range of load = 600 – 100 = 500gf

   Range of extension = 0.96 – 0.16 = 0.80cm

3. As the range of the load is greater than extension, so take the load axis parallel to larger side, while the extension axis to the smaller side of graph paper.

Selection of Scale

4. Since, the given data have only positive values, so due to this, take the origin at lower left corner of the graph paper.
5. Now find the smallest division which is to be projected along *X*-axis and *Y*-axis for load and extension respectively.

   Along *X*-axis (for load) 1SD (Smallest Division) = 0.2 cm

   Along *Y*-axis (for extension) 1SD (Smallest Division) = 100gf

Plotting of Data with Error Bars

6. Now, put the marking of points of the loads on the load axis and of extension on the extension axis of the graph paper.
7. Since, for the initial point of data, the value of the load is 100 gf and extension is 0.16 cm,put the dot on graph paper against the load 100 gf and extension 0.16 cm surrounded by a small circle.
8. As the measured accuracy is of ± 0.02 cm, so indicate the error bars against the upper and lower limiting values of extension as 0.16 + 0.02 and 0.16 – 0.02 or 0.18 and 0.14. So, in this way, the first data point is completely plotted.
9. In the similar manner, plot the remaining data points.

Note It should be noted that according to Hooke's law, all the data points should be in a straight line.

Joining the Points

10. Now, make a straight line by joining the data points. It should be noted that the points which do not lie on the straight line graph are distributed evenly above and below it.

Giving Name of the Graph

11. Note down the title of graph, i.e. **graph showing the relation between load and extension.**

Note Even from the data, it can be analysed that if we plot a graph between these two physical variables, *i.e.* load and extension, we will get a straight line because in the data as soon as load increases in the equal segments, the length also increases almost in the equal segments showing the linear relationship between them.

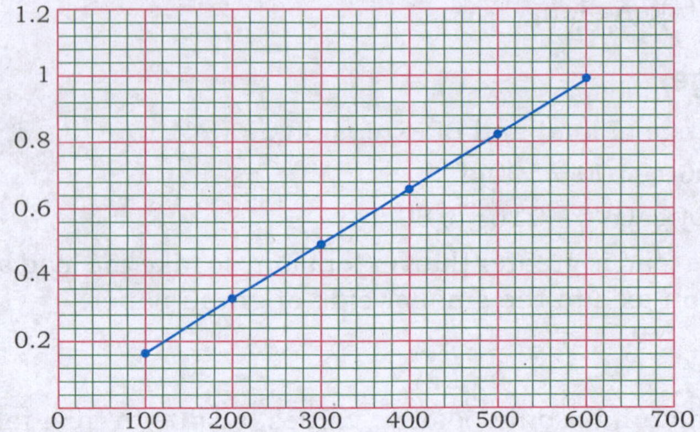

Graph showing the relation between load and extension

Result

The graph between the load and extension for the given set of data along with error bar has been shown through the graph. Therefore, from the given data and the plotted graph, we analysed that there is **linear relationship between the two physical variables, i.e. load and extension.**

PRECAUTIONS

1. While plotting the graph, a sharp pencil should be used.
2. The selection of the scale along the two axes should be properly done.
3. The considered data points should be joined either with a smooth curve or a straight line.
4. At the time of joining the data points of graph, enough care should be taken to join them smoothly. The curve and line should be thin.

Sources of Error

1. Improper choice of origin and the scale.
2. Improper marking of observation points.

Viva-Voce

Q 1 What is error bar in this experiment?

Ans. The graphical representation of the instrumental probable error by a bar around the plotted points is called error bar.

Q 2 Differentiate between independent and dependent variables.

Ans. Independent variable is one which varies arbitrarily, while the dependent variable is one which or whose value depends on independent variable.

Q 3 What do you mean by the term graph?

Ans. A graph is a visual representation of data often using lines, curves of bars to show the relationship between different quantities.

Q 4 What is the significance of the graph?

Ans. Graph helps us in achieving

(i) the calibration of certain instruments and to find out their exact readings.

(ii) to find out the value, which is not observed usually while performing the experiment.

Q 5 Give any example in which independent variable is taken along Y-axis instead of X-axis.

Ans. L-T^2 graph for a simple pendulum is an example in which independent variable is taken along Y-axis instead of X-axis.

Q 6 Which precautions are to be followed while performing this activity?

Ans. The errors in both the variables should be clearly shown and a clear rectangle should be shown around the plotted points.

Q 7 Define intrapolation of graph.

Ans. When the value of a physical quantity is determined whose value falls within the range of data is known as intrapolation of graph.

Activity 4

AIM

To measure the force of limiting friction for rolling of a roller on a horizontal plane.

Apparatus and Materials Required

A spring balance, a physical balance, set of weights, horizontal plane fitted with a frictionless pulley fitted at one end, thread, spirit level, wooden block with a hook on one side, weight box and lead shots (rollers).

Theory/Principle

The force of friction which comes into play between the two bodies when one tends to roll over the another surface is called **rolling friction**. It is always less than the sliding friction.

Consider a block of weight w' which has been placed over the lead shot spreaded on the horizontal surface as shown in figure.

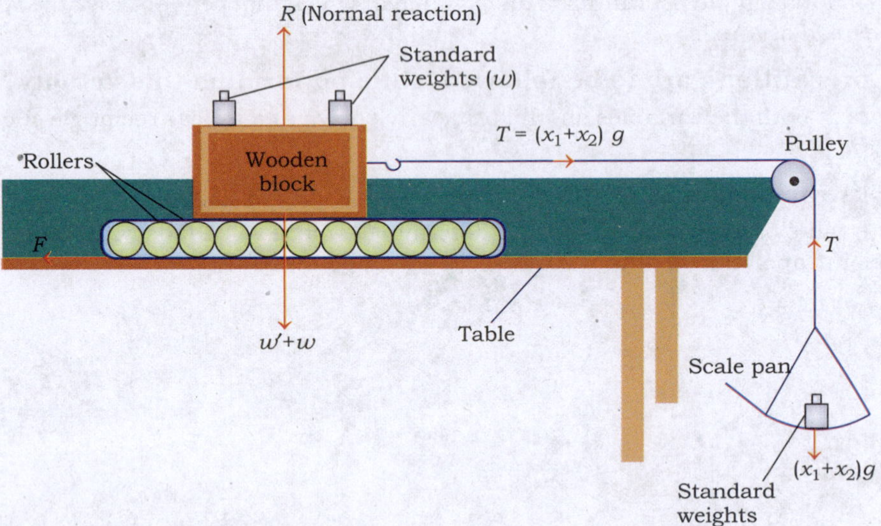

Experimental setup to study the rolling friction

The block is tied with a scale pan with the help of thread after passing through the pulley. Here, the force which will tend to pull the block towards the pulley is applied by the weight of the scale pan (including the weight put in it).

Procedure

Set up the Apparatus

1. With the help of a spirit level, check the horizontal surface and spread a layer of lead shots on it.
2. After checking the horizontal surface, measure the weight of the wooden block with the help of spring balance.
3. Determine the weight of the pan with the help of physical balance.

Observe the Motion of the Block Towards the Pulley

4. Add a small weight to the pan and notice that whether the wooden block kept on rollers starts moving or not.
5. If in case, the block does not start rolling, then from the weight box, add some more weights to the pan, from the weight box.
6. Repeat the step (4) till the block just starts moving.
7. When the block starts moving, note the total weight of the pan (including the weight put in it).
8. Now put some suitable weight over the wooden block and repeat the above steps (5) to (7) and note the respective weights in the observation table.
9. Repeat the process and increase the weights in steps over the wooden block and pan and then note the value of weights in the observation table.
10. Calculate the mean value of total weight (force) pulling the block and weights and record it.

Observations and Calculations

Weight of the wooden block, $w' = mg =$.......... N

Weight of the pan = (mass of the pan+ weight put in it) $= (x_1 + x_2) =$.........N

Table for the Measurement of Limiting Rolling Friction

S.N.	Weight of wooden block, w' (N)	Total weight being pulled $= (w' + w)$ = Normal reaction, R (N)	Weight in pan, x_1 (kg)	Weight of pan, x_2 (kg)	Total weight (force) pulling the block and standard weights, $(x_1 + x_2)$ (N)
1					$F_1 =$......... N
2					$F_2 =$......... N
3					$F_3 =$......... N
4					$F_4 =$......... N
5					$F_5 =$......... N

Result

Since, the total weight which is being pulled increases, the limiting value of rolling friction also increases.

PRECAUTIONS

1. *The scale pan should not provide the tension greater than the force of limiting friction.*
2. *The lead shots surface should be clean and dry.*
3. *The weights in the pan should be placed gently.*
4. *The portion of the string/thread between the pulley and hook should be horizontal.*
5. *Frictionless pulley should be used.*
6. *The scale pan should be tied in such a way that it does not touch the table.*

Sources of Error

1. The surface (table top) may not be horizontal.
2. Pulley may not be frictionless.
3. The thread between the hook and pulley may not be horizontal.

Viva-Voce

Q. 1 What is the relation between the rolling friction and the radius of the wheel?

Ans. Rolling friction inversely proportional to the radius of the wheel.

Q. 2 What do you mean by limiting friction?

Ans. The maximum value of the opposing force which comes into existence when one body is just at the verge of moving over the surface of another body, is called the limiting friction.

Q. 3 "The force of friction is known as self adjusting in nature". Explain this statement in brief.

Ans. The force of friction is known as self-adjusting in nature because it adjusts its magnitude and direction to keep itself always equal and opposite to the equal force applied to move the body at rest.

Q. 4 What can be the reason of keeping frictionless pulley in this activity?

Ans. It is usually done to keep the weight of the pan and weights in it to be fully effective, so friction in pulley reduces its effective value.

Q. 5 Differentiate between the sliding and rolling friction. Which one is greater either rolling friction or sliding friction?

Ans. Rolling friction comes into play when one object rolls over the surface of the other, while sliding friction is one which comes into play when one object slides over the surface of the other.

Sliding friction is greater than the rolling friction.

Q. 6 What is one of the factors which causes the friction?

Ans. Roughness of the surfaces is the cause of friction. It provides the interlocking between the two surfaces when the surfaces are in relative motion. So, when the body is pulled, elevations collide and provide friction.

Q. 7 State the factors on which the force of limiting friction depends.

Ans. Force of limiting friction depends upon the

(i) normal reaction (ii) nature of the two surfaces in contact.

Q. 8 The two segments of the thread joining the block and the pan passing over the pulley should lie in mutually perpendicular planes. Why? [NCERT]

Ans. If the segments of the thread do not lie in mutually perpendicular planes, there could be additional components of force that do not contribute to the motion of the block, leading to inaccuracies in the experiment.

Q. 9 The total weight pulling the block (including that of pan) should be such that the system just rolls without acceleration. Why we cannot add as much weight as we wish? [NCERT]

Ans. If the weight is too much, the block will accelerate, if it is too little, the block won't none. This balancing is crucial for accurately measuring the coefficient of friction.

Q.10 While negotiating a curve on a road, having sand spread over it, a two wheeler has to be slowed down to avoid skidding, why? [NCERT]

Ans. Sand reduces the friction between the tyres of the two wheeler and the road but friction is essential for providing the necessary centripetal force that keeps the vehicle on its curved path.

Activity 5

AIM

To study the variation in range of a projectile with angle of projection.

Apparatus and Materials Required

A measuring tape, large size protractor, PVC or a rubber pipe, a nozzle and source of water under pressure.

Theory/Principle

The horizontal distances between point of projection and point of return, covered by the projectile during its flight, is called its horizontal range. So, its range can be given by

$$R = \frac{u^2 \sin 2\theta}{g}$$

where, θ is the angle of projection and u is the velocity of projection.
Horizontal range R will be maximum, if

$$\sin 2\theta = 1 \quad \Rightarrow \quad \sin 2\theta = \sin 90^\circ$$

$$2\theta = 90^\circ \quad \Rightarrow \quad \theta = 45^\circ$$

$$\therefore \quad \text{Maximum horizontal range} = \frac{u^2}{g} \quad \Rightarrow \quad R_{max} = \frac{u^2}{g}$$

Procedure

Set up the Apparatus

1. Make the connection of a water pipe with the reservoir outlet and fix a metallic nozzle in the other end of pipe (held in hand), so that the velocity of projection of water coming out from the pipe remains constant.
2. Now, place the protractor in a slot in a horizontal base in order to make its plane vertical on the ground, so that its graduations can be easily seen.

Note For making a large protractor, take a circular plyboard or thick circular cardboard sheet of radius about 25 cm. Draw a diameter through its centre and cut it along the diameter to form two dees. On one of the dees, draw angles at an interval of 15° starting with 0°.

Determination of Range Corresponding to Certain Angle of Projection

3. Put the nozzle at the centre O of protractor. Open the tap to obtain the projectile and let the jet pass through some suitable marking of angle (say 15°) on protractor.
4. Notice that the path of the jet along which it moves should be a parabola and should fall back on the slab at some distance. Mark the point where the jet falls (i.e. point B).

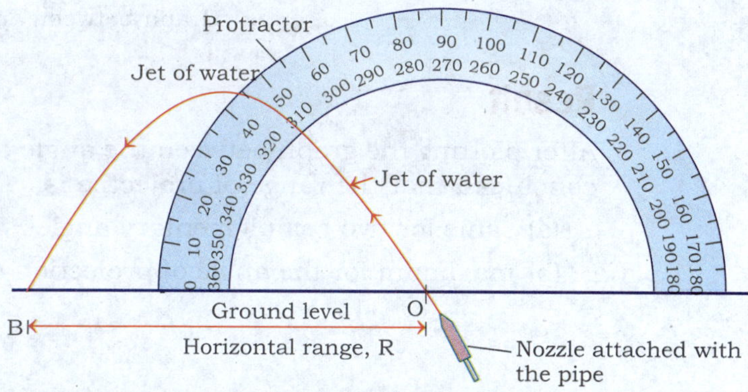

Set up to determine the horizontal range of a projectile corresponding to the angle of projection

5. Close the tap and with the help of measuring tape, measure the distance *OB*. This will give you the range (*R*) corresponding to the angle of projection 15°.
6. Now, vary the angle from 15° to 30°, 45°, 60°, 75° and with the help of measuring tape, measure the corresponding range (where the jet of water falls) for each angle of pojection in stepwise manner.
7. Note down the observations in a tabular form and plot a graph between range and angle of projection by taking them along *X* and *Y*-axes respectively.

Observations

Least count of measuring tape = ... cm.

Table for Studying the Variation in the Range of Projectile with Angle of Projection

S.N.	Angle of projection of projectile, θ	Range of projectile, *R* (cm)
1	15°	
2	30°	
3	45°	
4	60°	
5	75°	

Plotting Graph

Plot a graph between the angle of projection (θ) and corresponding range (*R*) by taking θ along *X*-axis and *R* along *Y*-axis.

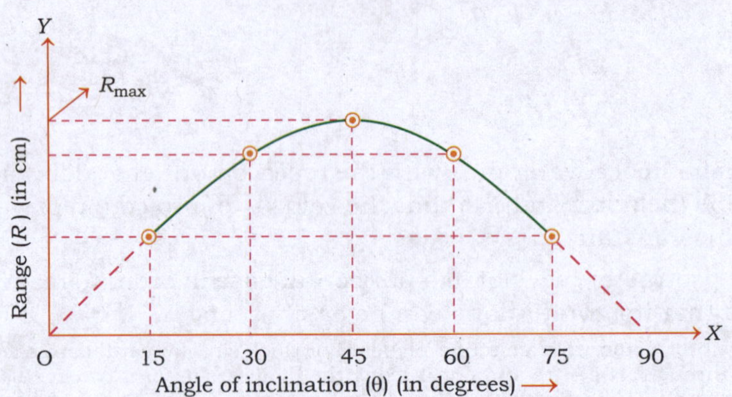

Graph between angle of projection and range

Result

After plotting the graph between the angle of projection (θ) and corresponding range (*R*), we have concluded that the range of projectile is

(a) same for two complementary angles (like for 15° and 75°, 30° and 60°).

(b) maximum for the angle of projection of .... degree. This angle will be almost 45°.

PRECAUTIONS

1. There should not be any leakage in the pipe and the pressure with which the water is released from the nozzle should not vary during the experiment.

2. There should be a constant water level in the reservoir in order to keep the velocity of projection constant.

3. The centre of area where the water strikes the ground should be considered for measuring the range of projectile.

4. The small nozzle should be used in order to get a thin stream of water.

5. The measurement of angle of inclination should be done carefully.

6. The trajectory of water should exactly lie on the plane of the protractor.

7. The point of return of the jet of water should be sharp.

Sources of Error

1. Velocity of water jet may change as the pressure of water may not remain constant.
2. The water from jet may not strike the ground at a sharp point.

Viva-Voce

Q. 1 Define the term horizontal range by a projectile.

Ans. The horizontal range is defined as the horizontal distance covered by a projectile. It is given by

$$R = \frac{u^2 \sin 2\theta}{g}$$

where, θ is the angle of projection & u is the velocity of projection.

Q. 2 On which factors, does the range of a projectile depend?

Ans. The range of a projectile depends on

(i) Initial velocity provided to projectile (ii) Acceleration due to gravity at that place
(iii) Angle of projection

Q. 3 What do you mean by projectile?

Ans. The phenomenon in which a body is projected in the upward direction at an angle θ with respect to the horizontal with an initial velocity and then afterwards, it is allowed to move under the action of gravity alone (it means no longer being propelled by any fuel).

Q. 4 State the condition for the maximum horizontal range of a given projectile.

Ans. Since, horizontal range will be maximum, if

$$\sin 2\theta = 1 \Rightarrow \sin 2\theta = \sin 90^\circ$$

$$\Rightarrow 2\theta = 90^\circ \Rightarrow \theta = 45^\circ$$

Therefore, maximum horizontal range, $R_{max} = \frac{u^2}{g}$

Q. 5 Give two examples of projectile.

Ans. A bomb released from an aeroplane and a javelin thrown by an athlete are the two examples of projectile. A boll thrown into the air and a kicked football.

Q. 6 Two bodies are projected with the same speed but at angles of projection θ and (90° − θ), will their time of flight be the same?

Ans. No, the time of flight, $T = \frac{2u \sin \theta}{g}$ $\because \sin(90 - \theta) = \cos\theta$

If T_1 and T_2 are the two times of flight, then $T_1 = \frac{2u \sin \theta}{g}$ and $T_2 = \frac{2u \sin(90° - \theta)}{g} = 2u \cos \theta$

$\therefore$ $T_1 \neq T_2$

Q. 7 A body is just released from a moving aeroplane. Will it move in a vertical path or in a parabolic path?

Ans. Parabolic path, because it will execute two dimensional motion, i.e. uniform horizontal motion and accelerated downward motion.

Q. 8 How are the two angles of projection for same range related with each other?

Ans. The range of same for two values of angles, the angle and its complementary angle, i.e. their sum is 90°, i.e. θ and (90° − θ).

Q. 9 Why do you get same range for angles of projection 15° and 75° ? [NCERT]

Ans. Consider the graph.

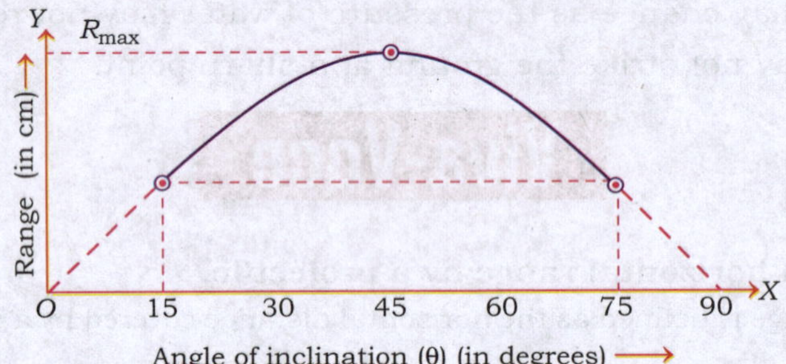

As we can see that, the projectile covers a parabolic path which shows that the horizontal range of water jet increases with increase in the angle of inclination of water pipe with the ground and starts decreasing as the angle of inclination of pipe increases beyond 45°. So, due to this, the corresponding ranges to the angle of inclination 15° and 75° are same.

Q.10 Why has a big protractor been taken? Would a protractor of radius about 10 cm be preferable. Explain? [NCERT]

Ans. A big protractor has been taken in this activity because a big protractor of large radius gives an exact and accurate value of angle of projection, so corresponding to this, the range of a jet of water is also accurate.

While in the case of protractor with radius 10 cm, the value of angle of projection becomes very difficult to measure. So, the protractor with radius 10 cm is usually not preferred.

Q.11 How would the range change, if the velocity of projection is increased or decreased? [NCERT]

Ans. According to the formula, $R = \frac{u^2 \sin 2\theta}{g} \Rightarrow R \propto u^2$

It means that horizontal range of the projectile is directly proportional to the square of its velocity. So, the range of projectile increases with increase in its velocity and decreases with decrease in its velocity.

Activity 6

AIM

To study the conservation of energy of a ball rolling down on an inclined plane (using a double inclined plane).

Apparatus and Materials Required

Two wooden blocks, plumb line, a half meter scale, spirit level, a double inclined plane, cotton/tissue paper, a steel ball of diameter about 2.5 cm.

Theory/Principle

According to the law of conservation of energy,

"Energy can neither be created nor destroyed but can be transformed from one form to another". Thus, sum of all forms of energy in the entire universe remains constant.

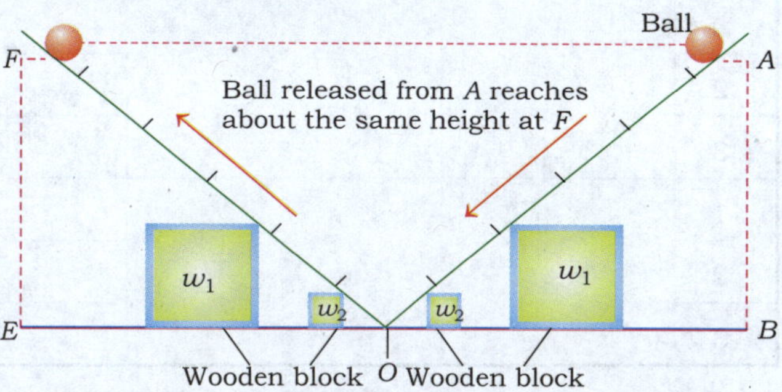

Set up for studying the conservation of energy of a ball using double inclined tracks

During the rolling motion of the steel ball on a perfectly smooth inclined plane, the continuous transformation of energy takes place. Thus, the sum of kinetic and potential energies of the steel ball remains constant provided there is no dissipation of energy due to air resistance, friction, etc. In the absence of any friction in the track (a case of an ideal track), the movement of the ball will remain to continue forever.

Therefore, **the law of conservation of mechanical energy can be verified by the equality of two vertical heights** *BA* **and** *EF*.

Procedure

Set up the Apparatus

1. Set up the experimental setup as shown in the above figure. The experimental table should be horizontal.
2. Clean the steel ball and inclined planes with cotton/tissue paper properly.

Releasing of Steel Ball

3. Release the steel ball from *A*, on either of the two inclined planes.
4. Find the vertical height *AB* (or *x*) of the point *A* from the table using a meter scale and plumb line. Note the observations.
5. After reaching the lowest point *O*, the ball starts heading towards point *F* of the other inclined plane. Note the point *F* upto which the ball reaches the inclined plane on the other side and find the vertical height *FE* (or *y*). Record the observations. At the time of observing the highest position of the steel ball on other plane, observer has to be very alert as the ball stays at the highest position only for an instant.
6. Shift the wooden block w_1 and w_2 kept under either of the two planes, towards the centre point *O* by a small distance. Now the angle of the slope of one of the planes would be larger than that of the other. Instead of changing the slope, the position of the point *A* (from which the ball is released) can be changed.

7. Release the ball again from point A on one of the two planes and mark the point F on the other plane upto which the steel ball rolls up. Also find the vertical height FE.
8. Repeat steps (6) and (7) for one more angle of the slope of the inclined plane.
9. Repeat the observations for another point of release on the same inclined plane and note the observations in the tabular form.

Observations

Table for studying the conservation of energy of a ball using double inclined tracks

S.N.	Reading on inclined plane from which the ball is rolled down		Reading on the inclined plane on which the ball rolls up			Difference, $(x - y)$ (cm)
	Position of mark A	Vertical height AB, x (cm)	Position of mark up to which the ball rolls up, F	Vertical height EF, y (cm)	Mean, y (cm)	
1			F_B =			
2			F_C =			
3			F_D =			
1			F_B =			
2			F_C =			
3			F_D =			

Result

Since, it can be seen from the observation table that the initial and final vertical heights are same within the limits of experimental error.

Therefore, the steel ball has same initial and final potential energies though during the motion, the potential energy gets converted into kinetic energy. It is clear that the sum of mechanical (kinetic + potential) energy possessed by a body rolling down an inclined plane remains the same. Hence, the **law of conservation of energy is verified**.

PRECAUTIONS

1. *The entire setup of apparatus should be made stable because even a small shake of the apparatus may cause a lot of dissipation of energy.*
2. *Both the wings of inclined plane must lie in the same vertical plane.*
3. *The tracks of inclined plane should be cleaned by cotton/tissue paper in order to avoid excessive friction, even a minute amount of dust or stain on track can cause much friction.*
4. *The position of the ball at point F should be noted carefully because the ball comes to rest at that point for a moment only.*

Sources of Error

1. The inclined plane may not be frictionless.
2. The planes may be shaky.
3. Setup must be neat and clean.

Viva-Voce

Q. 1 Why should the position of the ball at the highest point of climb not lasts longer?

Ans. The position of the ball at the highest point of climb does not last longer because any delay will change this position as the ball stays there for a moment. Thus, the delay will introduce some error.

Q. 2 Why should the inclined planes be smooth and hard?

Ans. The inclined planes should be smooth and hard in order to reduce the friction.

Q. 3 Suggest any two precautions in this activity.

Ans. The two precautions in this activity are

(i) The apparatus or set up of apparatus should be made stable.

(ii) The tracks of inclined plane should be cleaned by cotton.

Q. 4 How can you study the conservation of mechanical energy in this activity?

Ans. The study of conservation of mechanical energy in this activity is studied by the motion of a steel ball rolling on a double inclined plane.

Q. 5 While rolling the ball, what happens to the angle of inclination at both ends?

Ans. While rolling the ball, the angles of inclination at both the ends are not necessarily equal.

Q. 6 State one example in which kinetic energy is conserved.

Ans. During elastic collision, KE of the system remains constant.

Q. 7 Does the law of conservation of momentum hold good in this experiment?

Ans. Yes, if there are no forces of friction anywhere between ball and inclined plant are consider.

Q. 8 Can this activity be performed successfully with a steel ball of smaller diameter. [NCERT]

Ans. Yes, diameter of the ball does not matter but the rate of energy dissipation should be less.

Q. 9 If the ball is not reaching exactly upto the same height on the other wing, comment on the observations. [NCERT]

Ans. If the ball does not reach upto the same height on the other wing, it indicates a loss of energy. This happens due to factors like friction and imperfectly smooth transitions between the inclined planes.

Activity 7

AIM

To study dissipation of energy of a simple pendulum by plotting a graph between square of amplitude and time.

Apparatus and Materials Required

A meter scale, a clamp stand, stopwatch, thread, a split cork, a pendulum bob, chalk piece.

Theory/Principle

If a bob of simple pendulum oscillates, then its amplitude decreases and its energy also decreases. So, here the energy is dissipated due to the Stoke's viscous force or damping force experienced by the bob of the pendulum.

The maximum energy E and the maximum amplitude A are related as

$$E = \frac{1}{2}kA^2 \qquad \text{...(i)}$$

In case of an **ideal pendulum** (i.e. not any viscous force or damping force is acting on the bob hence, it is free to oscillate), the total energy remains constant because the amplitude remains constant. But in real practice, it is not possible because amplitude decreases with time due to several forces such as air drag, restoring force, etc., acting on the bob, hence energy also decreases with time.

Therefore, amplitude A falls with time for each successive oscillation.

The amplitude as a function of time can be given as

$$A(t) = Ae^{-\lambda t/2} \qquad \text{...(ii)}$$

where, λ is a constant which depends on damping and the mass of the bob and A is the initial amplitude.

From the above Eqs. (i) and (ii), it can be said that

The square of the amplitude A^2 (which is proportional to energy E of the simple pendulum) decays with the passage of time and hence, the energy is dissipated with time.

Eventually, if we plot a graph between the square of amplitude and time of oscillations by taking them along Y and X-axes respectively, then we will get an **exponential decay curve with the passage of time.**

Procedure

Set up the Apparatus

1. First of all, take a thread of a length about 150 cm and tie its one end to the hook of the bob.
2. Now pass other end of the thread through two half-pieces of a split cork in such a way that the length of the pendulum is 140 cm.
3. Now, firmly fix the cork in the clamp stand such that the line of separation of the split cork is at right angles to the line OA along which the pendulum oscillates.
4. Now, after inserting the cork in the clamp stand, fix the iron stand on the table in such a way that the bob hangs below the table without touching its edge and it should be about 2 cm above the floor.

5. Mark a vertical line with a piece of chalk or ink on the edge of the table along the vertical thread *OA*. This line should be marked just behind the thread. This line is marked to know the mean or rest position of the bob.

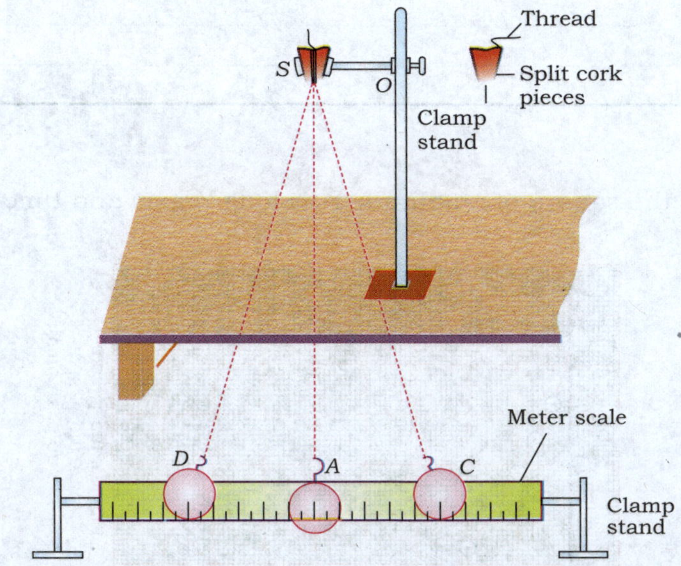

Setup of dissipation of energy of an oscillating simple pendulum

6. Now, put a transparent meter scale just below the pendulum so that the meter scale is in the plane of oscillations of pendulum and such that the zero mark of scale is just below the bob at rest. This meter scale is fixed with the help of two blocks or clamp stands.
7. Take a stopwatch and find its least count and zero error.

Relation between Amplitude and Time of Oscillations

8. Now, displace the bob from its mean position (about 10 cm away from its rest position) and leave it gently in such a way that it starts oscillating about its mean position.
9. Keep the bob oscillating for some time so that it can move along the straight line. After completion of few oscillations, when the bob reaches at the right extreme position i.e. point *A*, count zero and start the stopwatch at that instant.
10. Count one of oscillations when the bob reaches again at the right extreme position *A* and so on.
11. Note the value of amplitude of oscillation of the bob with the help of meter scale and the time of oscillations with the help of stopwatch when the bob completes 10, 20, 30,... oscillations. Now one can easily observe that the amplitude of oscillation of the bob decreases with the passage of time.
12. Note the observations in the tabular form.
13. Draw a graph between the square of amplitude and time of oscillations by taking them along *Y* and *X*-axes respectively, you will get a decreasing slope showing the amplitude decreases with the passage of time of oscillations of the bob.

Observations

Least count of the stopwatch = ... s.

Least count of meter scale = ... cm.

S.N.	Total number of oscillations	Amplitude, A (cm)	A^2 (cm^2)	Time, t (s)
1	10			
2	20			
3	30			
4	40			

Plotting Graph

Plot a graph between the square of amplitude A^2 along Y-axis and time t along X-axis.

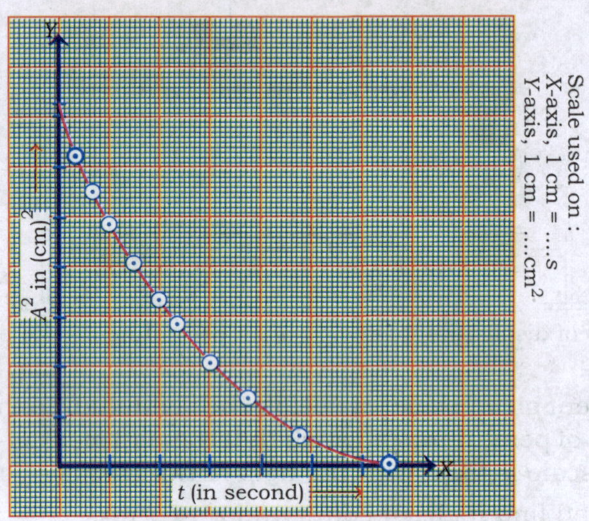

(Amplitude)^2-Time graph

Result

Since, we know that the energy E of a simple pendulum is directly proportional to the square of the amplitude A^2 and through the graph, we have noticed that the amplitude decreases with the passage of time and thus, the **energy of pendulum dissipates with the time.**

PRECAUTIONS

1. *The pendulum support should be rigid and the thread used must be inextensible.*
2. *The experiment should be performed at the place where the air drag is minimum.*
3. *Keep the bob oscillating for some time after giving some displacement to it. This helps the bob to oscillate in the same plane without any jerk.*
4. *The amplitude of oscillation should be small.*
5. *The split in the cork and the oscillation of the bob should be perpendicular to each other.*
6. *The bob should be suspended just above 2 cm from the ground.*
7. *In order to avoid the spinning of metallic bob, the pulling string should be used.*

Sources of Error

1. The thread may not be perfectly elastic.
2. There may be some personal errors involved in simultaneous noticing the amplitude and the stopwatch.

Viva-Voce

Q. 1 At what point during the oscillation of a simple pendulum, kinetic energy is maximum?

Ans. During the oscillation of a simple pendulum, the kinetic energy is maximum at the mean position.

Q. 2 Why the kinetic energy is zero at the extreme positions?

Ans. At the extreme positions, the bob of a simple pendulum is momentarily at rest. Thus, the kinetic energy of the bob is zero.

Q. 3 What is the relation between the damping force and velocity of the bob?

Ans. Damping force is proportional to the velocity of the bob.

$$fd = -bV$$

where, fd = Damping force

b = Damping coefficient

V = Velocity of bob

Q. 4 Why does the amplitude of simple pendulum decrease during the vibratory motion of the pendulum?

Ans. Amplitude decreases due to the damping forces (such as friction of the air, viscous force, etc.), as the damping forces oppose the motion of the pendulum.

Q. 5 Interpret the graph between A^2 and t you have drawn for a simple pendulum. [NCERT]

Ans. From the graph, it is observed that amplitude decays with the passage of time. Thus, the energy of pendulum dissipates with time.

Q. 6 Examine how the amplitude of oscillations changes with time. [NCERT]

Ans. The amplitude of oscillations decreases exponentially with time which reflects that energy initially dissipates rapidly and then dissipates slowly.

Q. 7 What does the decreasing amplitude of oscillation with time indicate in terms of variations in energy of simple pendulum with time? [NCERT]

Ans. The energy of a simple pendulum is directly proportional to the square of the amplitude. As the amplitude decreases exponentially with time, so the energy at the initial stage dissipates rapidly and further it dissipates slowly.

Q. 8 In what way does the graph between A and t differ from that between the A^2 and t graph, you have drawn. [NCERT]

Ans. The graph between A and t is more steeper than the graph between A^2 and t.

Q. 9 Compare the A^2 - t plots for

(a) oscillations with small damping and

(b) oscillations with large damping. [NCERT]

Ans.

(a) If the damping is small, then the amplitude of the forced vibration becomes very large and the applied frequency is close to the natural frequency.

(b) If the damping is large, then the amplitude of the forced vibration at resonance would be infinity and some damping is always present in the system and the amplitude remains finite.

Section B

Experiment 01

AIM

To determine Young's modulus of elasticity of the material of the given wire.

Apparatus and Materials Required

Two long identical pieces of wire, Searle's apparatus, a meter scale, a plumb line, slotted weights, screw gauge, spirit level.

Description of Apparatus

Searle's Apparatus

Searle's apparatus consists of two metal frames F_1 and F_2, which are hinged together in such a way that they can move relative to each other in vertical direction.

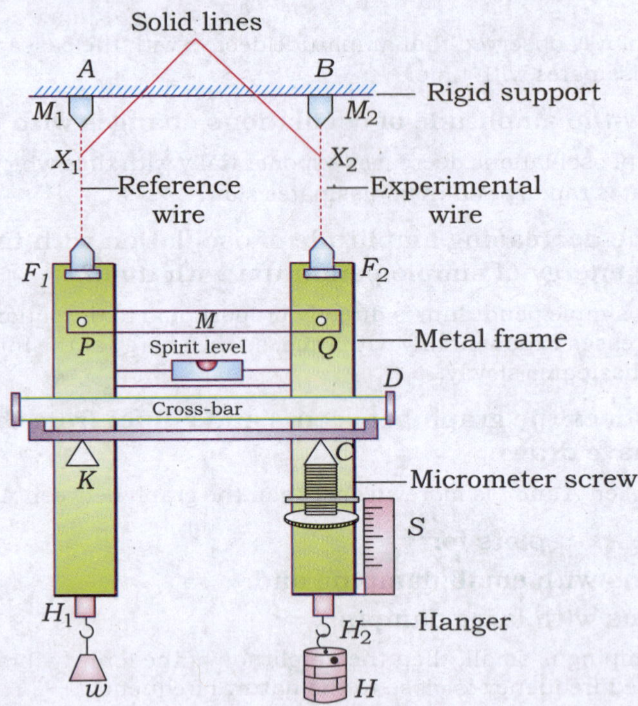

Here, a spirit level is used which is supported on a solid cross-bar frame *CD* which has been put stationary on the tip of the micrometer screw from the one end and on the knife edge (*K*) on the other end. This screw can be moved vertically and it has a disc having 100 equal divisions along its circumference.

There is a linear scale which is attached vertically and in case, if there would be any relative displacement between two hanged frames, then the spirit level will be no longer horizontal and the bubble of spirit level will get shifted from its centre. So, the distance through which the screw has to be moved gives the relative displacement between the two frames.

Theory/Principle

Searle's apparatus works on the principle of **Hooke's law**, according to which, "*stress developed in the wire (or any body) within the elastic limit of the material is directly proportional to the strain produced in it*".

i.e. $$\text{Stress} \propto \text{Strain} \Rightarrow E = \frac{\text{Stress}}{\text{Strain}}$$

where, E = coefficient of elasticity.

If a wire of length L and radius r is loaded with some suitable weight (Mg) due to which the increase in length of wire is ΔL.

Then, normal stress $= \dfrac{Mg}{\pi r^2}$ and the longitudinal strain $= \dfrac{\Delta L}{L}$

Therefore, Young's modulus, $$Y = \frac{\text{Normal stress}}{\text{Longitudinal strain}} = \frac{MgL}{\pi r^2 \Delta L}$$

where, ΔL = Extension of wire under load Mg, r = Radius of the wire

L = Length attached between the point of suspension and the frames.

By knowing ΔL, r and L, one can find the Young's modulus of elasticity of the material of the given wire.

Procedure

Set up the Apparatus

1. First of all, suspend the weights from the hooks in such a way that the two wires are stretched and can become free from any kinks.
2. Now, attach some constant weight (w) on the reference wire to keep it taut.
3. After this, measure the length of the experimental wire from the point of the support.

Measurement of Radius of Experimental Wire

4. Radius of experimental wire can be found using screw gauge. Firstly, determine the least count of screw gauge. It can be determined by dividing the pitch of the screw by the number of divisions on the circular scale.
5. Find the zero error in the screw gauge, if any zero error found, then consider it while measuring the diameter or radius of wire.
6. Determine the diameter of the wire (experimental one) at about 5 places and at each place in two mutually perpendicular directions.

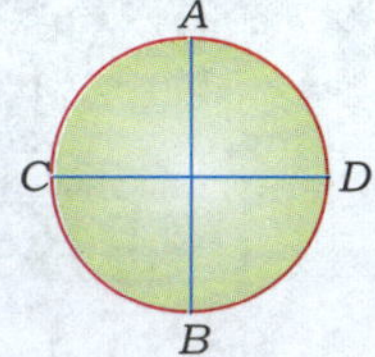

Measuring diameter of the wire in two mutually perpendicular direction.

7. After finding the diameter at different places of wire, determine the mean diameter and also the radius of the wire.
8. Knowing the breaking stress of the wire and the area of cross-section, find the breaking load of the wire. The maximum load on the experimental wire should not exceed one-third of breaking load otherwise the wire may break.

Measurement of Pitch and Least Count of Micrometer

9. Find the pitch and the least count of micrometer attached to the Searle's apparatus. Without hanger *B*, turn the micrometer screw gradually so that bubble of the spirit level stands exactly at the centre. Note the micrometer reading.

Measurement of Extension in Experimental Wire for Loading

10. Put a load of 0.5 kg on the hanger attached to the experimental wire and wait for sometimes (say 2 min) to allow the wire to expand fully. Now, the bubble in the spirit level will shift from the centre, bring the bubble back to centre by adjusting the micrometer screw, then note its reading.
11. Increase the load on experimental wire in steps of 0.5 kg and for each respective load, bring the bubble of the spirit level exactly to the centre by adjusting the micrometer screw.
12. Now, note the above readings.
13. Take about 8 observations for increasing load.

Measurement of Extension in Experimental Wire for Unloading

14. Now, decrease the load in steps of 0.5 kg and each time take micrometer screw reading as in step 10.
15. Note the readings on the micrometer screw each time for unloading in steps of 0.5 kg.

Note The micrometer reading may not be same for the same value of load during loading and unloading.

Observations

Length of the experimental wire = ... cm

Measurement of Diameter of Wire

Pitch of the screw gauge = ... cm

Number of divisions on the circular scale = ...

Least count of screw gauge = ... cm

Zero error of screw gauge = ...

Table for the Measurement of Diameter of Wire

S.N.	Reading along any direction			Reading along any perpendicular direction			Mean diameter, $D = \frac{a+b}{2}$ (cm)
	Linear scale reading, x (cm)	Circular scale reading, y (cm)	Observed diameter, a = x + (y + LC) (cm)	Linear scale reading, x′ (cm)	Circular scale reading, y′ (cm)	Observed diameter, b = x′ + (y′× LC) (cm)	
1							
2							
3							

Mean corrected diameter, $d = D$ + Zero correction = ...cm

Mean radius $= r = \frac{d}{2} =$ ... cm = ... m

Breaking stress of the wire = ...

Breaking load = ... kg

Measurement of Extension

Pitch of the micrometer screw = ... cm   Number of divisions on the circular scale = ...

Least count of the micrometer screw = ... cm

Acceleration due to gravity, $g = \ldots\ \text{cm/s}^2$

Table for the Extension Under Different Loads

S.N.	Load on hanger, M (kg)	Mircrometer screw reading			Extension for 1.5 kg, l' (cm)
		Load increasing, Z_1 (cm)	Load decreasing, Z_2 (cm)	Mean, $x = \frac{Z_1 + Z_2}{2}$ (cm)	
1	0.5			x_1	
2	1.0			x_2	
3	1.5			x_3	
4	2.0			x_4	$(x_4 - x_1)$
5	2.5			x_5	$(x_5 - x_2)$
6	3.0			x_6	$(x_6 - x_3)$

Calculations and Plotting Graph

Mean Length

The mean length can be determined by taking the mean of different values of extension obtained for 1.5 kg. From the table for the extension under different loads, the mean length can be given as

$$\text{Mean length, } \Delta L = \frac{(x_4 - x_1) + (x_5 - x_2) + (x_6 - x_3)}{3} = \frac{(2.0 - 0.5) + (2.5 - 1.0) + (3.0 - 1.5)}{3}$$

$$\Delta L = \ldots\ldots \text{cm for } 1.5 \text{ kg}$$

Young's Modulus by Using Formula

Young's modulus of experimental wire, $Y = \dfrac{MgL}{\pi r^2 \Delta L} = \ldots\ \text{Nm}^{-2}$

Young's Modulus by Using Graph

Plot a graph between load and extension by taking load along X-axis and extension along Y-axis. It will be noticiable that the graph will be a straight line.

Therefore, slope, $\tan\theta = \dfrac{DC}{FC} = \dfrac{BA}{EG} = \dfrac{\Delta L}{Mg} = \ldots \dfrac{m}{N}$

Thus, $$Y = \frac{L}{\pi r^2 \times \dfrac{\Delta L}{Mg}} = \frac{L}{\pi r^2 \times \tan\theta} = \ldots\ \text{Nm}^{-2}$$

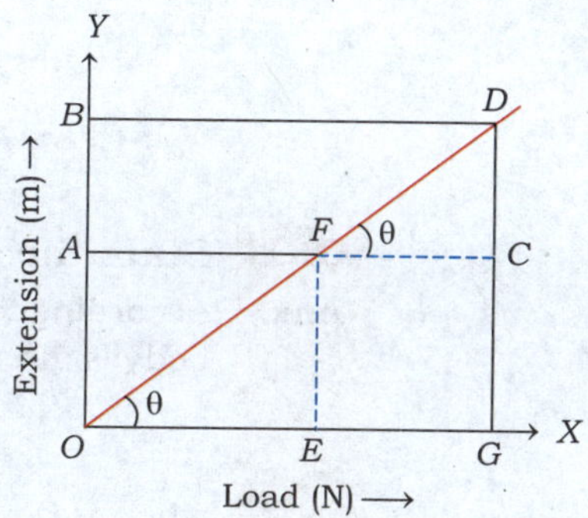

Load-extension graph for the given wire

Result

1. The Young's modulus of the material of given wire as determined by
   (i) using formula = ... Nm^{-2} (ii) using graph = ... Nm^{-2}
2. Straight line graph between load and extension shows that stress ∝ strain. This verifies Hooke's law.

Percentage Error

The percentage error of Young's modulus can be determined by knowing the two values of Y as given below.

Value of Y for the given material from the table of constant (actual value) = ... Nm^{-2}

Value of Y obtained from the experiment (measured value) = ... Nm^{-2}

$$\therefore \quad \text{Percentage error} = \frac{\text{Measured value} - \text{Actual value}}{\text{Actual value}} \times 100\%$$

PRECAUTIONS

1. The same wires should be hanged from the rigid support in all respect.

2. The Searle's apparatus screw should be moved in one direction to avoid backlash error.

3. Diameter should be measured at different places and also along the two mutually perpendicular directions, also check for its uniformity, it should be uniform throughout its whole length.

4. Load should be increased or decreased in regular steps.

5. Slotted weights should be added and removed gently.

6. Experimental and reference wires should be of same length, material and cross-section.

7. Adjust the spirit level only after sufficient time gap following each loading or unloading.

Sources of Error

1. The slotted weights may not be equal to the marked weights.
2. The support may not be perfectly rigid.
3. The wires used in the experiment may not have uniform cross-section throughout.
4. While loading or unloading, the diameter of wire may alter.
5. Kinks may not get removed from the experimental wire before starting the experiment.
6. Backlash error of the device used for measuring extension. This is an error occurred when the screw of the micrometer gets loosen and does not move forward.

Viva-Voce

Q. 1 State the Hooke's law as changed by Thomas Young.

Ans. According to Thomas Young, "within the elastic limit of the material, the stress developed in the body is directly proportional to the strain produced in it".

i.e. $\text{Stress} \propto \text{Strain} \quad \Rightarrow \quad E = \frac{\text{Stress}}{\text{Strain}}$

where, E = modulus of elasticity

Q. 2 How can you define Poisson's ratio?

Ans. Poisson's ratio is defined as the ratio between the lateral strain and the longitudinal strain.

Q. 3 What can be the reason of removing the kinks before starting the experiment?

Ans. If it is not done at the right time, then the kinks opened by the load will show more extension of wire.

Q. 4 Can you give the expression for the work done in stretching a wire?

Ans. Work done in stretching a wire can be given as

$$\text{Work done} = \frac{1}{2} \times \text{Stress} \times \text{Strain}$$

It becomes stored as potential energy of the molecules in stretched part of body.

Q. 5 Give the reasons for the requirement of two wires in Searle's apparatus?

Ans. By the use of these two wires in the Searle's apparatus,

(i) the small extensions can be effectively measured.

(ii) effect of change in length due to change in room temperature may be eliminated.

Q. 6 Define the term Young's modulus of elasticity.

Ans. Young's modulus of elasticity can be defined as the ratio of the normal stress to the longitudinal strain produced by it.

$$Y = \frac{\text{Normal stress}}{\text{Ionigitudinal strain}}$$

Q. 7 What is the reason of hanging both the wires from same rigid support?

Ans. Loading of experimental wire will equally yield suspension points of both the wires suspended from the same rigid support. It will eliminate the error due to unequal yielding of support.

Q. 8 Define elasticity and give its cause.

Ans. Elasticity is a property of matter due to which a body gets deformed on applying a force but regains its original shape or size on the removal of external deforming force.

The intermolecular forces between the molecules of substance gives rise to elasticity.

Q. 9 If the length of the wire used is reduced, what will be its effect on
(i) extension on wire (ii) stress on wire? [NCERT]

Ans. (i) If the length of a wire is used to reduced, the extension it experiences under a load will also be reduced.

(ii) If the length of the wire gets reduced, then there will be no change in the stress of wire.

Q.10 Use the wire of different radii (r_1, r_2, r_3) but of same material in this experiment. So, is there any change in the value of Young's modulus of elasticity of the material? Discuss your result. [NCERT]

Ans. According to question, consider three wires of different radii r_1, r_2 and r_3.

Since, we know that Young's modulus is depend upon the property of the material but not of the size of wire.

So, all the wires with their respective different radii will have same Young's modulus of elasticity.

Experiment 02

AIM

To find the force constant of a helical spring by plotting a graph between load and extension.

Apparatus and Materials Required

An iron stand with a heavy base, a vertical wooden scale, spring, a rigid support, a hook, a pointer, six 50 g slotted weights, a 50 g hanger, a pair of pliers, feviquick, a mirror strip.

Theory/Principle

The helical spring is a spring in which wire is wrapped in a coil that resembles a screw thread, works on the principle of **Hooke's law**. According to this law,

"The extension (i.e. strain) in the spring which is hanging from a solid support at one end only is directly proportional to the load applied (i.e. stress) on the free end, within its elastic limit."

Suppose on applying the force F on the lower end of the spring, its length increases by l. Due to elasticity, the spring will regain its original length after removing the force.

i.e.
$$\text{Load} \propto \text{Extension}$$
$$F \propto l \Rightarrow F = -kl$$

where, k is the constant of proportionality called as **force constant** or **spring constant** of the spring (Here –ve sign indicates that restoring force acts in opposite direction to the applied force). It may be defined as the restoring force set up per unit extension in the spring. Its unit is Nm^{-1} or dyne cm^{-1}.

Thus, by knowing the value of extension in length of the spring and the corresponding load suspended from it, one can find the force constant of that spring.

Procedure

Set up the Apparatus

1. Suspend the helical spring (having a pointer P and hanger H at its free end) from a rigid support, i.e. one end of the spring should be fixed on the top clamp rod with the help of pliers as shown in the figure given below.

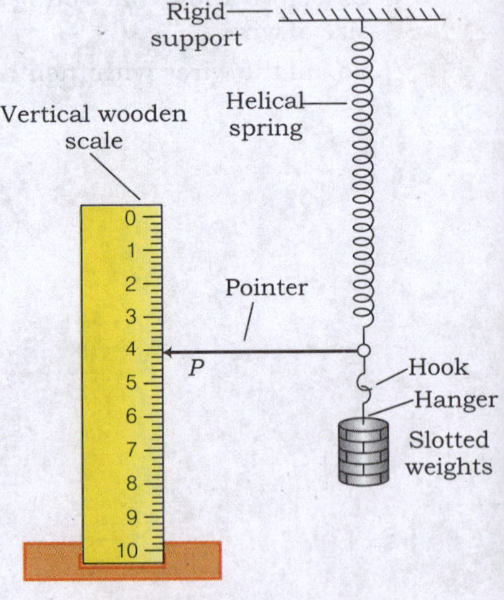

Extension of spring

Measurement of Extension in Length

2. Firstly, note down the initial position of the pointer on the scale when no weight is suspended from the hook i.e. zero value of the applied load.
3. Now, add a suitable weight (say 50 g) to the hanger and wait for the spring to be in equilibrium (i.e. wait for pointer to stop). Now, note the position of pointer again. After recording the position of pointer, keep on adding the weights on the hanger in steps of 50 g.

4. Note the corresponding positions of pointer and take the suitable number of readings.
5. Now, reduce the weight from hanger in the steps of 50 g and note the positions of pointer on vertical scale.
6. After recording the observations of change in length of spring during loading *a* (cm) and unloading *b* (cm), calculate their mean of the length of loading and unloading.

   Now, determine the difference between two consequent.

Observations

Least count of vertical scale = ... cm.

Mass of the hanger of slotted weight = ... g.

Mass of each slotted weight = ... g.

Extension in length, l ...... cm.

Table for Load and Extension

S. N.	Load on hanger, x (gf)	Reading of pointer tip on vertical scale			Extension, l (cm)
		Loading, a (cm)	Unloading, b (cm)	Mean, $c = \frac{a+b}{2}$ (cm)	
1	0			c_0	
2	50			c_1	$l_1 = c_1 - c_0 = \ldots$ cm
3	100			c_2	$l_2 = c_2 - c_0 = \ldots$ cm
4	150			c_3	$l_3 = c_3 - c_0 = \ldots$ cm

Plotting Graph and Calculations

After plotting the graph between load and extension by taking load along *X*-axis and extension along *Y*-axis, it is observed that the graph shows a straight line.

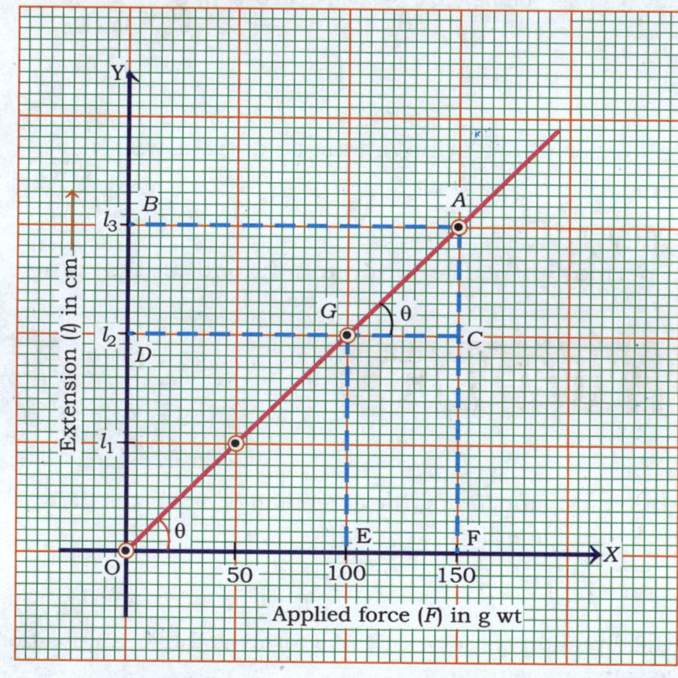

Scale *X*-axis

1 cm = 50 g wt of F

Scale *Y*-axis

1 cm = 0.5 cm of l

Load-extension graph for helical spring between F and l

Therefore, $$k = \frac{F}{l} = \text{slope of straight line,}$$

$$\tan\theta = \frac{AC}{GC} = \frac{BD}{EF}$$

The weight 1 gf can be converted into newton and length 1 cm into m as

$$1 \text{ gf} = 1 \times 10^{-3} \times 9.8 \text{ N}$$

and $$1 \text{ cm} = 1 \times 10^{-2} \text{ m}$$

Thus, $$k = ... \text{ Nm}^{-1}$$

Result

1. The load-extension graph for a given helical spring is a straight line.
2. The force constant for the given spring is ...... Nm^{-1}.

PRECAUTIONS

1. The spring support should be rigid.
2. The motion of the loaded spring should not be jerky, it should be strictly along vertical.
3. The amplitude of oscillations should be small.
4. Noting down of the reading should be done only when the tip of the pointer comes to rest.
5. The addition and removal of weights should be done in a gentle manner.
6. The values on the slotted weight should indicate their true mass.
7. The loading should be done under the elastic limit of the material of the spring to avoid the breaking.
8. The tip of the pointer should not touch the surface of the meter scale.
9. The half meter scale should be maintained parallel to the suspended spring.

Sources of Error

1. The slotted weights added on hanger may not have true or correct weight.
2. The pointer may not be horizontal.
3. The support of the spring may not be rigid.
4. The spring may get stretched permanently due to too much load on the hanger.

Viva-Voce

Q. 1 What is Hooke's law?

Ans. According to Hooke's law, "within the elastic limits, the extension of an elastic body is directly proportional to the tension (stretching force)".

i.e. $$F = -kx$$

where, k = spring constant.

Here the negative sign shows the direction of restoring force towards the mean position, while taking the magnitude, negative sign can be neglect.

Or

According to Hook's law Under the limit of electricity stress is directly proportional to the strain.

$$\text{Stress} \propto \text{Strain}$$

$$\text{Stress} = E \cdot \text{strain}$$

$$E = \text{Modulus of electricity}$$

Q. 2 If a spring is cut into equal parts, then what is the spring constant of each part with respect to original spring?

Ans. If the force constant of original (or given) spring is k, then the force or spring constant of each part with respect to original one would be $2k$.

$\because$ Extension $\propto$ Length of spring

$\therefore$ For full spring extension y, $k = \frac{F}{y}$

For half spring under same force extension is $\frac{y}{2}$, then

$$k' = \frac{F}{y/2} = \frac{2F}{y} = 2k \qquad \left(\because \frac{F}{y} = k\right)$$

Q. 3 What is the direct formula to determine the force constant of a spring?

Ans. When the spring oscillates about its mean position, then the time period of the loaded spring can be given as $T = 2\pi\sqrt{\frac{m}{k}} \Rightarrow k = \frac{4\pi^2 m}{T^2}$

where, T = time period, m = mass loaded and k = force constant

Q. 4 While performing the experiment, what is the reason for not allowing the tip of the pointer to touch the vertical scale?

Ans. While performing the experiment, it is not allowed to make the tip of the pointer to touch the vertical scale because due to the friction, the value of extension of the spring will be less than its actual value.

Q. 5 Assume the two springs with force constants k_1 and k_2, respectively are joined in series, then what will be the force constant of the combined system?

Ans. If k_1 and k_2 are the spring constants of the two springs, that are joined in series, then the force constant of the combined system will be given by $k = \frac{k_1 k_2}{k_1 + k_2}$.

Q. 6 Mention some factors on which the force constant of spring depends.

Ans. The spring (or force) constant of the spring depends upon the turn density, Young's modulus of elasticity of material of the wire of spring, length and area of cross-section of the spring.

Q. 7 What can be the reason for taking the readings for same load while load increasing and again while load decreasing?

Ans. If the readings get noted before the wire reaches the steady state, then the load increasing will be slightly less than the actual value and while load decreasing, it will be slightly more.

Q. 8 Two springs A (soft) and B (stiff), loaded with the same mass on their hangers, are suspended one-by-one from the same rigid support. They are set into vertical oscillations at different times and the time period of their oscillations are noted. In which spring, will the oscillations be slower? [NCERT]

Ans. The buoyancy of air and viscous drag due to it may slightly increase the time period of oscillations. This effect can be reduced by taking stiff spring of high density material. So, as per the question, when the two springs A which is soft and B which is stiff, loaded with the same mass on their hangers, if both of them are set into vertical oscillations, then time period of oscillation will be slower for load B.

Experiment 03

AIM

To study the variation in volume (V) with pressure (p) for a sample of air at constant temperature by plotting graphs between p and V, and between p and $1/V$.

Apparatus and Materials Required

Fortin's barometer, Boyle's law apparatus, vernier callipers, thermometer, set square, spirit level.

Description of Apparatus

Boyle's Law Apparatus

Which consists of two glass tubes about 25 cm long and 0.5 cm in diameter. Its one tube AB is closed at one end while the another tube CD is opened.

These two tubes are drawn into fine opening at the other ends A and D. The ends of both the tubes are connected by a thick walled rubber tube. The tube AB is fixed vertically along the meter scale S and the other tube CD can be moved vertically along a vertical rod and can be fixed to it at any altitude with the help of the screw.

Both the tubes and the rubber tubing are filled with mercury. The height of mercury in both the tubes is measured by the vertical scale with the help of set square. The closed end tube has some air trapped in it. Due to this,the volume of air is proportional to the length of air column because it is of uniform cross-section. The whole apparatus is fixed on a horizontal platform with a horizontal stand provided with levelling screws.

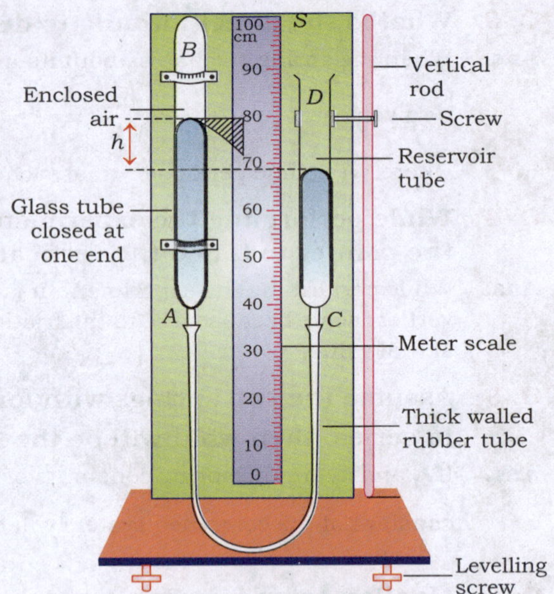

Boyle's Law of Apparatus

Theory/Principle

Boyle's Law

According to this law, *"at a constant temperature, the pressure exerted by an enclosed mass of gas is inversely proportional to its volume."*

i.e. $$p \propto \frac{1}{V} \Rightarrow p = \frac{K}{V}$$

It means that at constant temperature, the volume of the given mass of a gas varies inversely with its pressure. So, it signifies that the **graph between p and V will be a curve, i.e. a rectangular hyperbola and between p and $1/V$ will be a straight line.**

Procedure

Measurement of Pressure

The pressure of the enclosed air in tube *AB* is measured by noting the difference (h) in the mercury level (X and Y) in the two tubes *AB* and *CD* with the help of set square by setting one of its edges tangential to the curved surface of the mercury and other parallel to the vertical scale. Since, liquid in interconnected vessels have same pressure at any horizontal level,

$$p \text{ (pressure of enclosed air)} = Z \pm h \qquad \text{(where, } Z \text{ is the atmospheric pressure)}$$

$Z \pm h$ will be considered according to the levels X and Y taking into account whether the pressure of air in tube *AB* is more than atmospheric pressure or less, that means these two are added algebrically.

Measurement of Volume of Trapped Air

In case the closed tube is not graduated,

Volume of air in tube = Volume of air in length *PR* – Volume of air in curved portion

Let r be the radius of the tube.

Volume of curved portion = Volume of the hemisphere of radius,

$$r = \frac{1}{2} \times \frac{4}{3}\pi r^3 = \frac{2}{3}\pi r^3$$

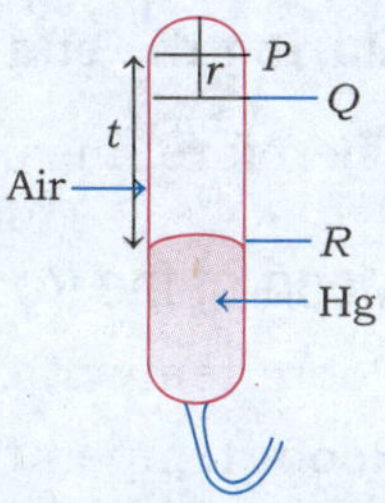

Volume of $PQ = \pi r^2 \times r = \pi r^3$

Error in volume $= \pi r^3 - \frac{2}{3}\pi r^3 = \frac{1}{3}\pi r^3$

This should be subtracted from the measured length l.

Measurement of Volume of Air for a Given Pressure

Initial Observations

1. Firstly, set up plank of Boyle's law apparatus vertically with help of levelling screws and spirit level.
2. Note the room temperature by using a thermometer.
3. Note the atmospheric pressure using Fortin's barometer.
4. After measuring the air enclosed in tube *AB*, adjust the height of tube *CD* such that mercury level in both the tubes is at same level.
5. After noting down the reading of mercury levels in tube *AB* and *CD* against scale *S*, note down the volume of enclosed gas in graduated tube *AB*. The same procedure will be followed as discussed in part (ii) to measure the volume.

Raising the Tube *CD*

6. Raise the tube *CD* upwards by about 2 cm. Mercury level in tube *AB* will also move upwards a little, reducing the volume of enclosed air. Note down the reduced volume.
7. Moreover, pressure of air in tube *AB* increases and mercury level in *AB* remains lower than that in *CD*.
8. Position of mercury level in tube *CD* is noted against the vertical scale using the set squares. Here, the set square is used to read the meniscus of the mercury, thereby the difference in the mercury level X and Y can be determined.
9. Now repeat the steps (6), (7) and (8) few more times by moving tube *CD* upward by 2 cm each time.

Lowering the Tube *CD*

10. Also, lower the tube *CD* and bring the mercury level with the same horizontal line as in tube *AB*.
11. Move the tube *CD* downwards by few centimetres.
12. Notice that the mercury level in tube *AB* will also come down (which shows a little increase in volume of enclosed air).
13. After noting down the value of increased volume, notice that the pressure of air in tube *AB* decreases and mercury level in tube *AB* should remain higher than that in tube *CD*.
14. Now, repeat the above steps (11) and (12) few more times by lowering the tube *CD* each time by 2 cm.
15. Note all these observations in a tabular form.

Observations

Mean of the Atmospheric Pressure

During the beginning of experiment, atmospheric pressure, Z_1 = ... cm of Hg

During the end of experiment, atmospheric pressure, Z_2 = ... cm of Hg

Therefore, mean atmospheric pressure, $Z = \frac{Z_1 + Z_2}{2}$ = ... cm of Hg

Mean of the Room Temperature

Room temperature during the beginning of experiment, t_1 = ... °C

Room temperature at the end of the experiment, t_2 = ... °C

Mean temperature, $T = \frac{t_1 + t_2}{2}$ = ... °C

Correction in the Level of Mercury due to Curved Portion of the Tube *AB*

Reading at the top end of the closed tube *AB*, x_1 =...... cm

Reading where the curved portion of tube *AB* begins, x_2 = ... cm

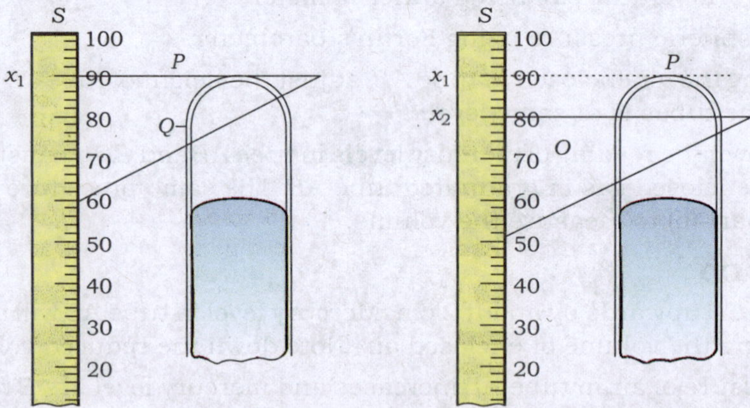

Correction for the close tube

Now, correction $= \frac{1}{3}(x_1 - x_2) = ...$ cm

Or

The correction in level can also be determined with the same method as discussed in part of the procedure, i.e. correction for level, $l = \frac{1}{3}r$, where r = radius of the tube.

Table for Measurement of Pressure and Volume of Enclosed Air

S.N.	Level of mercury		Pressure difference, $h = X - Y$ (cm of Hg)	Pressure of air in tube AB, $p = Z \pm h$ (cm of Hg)	Volume of air, V (cm)^3	$\frac{1}{V}$ (cm^{-3})	pV
	In tube *AB* (closed one), X (cm of Hg)	In tube *CD* (opened one), *Y* (cm of Hg)					
1							
2							
3							
4							

Note In order to achieve the aim of this experiment, you should focus on its centralised core concept, i.e. while taking the readings in the observation table, the value of V should be decreased with respect to the increasing value of p while the value of $1/V$ should be increased with respect to the increasing value of p. So, it will give you the constant value of pV, which is an ultimate result.

Plotting graph

With the help of the observation table,

1. Plot the graph between p and V by taking p along X-axis and V along Y-axis. The graph will be a rectangular hyperbola.
2. Plot a graph between p and $1/V$ by taking p along X-axis and $1/V$ along Y-axis. The graph will be a straight line passing through the origin.

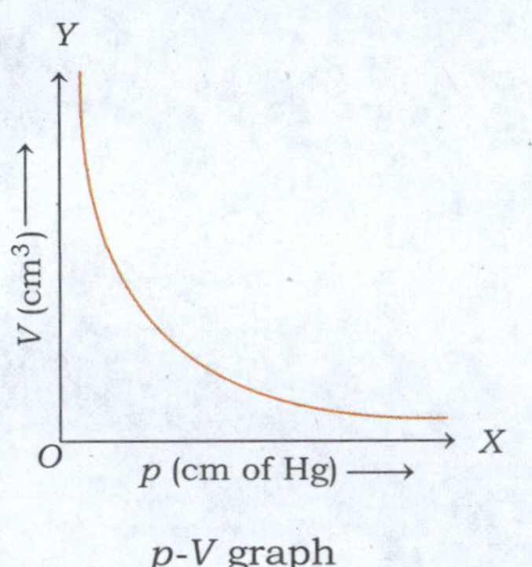

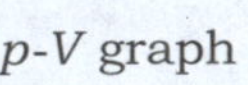

p-V graph

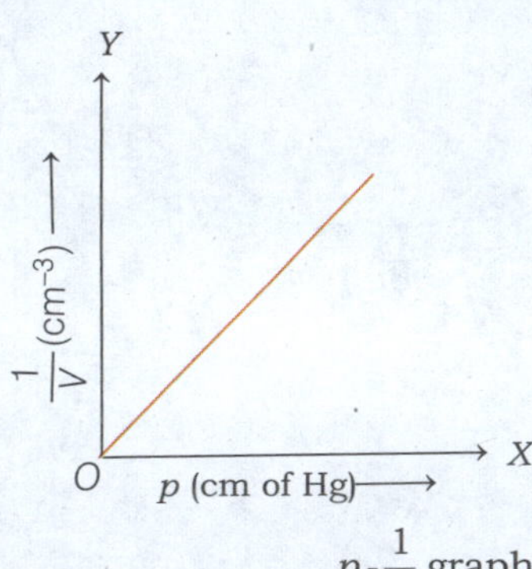

p-$\frac{1}{V}$ graph

Result

1. In the observation table, the value of pV is constant.
2. Within the experimental limits, the graph between p and V is a rectangular hyperbola. i.e. pV = constant.
3. Within the experimental limits, the graph between p and $1/V$ is a straight line. i.e. $p \propto \frac{1}{V}$.

PRECAUTIONS

1. *Before starting the experiment, apparatus should be levelled on prank gently.*
2. *The correction for the curved portion of the closed tube should be taken under the consideration while measuring the volume of air.*
3. *The open tube should be plugged with cotton when not in use.*
4. *The readings should be taken carefully in order to get an exact desired graph either in between p and V or in between p and 1 / V.*
5. *Mercury used should be clean and not leave any trace on the glass.*
6. *The apparatus should not be shifted in between observations.*
7. *The apparatus must be well covered when not in use to avoid any contamination.*

Sources of Error

1. The room temperature and the atmospheric pressure may get changed while performing the experiment.
2. The closed end of the tube *AB* may not be hemispherical.
3. The air in tube *AB* may not be dry.
4. The readings may not be taken carefully which can result into an error in the ultimate result.
5. The mercury may be oxidised due to exposure to atmosphere.
6. The diameter of the glass tubes may or may not be the same.

Viva-Voce

Q. 1 State Boyle's law.

Ans. It states that the pressure (p) of an enclosed gas (i.e. for a given mass of gas) is inversely proportional to its volume (V), provided that the temperature of gas remains constant.

i.e. $$p \propto \frac{1}{V} \Rightarrow pV = \text{constant}$$

Q. 2 What can be the reason of making the Boyle's law apparatus vertical?

Ans. It is necessary to make the Boyle's law apparatus vertical because, if it is not vertical, then the reading of mercury column will not be accurate.

Q. 3 Why should the air enclosed in tube *AB* be dry?

Ans. Air enclosed in tube *AB* should be dry because the behaviour of water vapours at room temperature is different than the behaviour of air. Moisture in air will exert its own pressure on the mercury column.

Q. 4 While performing the experiment, what is the reason of moving the tube *CD* upward or downward slowly?

Ans. It is usually done because while moving the tube *CD* in upward direction, the pressure on the gas enclosed in tube *AB* increases and while moving the tube *CD* in downward direction, the pressure decreases.

Q. 5 What is the use of mercury in Boyle's law apparatus?

Ans. Since, the pressure difference is in terms of difference of mercury levels in tube *AB* and *CD*. So, when this difference gets added algebraically to atmospheric pressure, it gives the pressure of air in tube *AB* in cm of Hg.

Q. 6 Name the laws which govern the gas behaviour.

Ans. They are Boyle's law, Charles' law, Gay-Lussac's law, Avogadro's law, Dalton's law of partial pressures and Graham's law of diffusion.

Q. 7 Give any one postulate of kinetic theory of gases.

Ans. The intermolecular forces are so small that the molecules may be considered to be moving freely in the gas.

Q. 8 Why should the mercury used in Boyle's law apparatus be clean and dry?

Ans. Mercury used in the apparatus should be clean and dry because pressure being measured in the terms of height of mercury column and the contamination will change the density of mercury and ultimately, the value of pressure.

Q. 9 Give the relation or dependency of the pressure on the radius of tube *AB* and *CD*.

Ans. The pressure does not depend upon the radius or area of tube.

Q. 10 Why should the upper meniscus of the mercury in the two tubes recorded carefully using a set-square?

Ans. While measuring the upper meniscus of the mercury in the two tubes, the set square is usually placed tangentially to the upper meniscus of mercury in order to determine its level (without any error).

Q.11 If we perform experiment with a tube of insufficient length, will the liquid overflow?

Ans. No, the liquid meniscus will adjust its radius of curvature.

Q.12 Why does the meniscus of water appear to be inverted when seen through the telescope?

Ans. This is because the final image formed by a compound microscope is inverted wrt object.

Q.13 The apparatus when not in use should be kept covered to avoid the contamination of mercury in the open tube. How will the oxidation of mercury affect the experiment? [NCERT]

Ans. When the apparatus is not in use, then it should be kept covered because pressure is measured in terms of height of mercury column and the contamination of mercury will change its density and in turn the value of pressure. If mercury oxidises, there might be change in mass or volume of liquid mercury, which could impact experiments.

Q.14 If the diameter of tube *AB* is large, then why would the estimation of curved portion be unreliable? [NCERT]

Ans. If the diameter of the tube becomes large, then it will lead to the increase in the volume of curved portion. It means that the error in its volume will get increased which ultimately will lead to the error in its length.

Q.15 Comment on the two methods used for the estimation of volume of the curved portion of closed tube. What are the assumptions to be made for the two methods? [NCERT]

Ans. Both the methods used in the experiment were to analyse the variation of volume with pressure. First method includes the volume of trapped air and second one includes the measurement of volume of air for a given pressure.

Experiment 04

AIM

To determine the surface tension of water by capillary rise method.

Apparatus and Materials Required

Travelling microscope, beaker, cork along with pin, three glass capillary tubes of different radii, clamps and stand, thermometer, water, plumb line, dilute caustic soda solution, dilute nitric acid, a fine moving stand of adjustable height.

Theory/Principle

1. **Surface Tension** It is the property of a liquid by virtue of which its free surface at rest behaves like an elastic skin or a stretched rubber membrane with a tendency to contract, so as to occupy minimum surface area.

$$\text{Surface tension} = \frac{\text{Force}}{\text{Length}}$$

Its SI unit is newton per metre (Nm^{-1}) and dimensional formula is $[M^1L^0T^{-2}]$.

2. **Capillarity** When a capillary tube is dipped in a liquid, the liquid level either rises or falls in the capillary tube. The phenomena of rise or fall of a liquid level in a capillary tube dipped in it, is called capillarity or capillary action.

Due to this, the weight of the column of the liquid below the meniscus is usually supported by the upward force of surface tension.

Therefore, the surface tension is given by, $T = \dfrac{r(h + r/3)\rho g}{2\cos\theta}$

where, h = Height of the liquid column, r = Inner radius of the capillary tube,

θ = Angle of contact i.e. angle between tangent to the liquid surface at the point of contact and solid surface inside the liquid.

Hence, by knowing the values of h, r and θ, one can find the surface tension of water by capillary rise method.

Procedure

Arrangement of the Apparatus

1. First of all, put the stand of adjustable height on the table and let its base be in horizontal direction with the help of levelling screws.
2. Use the clean water (dust free) in an open dish or beaker and measure its temperature and put it on the top of the stand.
3. Now, after putting the water, take few capillary tubes of different radii and make them clean successively in caustic soda and nitric acid solution and rinse thoroughly with water and then dry them.
4. In the accordance of increasing radius, clamp the capillary tubes in a metallic plate.

5. Also, mount a pointer on the same plate parallel to the capillary tubes.
6. Along with capillary tubes, also clamp the horizontal handle of metallic plate in a vertical stand in such a way that the capillary tubes and the pointer becomes vertical. This can be easily done by using plumb line.
7. After clamping the handle, manage the height of metallic plate in such a way that the capillary tubes dip in the water in a beaker. Even, besides this, adjust the position of pointer in such a way that its tip should just touch the water surface.

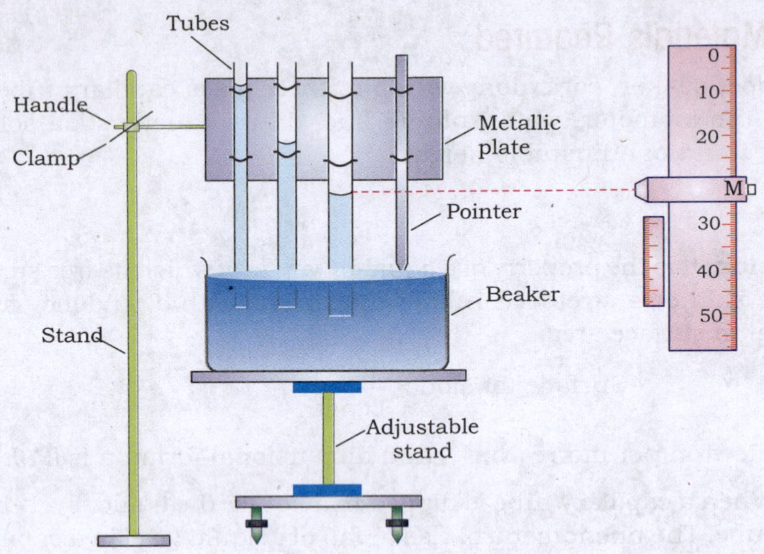

Experimental set up to determine the surface tension of water by capillary rise

To Determine the Capillary Rise

8. For the horizontal and vertical scale of travelling microscope, determine the least count.
9. Now, move the microscope to a particular height by making its axis horizontal and pointed tip in the direction of capillary tubes.
10. Bring the microscope in front of first capillary tube (which has maximum rise).
11. After this, with help of microscope, let the horizontal wire to just touch the central part of concave meniscus but it looks convex through the microscope. Take the reading on the vertical scale of the microscope.

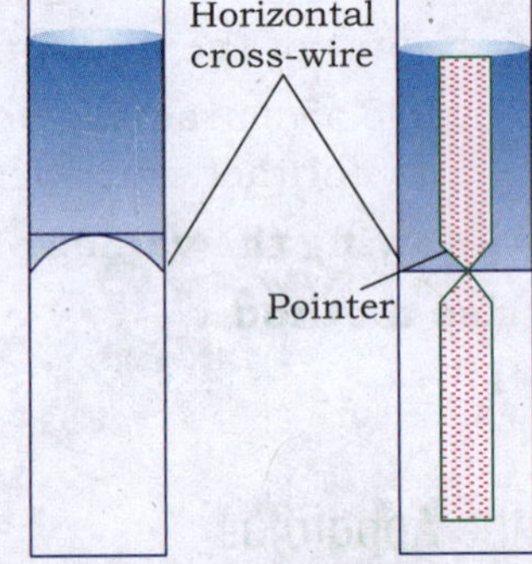

Enlarged view of water meniscus through microscope

12. Again, after moving the microscope horizontally, bring it towards the second capillary tube and then note the position of the microscope on vertical scale.
13. In the same manner, repeat the steps (11) and (12) for the third capillary tube.
14. Now, the microscope is to be moved further horizontally to bring it just in front of the tip of the needle.

15. Lower the microscope and make its horizontal wire touch the tip of the pointer. Now, the horizontal cross-wire lies symmetrically between the tip of the needle and its inverted image in the water. The corresponding reading on the vertical scale of the microscope is noted.
16. The difference between reading of the meniscus and reading of the tip of the needle will give the capillary rise of the given liquid.

To Determine the Internal Diameter of the Capillary Tube

17. In order to find out the internal diameter of the capillary tube, put the first capillary tube on the stand with adjustable height.
18. Now, the microscope should be focused on the end dipped in water.
19. Notice that a white circle surrounded by a green circular strip will be formed.
20. After the formation of circular strip, let the horizontal wire to touch the inner circle at D and B.

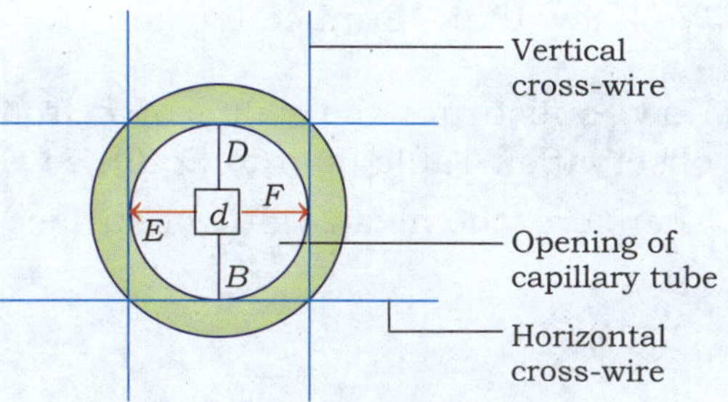

Determination of internal diameter of capillary tube

21. Now, note down the readings as the difference will give the vertical internal diameter BD of the capillary tube.
22. In the similar way for finding the internal diameter EF, repeat the steps (20) and (21) to make the vertical cross-wire touch the inner circle at E and also at F. Repeat this procedure to measure the internal diameters of the rest two capillary tubes.
23. Note the observations in a tabular form.

Observations

Least count of travelling microscope, LC = ... mm

Table for the Measurement of Capillary Rise

S. N. of capillary tube	Reading of meniscus, H_1 (cm)			Reading of the pin touching the water surface, h_2 (cm)			Height of the liquid rise, $h = h_1 - h_2$(cm)
	Main scale reading, x (cm)	Vernier scale reading, y (cm)	$h_1 = (x + y \times LC)$ (cm)	Main scale reading, x' (cm)	Vernier scale reading, y' (cm)	$h_2 = (x' + y' \times LC)$ (cm)	
1							
2							
3							

Table for the Measurement of Internal Diameter of the Capillary Tubes

S. N. of capillary tube	Microscope reading along diameter, EF (cm)		Diameter, $D' = \beta - \alpha$ (cm)	Microscope reading along diameter, BD (cm)		Diameter, $D'' = \beta' - \alpha'$ (cm)	Mean diameter, $D = \frac{D' + D''}{2}$ (cm)
	One end, α (cm)	Other end, β (cm)		One end, α' (cm)	Other end, β' (cm)		
1							
2							
3							

Mean radius, $r = \frac{\text{Mean diameter}}{2}$ = ... cm

Temperature of water, t ..... °C

Density of water at observed temperature, ρ = ... g cm^{-3}

Calculations

We know that, Surface tension, $T = \frac{r(h + r/3)\rho g}{2\cos\theta}$ ...(i)

Now, substitute the value of h from the observation Table (i) and the value of r from the observation Table (ii) into Eq.(i), so we will get the value of T (surface tension).

Therefore, the mean value of surface tension,

$$T = \frac{T_1 + T_2 + T_3}{3} = \text{..... dyne cm}^{-1}$$

Result

The surface tension of water at $t°$ C = ... dyne cm^{-1}.

PRECAUTIONS

1. *While dipping in the water, the capillary should be kept vertical.*
2. *The liquid column's height should be measured from the lowest point of concave meniscus.*
3. *The adjusting screws of the microscope should be moved in one direction at a time in order to avoid a backlash error.*
4. *Impure water should not be used as sometimes it has some traces of grease, so that the fresh tap water is preferred.*
5. *Temperature of water should be noted regularly. The rise in temperature affects the value of surface tension.*
6. *The water in the beaker should be filled upto its brim, so that glass edge does not obstruct the view of the tip of the pointer.*
7. *While focussing the microscope during the experiment, the adjusting screws of microscope should move in one direction only.*

Sources of Error

1. The adjusting screws of microscope may not be moved in one direction at a time.
2. Placement of capillary tube may not be vertical which introduces an error in the measurement of the height of the liquid column in the tube.
3. Change in temperature while performing the experiment may cause the error.
4. Water and capillary tube may not be free from grease and dirt.

Viva-Voce

Q. 1 What do you think about the reason of existence of a pressure difference on the two sides of a curved liquid surface?

Ans. There is always a pressure difference on the two sides of a curved liquid surface because curved free liquid surface has more area, due to which it tends to become flat in order to minimise the surface area. Thus, the pressure is not the same above and below the surface.

Q. 2 How can you define the term capillarity?

Ans. The phenomena of rise or fall of a liquid level in a capillary tube dipped in the liquid, is called capillarity.

Q. 3 While performing the experiment, how do you decide that a liquid will rise or get depressed in a capillary?

Ans. While performing the experiment, if a liquid wets the surface of container, then it will rise and if it does not stick to the container surface, then it will get depressed.

Q. 4 What is surface tension?

Ans. It is the property of a liquid by the virtue of which its free surface at rest behaves like an elastic skin or a stretched rubber membrane with a tendency to contract in order to occupy the minimum surface area.

Q. 5 What can be the reason of preferring the fresh tap water rather than the pure distilled water for the determination of surface tension?

Ans. The fresh tap water is preferred instead of pure distilled water for the determination of surface tension because the distilled water is slightly greasy and its surface tension is less.

Q. 6 What can you say about the variation of surface tension of water with respect to the temperature?

Ans. Surface tension of water decreases with increase in its temperature.

Q. 7 Differentiate between force of cohesion and force of adhesion.

Ans. The force of attraction between the molecules of same substances is called force of cohesion, while the force of attraction between the molecules of different substances is called force of adhesion.

Q. 8 Is it possible for all liquids to rise in a capillary tube?

Ans. No, it is not possible for all liquids to rise in a capillary tube, since liquids which make a convex meniscus in capillary tube are depressed, e.g. mercury is depressed in a glass capillary tube.

Q. 9 What is the reason of measuring the internal diameter of the capillary tube in two mutually perpendicular directions?

Ans. The internal diameter of the capillary tube is usually measured in two mutually perpendicular directions to take the mean value which in turn will eliminate the error.

Q.10 If the liquid is heated, what happens to the surface tension?

Ans. Surface tension decreases with increase in temperature.

Q.11 Why does the meniscus of water appear to be inverted when seen through the telescope?

Ans. This is because the final image formed by a compound microscope is inverted with respect to the object.

Q.12 **If the radius of the capillary tube is reduced, the rise of liquid will be more or less?**

Ans. Rise of liquid will be more as rise of liquid h is inversely proportional to the radius r of the capillary tube.

Q.13 **Can you measure surface tension of oil using this method?**

Ans. Yes, if the liquid wets the tube (i.e., has a concave meniscus and angle of contact < 90°).

Q.14 **Why is the meniscus of a liquid will be concave or convex?**

Ans. Meniscus are a manifestation of a capillary action, by which either surface adhesion pulls a liquid up to form a concave meniscus or internal cohension pulls the liquid down to form a convex meniscus.

Q.15 **Suppose the length of the capillary tube taken is less than the height upto which the liquid could rise. What do you expect if such a tube is inserted inside the liquid? Explain your answer.** [NCERT]

Ans. If the length of the capillary tube taken is less than the height, then the liquid will rise upto the upper edge of capillary tube. Its surface will become less covered and becomes plane.

Thus, the radius of curvature increases, $h \propto \frac{1}{R}$ as $R \to \infty$, then $h \to 0$

Q.16 **Two matchsticks are floating parallel and quite close to each other. What would happen if a drop of soap solution or a drop of hot water falls between the two sticks? Explain your answer.** [NCERT]

Ans. When a drop of soap solution or a drop of hot water is made to fall between the two matchsticks floating parallel and close to each other, then the force per unit length between the two matchsticks decreases due to the decrease in the surface tension and the force on the farther end of both the matchsticks get increased due to which they both will flow away from each other.

Experiment 05

AIM

To determine the coefficient of viscosity of a given viscous liquid by measuring terminal velocity of a given spherical body.

Apparatus and Materials Required

A screw gauge, stopwatch, clamp with stand, thermometer, transparent viscous liquid, a cylindrical glass pipe about 1.25 m in length and 4 cm in diameter, a forcep, a meter scale and thread, some steel balls of known diameter, two large corks, a cork borer.

Theory/Principle

Viscosity is the property of a fluid by the virtue of which an internal resistance comes into play when the fluid is in motion and opposes the relative motion between its different layers.

Coefficient of Viscosity

Suppose a fluid flows over a fixed surface. The upper layers of the fluid move with some increasing velocity while the layer of the fluid in contact with surface does not move. So, due to this, a dragging force F comes into action which acts tangentially to every layer. Thus, force is given by

$$F = \frac{-\eta A dv}{dx}$$

i.e.

$$\eta = \frac{-F}{A \cdot \frac{dv}{dx}}$$

where, η is called coefficient of viscosity and the negative sign shows that the force is acting in the opposite direction of velocity.

Thus, coefficient of viscosity is defined as the tangential force required to maintain a unit velocity gradient between the two layers each of unit area.

SI unit of coefficient of viscosity is newton-second metre^{-2} (N-sm^{-2})) or poise (P) and dimensional formula is $[ML^{-1}T^{-1}]$.

Stoke's Law

Sir George G Stokes, an English scientist found that the backward dragging force F acting on a small spherical body of radius r, moving through a fluid of coefficient of viscosity η with velocity v is given by

$$F = 6\pi\eta r v$$

So, this is called **Stoke's law**.

Terminal Velocity

It is the maximum velocity acquired by the body, falling freely in a viscous medium.

Suppose a spherical body of radius r falls through a viscous fluid of viscosity η with terminal velocity v and if the densities of the body and fluid are σ and ρ respectively, then

Weight of the spherical body = Upward thrust + Force of viscosity

$$\frac{4}{3}\pi r^3 \sigma g = \frac{4}{3}\pi r^3 \rho g + 6\pi\eta r v$$

[∵ Weight or thrust = mg and mass = volume × density]

Therefore, terminal velocity is given by

$$v = \frac{2}{9}\frac{r^2(\sigma - \rho)}{\eta} g$$

The terminal velocity depends directly on the square of the diameter of spherical body. Therefore, if several spherical bodies of different radii will allow to fall through a viscous fluid, then the graph between v and r^2 will be straight line.

Procedure

Setting up the Apparatus

1. Take a wide bore tube of transparent glass of diameter about 4 cm and of length approximately 1.25 m. Clean the tube and then fix it with the stand by using a clamp.

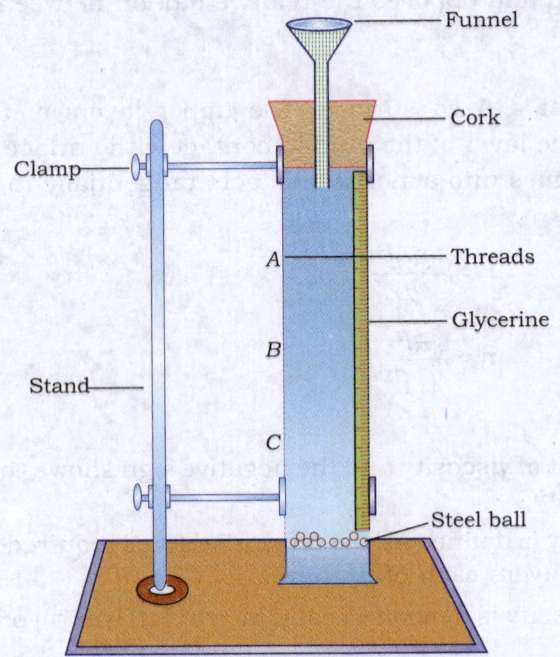

Experimental set up to determine the coefficient of viscosity

2. Fit a rubber stopper or cork at one end of the wide tube and ensure that it is air tight and make bore with the help of cork borer.
3. Fit a short inlet tube (Funnel) in the cork and fill the tube with the given transparent viscous liquid (say glycerine). It should be ensured that there is no air bubble inside the viscous liquid in the wide bore tube.
4. Find out the least count of the vertical scale and stopwatch.
5. Using thermometer, note down the room temperature.
6. Put three threads A, B and C around the wide bore tube dividing it into four portions such that $AB = BC$, each about 30 cm. The thread A should be around 40 cm below the mouth of the wide bore tube (length sufficient to allow the ball to attain terminal velocity).

Put the Steel Balls into the Glass Tube

7. Take some steel balls of different radii and clean and dry them properly. Measure the diameter of each ball with the help of screw gauge.
8. Now, rinse these balls thoroughly with the same viscous liquid (glycerine) in a petri dish or a watch glass, so that no air bubble(s) on their surfaces can be developed.
9. By using a forceps hold one of the balls of radius r_1 near the top of tube and allow the balls to fall freely through the funnel along the axis of the liquid column.

Time Taken to Reach from One Thread to Another

10. The ball falls down in the liquid with accelerated velocity upto some distance and then it falls down with uniform velocity.
11. Take two stopwatches and when the spherical ball passes through the thread *A*, start both of them simultaneously. Stop one of the watches as the ball passes through the thread *B*. Allow the second stopwatch to continue and stop it when the ball crosses the thread *C*.
12. Note the times t_1, i.e. time taken by the falling ball to travel from *A* to *B* and t_2, i.e. the time taken by it in falling from *A* to *C* as indicated by the two stopwatches. If terminal velocity had been attained before the ball crosses *A*, then $t_2 = 2t_1$. If it is not, so repeat the experiment with steel ball of same radii after adjusting the positions of threads.
13. Repeat the experiment for other balls of different diameters.
14. Obtain terminal velocity for each ball.
15. On plotting a graph between the square of the radius r^2 and terminal velocity v, a straight line will be obtained.

Observations

1. Internal diameter of the wide bore tube = ... cm = ... m
2. Length of wide bore tube = ... cm = ... m
3. Distance between *A* and *B* = ... cm = ... m
4. Distance between *B* and *C* = ... cm = ... m

   Average distance *h* between two consecutive threads = ... cm = ... m
5. Acceleration due to gravity at the place of experiment = ... g-ms^{-2}
6. Least count of stopwatch = ... s
7. Temperature of experimental liquid (glycerine), θ = ... °C
8. Density of material of steel balls, σ = ... kgm^{-3}
9. Density of the viscous liquid used in the tube = ... kgm^{-3}
10. Density of experimental viscous liquid, ρ = ... kgm^{-3}

Observations of Temperature

Temperature of viscous fluid at the time of beginning of the experiment, t_1 = ...°C

Temperature of viscous fluid at the end of experiment, t_2 = ...°C

Mean temperature, $t = \frac{t_1 + t_2}{2}$

Table for Measurement of Time of Fall of Steel Balls

S. N. of steel ball	Diameter of spherical balls		Square of the radius of the balls, r^2 (m^2)	Time taken for covering distance $h = \ldots$ cm between threads				Terminal velocity, $v = \frac{h}{t}$ (ms^{-1})
	d (cm)	$r = \frac{d}{2}$ (m)		A and B t_1 (s)	A and C t_2 (s)	B and C $t_3 = t_2 - t_1$ (s)	Mean time, $t = \frac{t_1 + t_3}{2}$ (s)	
1								
2								
3								
4								
5								
6								

Calculations and Plotting Graph

Plot a graph between r^2 and v by taking r^2 along X-axis and v along Y-axis, we will get a straight line. Since, the slope of the graph,

$$\tan\theta = \frac{BC}{AB} = \frac{v}{r^2}$$

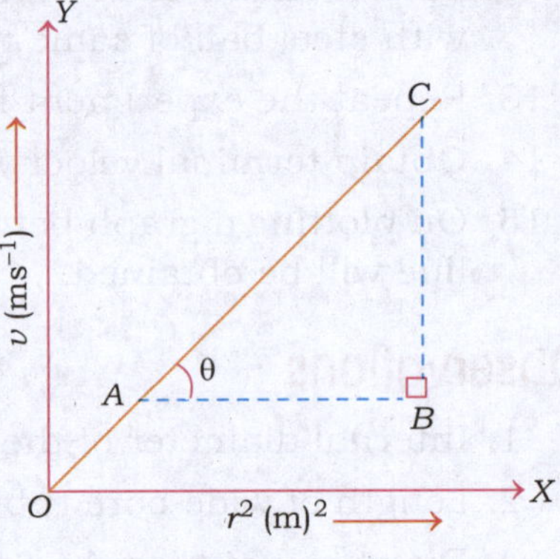

Graph between r^2 and v

Also, coefficient of viscosity, $$\eta = \frac{2}{9}\frac{(\sigma - \rho)}{\left(\frac{v}{r^2}\right)} g$$

It can be rewritten as, $$\eta = \frac{2}{9}\frac{(\sigma - \rho)}{\tan\theta} g = \ldots \text{poise } [\text{Nsm}^{-2}]$$

$$\text{Error} = \frac{\Delta\eta}{\eta} = \frac{2\Delta r}{r} + \frac{\Delta\text{slope}}{\text{slope}}$$

Standard value of η =.....Nsm^{-2} Percentage error in η =........ %

$\therefore$ The final value of coefficient of viscosity, η = ... P

Result

The coefficient of viscosity of liquid at temperature (0° C) = ... ± ...... Nsm^{-2}.

PRECAUTIONS

1. The steel balls used in the experiment must be perfectly spherical.
2. The temperature of the liquid should be measured in the beginning as well as in the end of the experiment because it affects the viscosity of the fluid.
3. The diameters should be measured in two mutually perpendicular directions.
4. Noting down of the velocity should be done when it becomes constant.
5. The steel balls should fall without touching the sides of the tube and they should be wetted with the same viscous fluid as filled in the tube.

Sources of Error

1. The liquid of non-uniform density may have used.
2. The lead shots or steel ball may not be of small size.
3. The bore in the cork may not be at the centre.
4. The noted velocity may not be constant.

Viva-Voce

Q. 1 Explain Stoke's law.

Ans. According to Stoke's law, if a small sphere of radius r is moving with a uniform velocity v through an infinite homogeneous and incompressible fluid of coefficient of viscosity η, then it experiences a dragging force given by

$$F = 6\pi\eta rv$$

This is known as Stoke's law.

Q. 2 What is the reason for the steel balls to be of same radii?

Ans. The terminal velocity is directly proportional to the square of the radius, therefore the large size steel balls will fall very fastly and the time of fall may not be measured accurately.

Q. 3 What is the coefficient of viscosity?

Ans. Coefficient of viscosity is numerically equal to the tangential force required to maintain a unit velocity gradient between the two layers each of unit area.

Q. 4 How does the viscosity of liquid and gas change?

Ans. The viscosity of a liquid decreases with increase in temperature, while that of gas increases with increase in temperature. The viscosity of liquid increases with increase in pressure whereas the viscosity of gas does not change with pressure.

Q. 5 What can be the reason of increasing of radius of bubble during its upward movement?

Ans. There is always increase in the radius of the bubble during its upward movement because as the bubble moves up, the pressure of liquid outside it decreases. So, in order to maintain the equilibrium with excess of pressure inside it due to surface tension, the bubble expands.

Q. 6 Which runs faster; a cold water or a hot water? Give one reason.

Ans. Hot water runs faster than a cold water because the viscosity of hot water is lesser than that of cold water.

Q. 7 Define terminal velocity. Also, mention its expression.

Ans. The maximum velocity acquired by the body, falling freely in a viscous medium is called the terminal velocity.

It is given by
$$v = \frac{2}{9}\frac{r^2(\sigma - \rho)}{\eta}g$$

Q. 8 What kind of liquid should be used in this experiment and why?

Ans. A clean and the transparent liquid should be used in this experiment because the motion of the ball must be visible in the liquid.

Q. 9 Why do the air bubbles not attain the terminal velocity when they move up?

Ans. When the air bubbles move up, then their radii increase due to which the upthrust on them also increases. So, due to this reason, the air bubbles do not attain the terminal velocity during their upward movement.

Q. 10 Why is the diameter of the falling sphere kept small?

Ans. To minimize disturbance and ensure smooth laminar flow.

Q.11 What is the effect of temperature on the coefficient of viscosity of liquid? [NCERT]

Ans. The coefficient of viscosity decreases with increase in temperature because the forces of cohesion between the liquid molecules decreases with increase in temperature.

Q.12 Do all the raindrops, strike the ground with the same velocity irrespective of their size? [NCERT]

Ans. Since, we know that the terminal velocity is directly proportional to the square of radius but as per the question, the velocity is independent of the size of raindrop. Therefore, all the raindrops strike the ground with same velocity irrespective of their size.

Q.13 Is Stoke's law applicable to the body of shapes other than spherical? [NCERT]

Ans. According to Stoke's law, viscous force $F = 6\pi\eta r v$, which is only applicable for spherical bodies. So, we can say that Stoke's law is only applicable to the body of spherical shape.

Experiment 06

AIM

To study the relationship between the temperature of a hot body and time by plotting a cooling curve.

Apparatus and Materials Required

Two thermometers, clamp and stand, Newton's law of cooling apparatus, a beaker, a burner, wire gauge, tripod stand, stopwatch, two rubber stoppers with holes, a cotton thread.

Description of Apparatus

Newton's Law of Cooling Apparatus

The apparatus for Newton's law of cooling is shown below.

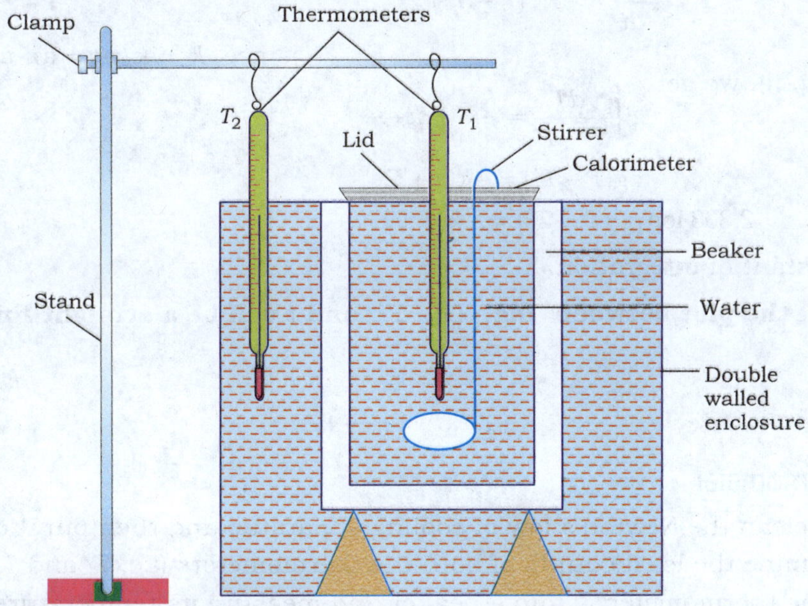

Newton's law of cooling apparatus

As shown in figure, the law of cooling apparatus has a double walled container, which can be closed by an insulating lid. Water filled between double walls ensures that the temperature of the environment surrounding the calorimeter remains constant. Temperature of the liquid and the calorimeter also remain constant for a fairly long period of time, so that temperature measurement is feasible. Temperature of water in calorimeter and that of water between double wallls of container is recorded by two thermometer.

Theory/Principle

According to Newton's Law of Cooling,

"The rate of cooling (i.e. rate of loss of heat) of a body is directly proportional to the temperature of the body above its surroundings provided that the difference in the temperature of the body and its surroundings is not very large.

$$\frac{dQ}{dt} \propto (T - T') \Rightarrow \frac{dQ}{dt} = -k(T - T')$$

The negative sign shows that the body is losing its temperature.

where, $\frac{dQ}{dt}$ = rate of loss of heat, k = constant

$(T - T')$ = difference in temperature of the body and its surroundings

Consider if a body of mass m, specific heat s and temperature T is placed in surroundings of temperature T', then

$$\text{amount of heat loss, } Q = msT$$

Therefore, $$\text{rate of cooling, } \frac{dQ}{dt} = ms\frac{dT}{dt} \Rightarrow ms\frac{dT}{dt} = -k(T - T')$$

Thus, $$\frac{dT}{dt} = -k'(T - T') \quad \text{...(i)}$$

[since, $k' = k/ms$ = an another constant]

On integrating Eq. (i), we get

$$\int \frac{dT}{T - T'} = -k' \int dt$$

$$\log(T - T') = -k't + C$$

$$2.303 \log_{10} (T - T') = -k't + C \quad \text{...(ii)}$$

where, C is a constant of integration.

Eq. (ii) shows that **the plot between $\log_{10}(T - T')$ and t will be a straight line with negative slope.**

Procedure

Calibrate the Thermometer

1. First of all, clean the Newton's law of cooling apparatus and then put it on the table.
2. Then, determine the least counts of both the thermometers (i.e. T_1 and T_2).
3. Now, put one thermometer T_1 into a beaker and measure its temperature.
4. Put the thermometer T_2 in the double walled container with the help of clamp stand and measure its temperature.
5. Now, the initial readings of the thermometers T_1 and T_2 are noted thereby the calibration in one thermometer giving incorrect reading with respect to other can be achieved. The difference between the readings gives the correction.

Note the Falling Temperature of the Hot Liquid

6. Find the least count of stopwatch used and then put the water into the double walled container at room temperature.
7. Now, with the help of the clamp stand, fix the other thermometer T_2 in the water contained in double walled container and note the initial reading of the thermometer T_2 (i.e. the value of θ_1) in the beginning of the experiment.

8. Heat some water separately to a temperature of about 40°C above the room temperature. Pour hot water into calorimeter up to its top.
9. Put the calorimeter along with hot water, back in the enclosure and cover it with lid.
10. Now, fix the thermometer T_1 and the stirrer in the calorimeter through the holes in the lid. The rubber stoppers in the holes are fixed to provide the proper air tight.
11. Now wait for some time and note the initial temperature of the water between enclosure of double walled with the help of thermometer T_2, when the difference of readings of two thermometers T_1 and T_2 is about 30 °C and simultaneously start the stopwatch.

    Note the initial reading of the thermometer T_1 after every one minute. This temperature will be noted as T(°C) in the observation table.
12. Now, try to keep on stirring gently and constantly.
13. So, the moment, when the fall of temperature of about 5 °C above that of enclosure, the temperature of the enclosure by the thermometer T_2 should be noted after every two minutes. This temperature will be noted as T' in the observation table.
14. When the fall of temperature becomes very slow, stop noting the temperature and then stop the stopwatch.
15. Note the temperature of the surrounding water with the help of thermometer T_2 at the end of the experiment. This value of temperature be θ_2.
16. Find the difference temperature of water $(T - T')$ and also $\log_{10}(T - T')$ for each reading, using logarithm tables.
17. Plot a graph between time t, taken along X-axis and $\log_{10}(T - T')$ taken along Y-axis. Interpret the graph.

Observations

Calibration in Thermometer

Initial reading of the thermometer T_1, a = ... °C

Initial reading of the thermometer T_2, b = ...°C

Correction to be applied on thermometer T_2, $(a - b)$ = ...°C

Observations after Calibration

Least count of stopwatch = ... s

Least count of both the thermometers = ... °C

Initial temperature of water in the enclosure,

θ_1 = ...°C

Final temperature of water in the enclosure,

θ_2 = ...°C

Mean temperature, $\theta_0 = \dfrac{\theta_1 + \theta_2}{2}$ = ...°C

Table for Measuring the Change in the Temperature of Water with Time

S.N.	Time for cooling, t (s)	Temperature of water in calorimeter, T (°C)	Temperature of water in enclosure, T' (°C)	Difference of water temperature, $T - T'$ (°C)	$\log_{10}(T - T')$
1					
2					
3					
⋮					
20					

Plotting graph

(i) After plotting a graph between temperature $(T - T')$ and time (t) by taking the temperature difference $(T - T')$ along Y-axis and time for cooling (t) along X-axis, we get a curve known as cooling curve.

(ii) After plotting a graph between $\log_{10}(T - T')$ and time (t) by taking $\log_{10}(T - T')$ along Y-axis and (t) along X-axis, we get a straight line.

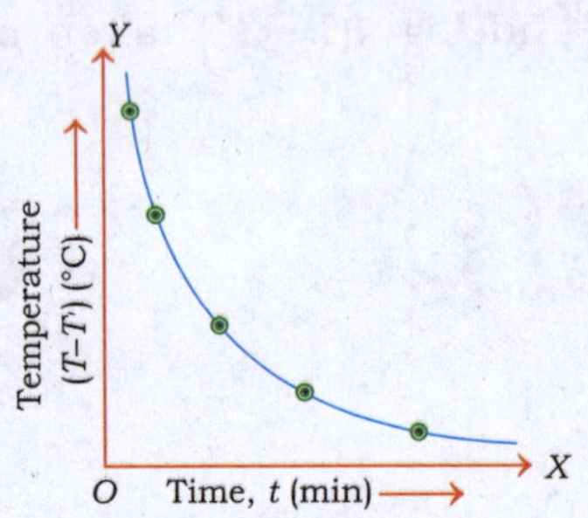

Graph between temperature $(T - T')$ and time (t) for cooling

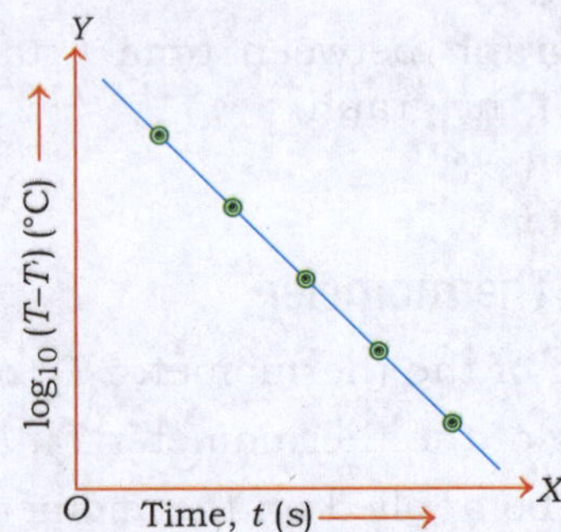

Graph between $\log_{10}(T - T')$ and time (t) for cooling

Result

Since, the cooling curve for water is shown as follows

(i) $(T - T')$ *versus* (t) graph is an exponential curve.

(ii) $\log_{10}(T - T')$ *versus* (t) graph is a straight line.

Also, it has been noticed that, the temperature falls quickly in the starting and then slowly as the difference of temperature goes on decreasing. Hence, the cooling curve is an exponential decay curve. So, this is a required condition with Newton's law of cooling.

PRECAUTIONS

1. *Stirring of water in the calorimeter should be done continuously and gently.*
2. *The openings for the insertion of thermometers should be air tight.*
3. *Circulation of water should be done between the double walls in order to obtain the surroundings of a constant temperature.*
4. *The initial temperature of the water kept in calorimeter must be about 30°C, slightly above the room temperature.*
5. *One of selected thermometers should be calibrated when the difference in the initial readings is observed.*
6. *The calorimeter having the hot liquid should be covered with the help of lid thereby the evaporation of water can be prevented.*
7. *The calorimeter in between the walls should be suspended in such a way that it would not touch the walls. Otherwise the hot liquid kept in the calorimeter will cool rapidly due to the process of conduction.*

Sources of Error

1. The temperature of surroundings may get changed.
2. The water in the calorimeter may not be stirred continuously.
3. Stopwatch may not be stopped at the desired moment.
4. The opening for thermometer may not be air tight.

Viva-Voce

Q. 1 What is radiation?

Ans. Radiation is the mode of transmission of heat from a hot body to a cold body or surroundings without requiring an intervening medium.

Q. 2 What are the factors on which the heat radiated by a body depends?

Ans. The heat radiated by a body depends upon

(i) nature and area of its surface (ii) temperature of the body (iii) temperature of surroundings

Q. 3 What do you mean by a black body? Also, define black body radiation.

Ans. A body which completely absorbs thermal radiations of all wavelengths falling upon it is called a black body. So, when such a body is heated, it emits the radiations of all possible wavelengths. The radiations which are emitted by a black body is called black body radiation.

Q. 4 Why does the space between the double walls of the surrounding vessel should be filled with flowing water?

Ans. In order to make a constant temperature of the surroundings of the calorimeter, the space between the double walls of the surrounding vessel should be filled with flowing water.

Q. 5 State the Wien's law.

Ans. Wien's law states that the product of wavelength corresponding to maximum intensity (λ_m) and absolute temperature (T) of a black body is equal to a constant. i.e. $\lambda_m T = \delta$

where, δ = Wien's constant.

Q. 6 What is the shape of cooling curve?

Ans. The cooling curve is an exponential decay curve (it is a hyperbolic curve).

Q. 7 How is Newton's law of cooling different from Stefan's law of heat radiation? [NCERT]

Ans. According to Stefan's law of heat radiation, "the total amount of radiant energy emitted by unit area of perfectly black body in one second is directly proportional to the fourth power of its absolute temperature". i.e. $E \propto T^4$

While according to Newton's law of cooling, the rate of cooling of a body is directly proportional to the temperature difference between the body and its surroundings, provided that the temperature difference is small. i.e. $\frac{dQ}{dt} \propto (T - T_0)$

Q. 8 Find the specific heat of a liquid/solid by using Newton's law of cooling apparatus. [NCERT]

Ans. According to Newton's law of cooling, $\frac{dQ}{dt} \propto (T - T_0)$ and we know that for a body of mass m, specific heat s, temperature T kept in surroundings of temperature T_0, $Q = msT$

Therefore, rate of cooling, $\frac{dQ}{dt} = ms\frac{dT}{dt}$. So, by this formula, the value of specific heat (s) can be calculated.

Q. 9 Does the Newton's law of cooling hold good for all the temperature differences? [NCERT]

Ans. It should be noted that the Newton's law of cooling holds good for the temperature difference between the body and its surroundings which should not be more than 30°C . Hence, $(T - T_0)$ should not be more than 30°C .

Experiment 07

AIM

To determine specific heat capacity of a given solid by the method of mixtures.

Apparatus and Materials Required

Stirrer, a copper calorimeter, a hypsometer, a lid, physical balance, weight box, a heating device i.e. burner, two half degree thermometers, beaker, clamp stand, tipod stand, cold water, the powder of solid whose specific heat capacity is to be determined..

Theory/Principle

If a body have mass m and specific heat s, then the amount of heat lost / gained by it, when its temperature changes by Δt is given as $\Delta Q = ms\Delta t$.

Specific Heat Capacity

It is defined as the quantity of heat required to raise the temperature of unit mass of a substance through 1°C. Its SI unit is $Jkg^{-1}K^{-1}$.

Principle of Calorimetry

According to this principle,

"If the bodies of different temperatures are brought in thermal contact, then the amount of heat lost by the body at higher temperature is equal to the amount of heat gained by the body at the lower temperature, at equilibrium, provided that no heat is lost into the surroundings."

$\therefore$ Heat lost by the hotter body = Heat gained by the colder body

Procedure

Calibrate the Thermometer

1. First of all, place the two thermometers in a beaker containing water. Note their readings.
2. Keep the first thermometer fixed and determine the correction to be applied to the other one. This is called calibration.

Setting up the Contents of Hypsometer and Weighing the Empty Calorimeter

3. Now, place the second thermometer B in the copper tube of hypsometer consisting the powder of given solid whose specific heat capacity is to be found. It is to be checked that the second thermometer which has been placed in the copper tube gets completely surrounded by the powder of solid.
4. Also, pour the water in one half of the boiler of the hypsometer and put it on a burner. The hypsometer along with the burner and the calorimeter are separated by a wooden screen which is used to give the proper insulation.
5. The manometer fixed with the hypsometer is used to measure the pressure inside the hypsometer by taking into account that the mercury level in the two limbs of the manometer should be same. In case when pressure inside the hypsometer gets increased, then some pressure is released through the steam outlet.

6. Measure the weight of empty calorimeter along with the stirrer and lid with the help of a physical balance. It should be ensured that the calorimeter is clean and dry.

Note While using the physical balance, it should be ensured that balancing of the pans has been done.

7. After measuring the weight of calorimeter, record its respective reading (m_0).

Weighing the Calorimeter Along with Water

8. Pour the given water in the one-third part of the calorimeter. The temperature of the water must be about 5-6°C below the room temperature and ensure that no vapour gets condensed over the calorimeter. Also, make sure that the quantity of water taken would be sufficient to completely submerge the given solid in it. Now, weigh the filled calorimeter with water along with the stirrer and the lid again and note its mass m_1.
9. Place the calorimeter in its insulating cover. Now, a thermometer *C* should be suspended in the calorimeter in such manner that its bulb does not touch the bottom of the calorimeter. Note the temperature (T_C) of the calorimeter along with its content.

Heating the Hypsometer Containing Powder of Solid

10. Now, take powder of solid in a hypsometer.

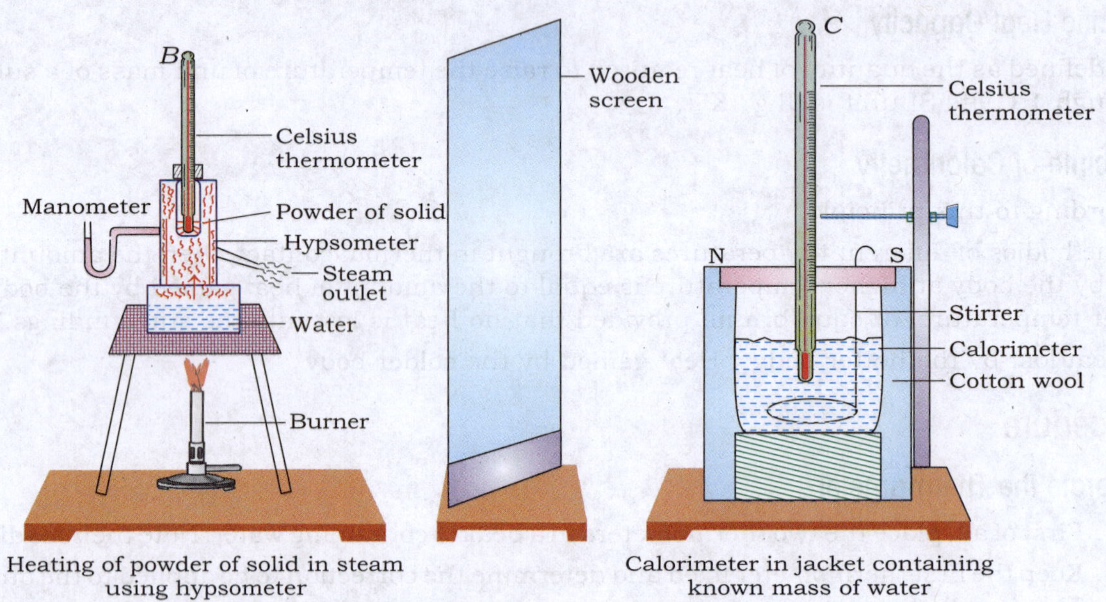

Heating of powder of solid in steam using hypsometer

Calorimeter in jacket containing known mass of water

11. Provide some heat to hypsometer for about 8 min till the temperature of body (or solid) remains steady, then note the temperature of solid with the help of thermometer *B*. This is called **steady temperature** (T_H).

Shifting of Solid from Hypsometer to Calorimeter

12. After recording the temperature, shift the solid from the hypsometer to the calorimeter fastly.
13. Mix the ingredients and note down the final temperature (T_2) of the mixture (i.e. water and solid).
14. Now, remove the first thermometer from calorimeter and measure the weight of the calorimeter along with its contents (i.e. water and solid and lid).

Observations

Calibrate the Thermometer

Reading of the first thermometer, T_C = ...°C

Reading of the second thermometer, T_B = ...°C

Correct reading of second thermometer, $T_C - T_B$ = ...°C

Observations After Calibration of Thermometer

1. Temperature of thermometer $C (T_C)$ = ...°C
2. Temperature of thermometer $B (T_B)$ = ... °C
3. Mass of the empty calorimeter with stirrer (m_0) = ...g
4. Mass of the calorimeter with water, (m_1) = ... g
5. Mass of solid (m_2) = ... g
6. Steady temperature of hot solid (T_H) = ... °C
7. Corrected temperature of hot solid $(T) = T_H - (T_C - T_B)$ = ... °C
8. Temperature of cold water (T_1) = ... °C
9. Temperature of mixture (T_2) = ... °C
10. Specific heat capacity of material of calorimeter (s_a) = ... J $kg^{-1} °C^{-1}$
11. Specific heat capacity of water (s) = ... J $kg^{-1} °C^{-1}$

Calculations

1. Mass of the water in calorimeter, $(m_1 - m_0)$ = ... g = ... kg
2. Mass of hot solid, $(m_2 - m_1)$ = ... g
3. Rise of temperature of cold water and calorimeter, $(T_2 - T_1)$ = ... °C
4. Fall in temperature of solid, $(T - T_2)$ = ... °C
5. Heat gained by calorimeter, stirrer and cold water = $[w + (m_1 - m_0)(T_2 - T_1)]$ = ...

   Here, w = weight of the calorimeter along with its contents.
6. Heat lost by solid = $(m_2 - m_1) \times s \times (T - T_2)$ = ...

   According to principle of calorimeter,

$$\text{Heat lost} = \text{Heat gained}$$

$$\Rightarrow \quad s = \frac{[w + (m_1 - m_0)(T_2 - T_1)]}{[(m_2 - m_1)(T - T_2)]}$$

where, s = specific heat of a given solid

Result

Specific heat of given solid by the method of mixture is .... cal $g^{-1} °C^{-1}$.

PRECAUTIONS

1. In order to avoid any heat loss due to radiation, outer surface of calorimeter must be polished.
2. Till the time, the final temperature is not measured, thermometer should not be taken out after being placed in the liquid.
3. Amount of water taken in hypsometer should be sufficient.
4. Cold water temperature should not be below the dew point.
5. Physical balance should be in proper working condition and ensure that there is no zero error.
6. The two thermometers used should be of the same range and least count.
7. The solid used should not be chemically reactive with the liquid or water used.
8. While measuring the temperature, the thermometers should always be held in vertical position.
9. The line of sight should be perpendicular to the mercury level while recording the temperature. This helps to keep away from the parallax error.
10. The calorimeter should be always kept in its insulated cover and at a sufficient distance from the source of heat and should not be exposed to sunlight, so that it absorbs no heat from the surrounding.

Sources of Error

1. The bulb of thermometer may not be dipped completely inside the powder of solid.
2. Some heat may get lost while transferring the solid.
3. Radiation process can not be completely eliminated.

Viva-Voce

Q. 1 Define the term heat capacity.

Ans. Heat capacity is defined as the amount of heat required to raise its temperature through one degree. So, if we consider ΔQ be the heat supplied to a body of mass m to raise its temperature by ΔT, then $\Delta Q = mc\Delta T$.

Q. 2 What is calorimeter?

Ans. It is a device in which measurement of heat can be made. It consists of a metallic vessel with a stirrer of same material. The vessel is kept inside a wooden jacket which is thermally insulated from the surroundings.

Q. 3 Mention the purpose of using hypsometer.

Ans. Hypsometer is a device in which we heat a solid. So, in order to provide a same constant temperature to solid, we use hypsometer.

Q. 4 Give the name of the substance which has the highest value of specific heat capacity.

Ans. The substance which has the highest value of specific heat capacity is **water.**

Q. 5 Which two precautions has to be followed while performing this experiment?

Ans. The two precautionary measures which has to be followed while performing this experiment are as follows

(i) Till the time, the final temperature is measured, thermometer should not be taken out after being placed in the liquid.

(ii) Readings should be taken through thermometer only when it shows steady temperature.

Q. 6 State the reason, why is a manometer attached with the hypsometer?

Ans. As, we know that boiling point of water depends on the atmospheric pressure. So, in order to keep an eye on the idea of pressure in the hypsometer, manometer is attached with it.

Q. 7 Mention the SI unit of specific heat capacity.

Ans. The SI unit of specific heat capacity is joule per kilogram per kelvin rise in temperature, i.e. ($J\ kg^{-1}\ K^{-1}$).

Q. 8 Why should the solid be quickly transferred into water after heating?

Ans. To avoid loss of heat to the surroundings.

Q. 9 What do you mean by latent heat?

Ans. Latent heat of a substance is defined as the amount of heat required to change the state of unit mass of the substance at a constant temperature.

Q.10 Why do the specific heat of the substance is more in its liquid state as compared to that in the solid state?

Ans. The specific heat of the substance is more in its liquid state than that in its solid state because in liquid state, the molecules may have more degree of freedom.

Q.11 What is the significance of the high specific heat of body?

Ans. It is comparatively difficult to heat a body of high specific heat and once heated it loses heat slowly.

Q.12 What do you think, what quantities can be measured with the help of calorimeter?

Ans. Thermal capacity, water equivalent of calorimeter and latent heat.

Q.13 Why do we generally use a calorimeter made of copper? [NCERT]

Ans. We use a calorimeter made of copper because copper has very low value of specific heat. So, due to this, a large increase in temperature takes place when some quantity of heat is supplied to it.

Q.14 Is specific heat a constant quantity? [NCERT]

Ans. No, specific heat is not a constant quantity because it depends on the nature of the substance and its temperature.

Q.15 Why is it important to stir the contents before taking the temperature of mixture? [NCERT]

Ans. It is important to stir the contents before taking the temperature because when we record this temperature, it is used in the form of calculation as per the principle of calorimetry. So, it is must to stir the contents before taking the temperature of mixture.

Q.16 What is water equivalent? [NCERT]

Ans. The water equivalent of a body is defined as the mass of the water which requires the same amount of heat as is required by the given body for the same increase of temperature.

Q.17 What is thermal equilibrium? [NCERT]

Ans. Thermal equilibrium is a stage where the thermodynamical systems which are in equilibrium has the same temperature.

Experiment 8

AIM

To study the relation between frequency and length of a given wire under constant tension using a sonometer.

Apparatus and Materials Required

A meter scale, a set of six tuning forks of known frequencies, a sonometer, hanger with 500 g weight, seven 500 g slotted weights, rubber pad, paper rider and two wooden bridges.

Description of Apparatus

Sonometer

Sonometer is a device used for demonstrating the relationship between the frequency of the sound produced by a plucked string and the tension, length and mass per unit length of string. This apparatus consists of a hollow wooden box with a peg at its one end and pulley at another end.

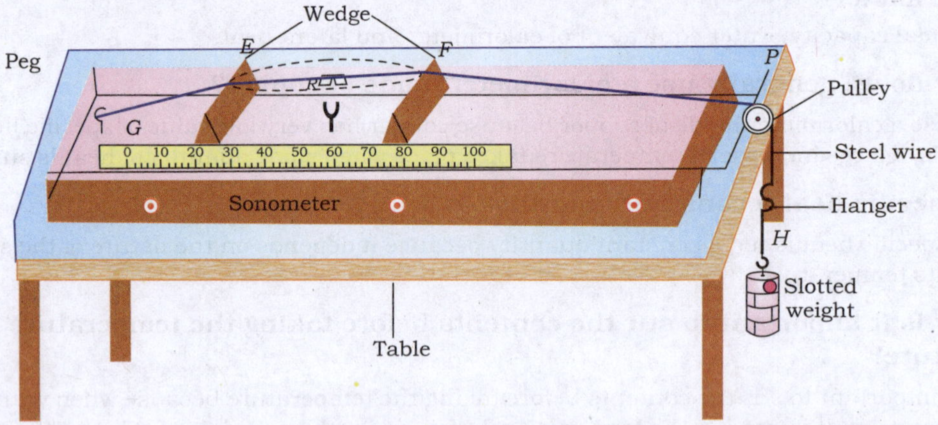

A sonometer set-up on the table

It is shown in the figure that one end of a metal wire is attached to the peg and one passes over the pulley. A hanger is suspended from the free end of the wire, so by placing the slotted weights on it, tension is applied to the wire. After putting the two bridges under the wire, the length of the vibrating wire can be fixed. So, at the end, by keeping the position of one bridge fixed and by changing the position of other bridge, the vibrating length can be altered. To perform the experiment, a sonometer setup should be fixed on the table as shown in figure.

Theory/Principle

Resonant Vibrations

When a body is set into vibrations of large amplitude or frequency by keeping an another vibrating body of same natural frequency near it, then the phenomenon of **resonance** takes place. The resulting vibrations produced are called **resonant vibrations**.

Laws of Vibrating String

The frequency of the vibrating string is determined by some laws which on combining give the relation between frequency, tension, length and mass per unit length of the vibrating string. These laws of vibrating string are as follows:

First Law (The law of length)

According to this law, the frequency (ν) of a stretched vibrating string is inversely proportional to the length (L) of the string provided the mass per unit length or linear mass density (m) and tension (T) in the string remains constant.

$$\nu \propto \frac{1}{L} \quad \ldots\text{(i)}$$

Second Law (The law of tension)

According to this law, the frequency (ν) of the stretched vibrating string is directly proportional to the square root of tension (T) in the string provided the mass per unit length (m) and length (L) remains constant.

$$\nu \propto \sqrt{T} \quad \ldots\text{(ii)}$$

Third Law (The law of mass)

According to this law, the frequency (ν) of the stretched vibrating string is inversely proportional to the square root of the linear mass density, i.e. mass per unit length (m) of the string provided the length (L) of the string and tension (T) in the string remains constant.

$$\nu \propto \frac{1}{\sqrt{m}} \quad \ldots\text{(iii)}$$

On combining Eqs. (i), (ii) and (iii), we get

$$\nu \propto \frac{1}{L}\sqrt{\frac{T}{m}}$$

$$\nu = \frac{1}{2L}\sqrt{\frac{T}{m}} \quad \ldots\text{(iv)}$$

[Here, $\frac{1}{2}$ is the constant of proportionality for a string vibrating in a single segment.]

where, m = mass per unit length of the string, L = length of vibrating string

T = tension in the string = Mg,

M = mass of suspended weights including the mass of hanger

Since, from Eq. (i), $\nu \propto \frac{1}{L}$ i.e. νL = constant

So, the graph between ν and $\frac{1}{L}$ will be a straight line, while the graph between ν and L will be a curve, i.e. hyperbola.

Procedure

Setting up the Sonometer

1. First of all, fix the sonometer on the table in such a manner that its one end carrying pulley sets on the edge of the table, so that the hanger can be suspended without touching the table.
2. Make the groove clean in order to confirm that it has minimum friction.
3. Now, place the two wooden blocks or bridges E and F to remove the kink in the wire.

Attaining the Resonance

4. Now, stretch the wire by putting a suitable load on the hanger.
5. Now, set the tuning fork of frequency ν_1 into vibrations by striking it against the rubber pad.
6. Pluck the sonometer wire and compare the sound produced by tuning fork and the sound produced by the plucked wire.
7. Record the difference between the two sounds.
8. Adjust the bridge F to vary the length of the vibrating wire till these two sounds appear alike. This condition is called **resonance**.
9. In order to attain the final adjustment, take a small piece of paper and then fold it to give it the V-shape looking like a paper rider. Now, place this paper rider at the middle of the wire EF.
10. Now, vibrate the tuning fork and touch the lower end (or stem) of its handle with sonometer board.
11. Keep on adjusting the bridge F. The wire vibrates and paper rider falls down. This indicates the condition of resonance.

Measure the Length of Resonating Wire

12. With the help of a meter scale, measure the length of the wire between the edges of two bridges E and F and then note it. This is called **resonant length** of the wire because in this condition, the frequency of vibration of wire equals to that of tuning fork.
13. Note the length of the wire.

    Repeat the above process again but this time bringing the bridges very close to each other and then move them apart.
14. Now, take the remaining tuning forks and repeat the above procedures in the order of increasing frequency but keeping the load on the hanger unchanged.
15. Note the observations in a tabular form.
16. After taking the observations, plot the graphs between ν and L and ν and $\frac{1}{L}$.

Observations

Table for Variation of Frequency with Length

S. N.	Frequency of tuning fork f (Hz)	Resonant Length of the sonometer wire		Mean $\frac{L_1 + L_2}{2} = L$	$\frac{1}{l}$ cm^{-1}	$f \times L$
		Length increasing L_1 (cm)	Length decreasing L_2 (cm)			
1.	256					
2.	288					
3.	320					
4.	384					
5.	480					

Plotting graph

1. With the help of observation table, when we plot the graph between the frequency (ν) and the length (L) by taking them along X-axis and Y-axis respectively, we get a curve, i.e. hyperbola.

2. In the similar manner, if we plot a graph between the frequency (ν) and reciprocal of length $\left(\frac{1}{L}\right)$ by taking them along X-axis and Y-axis respectively, we get a straight line.

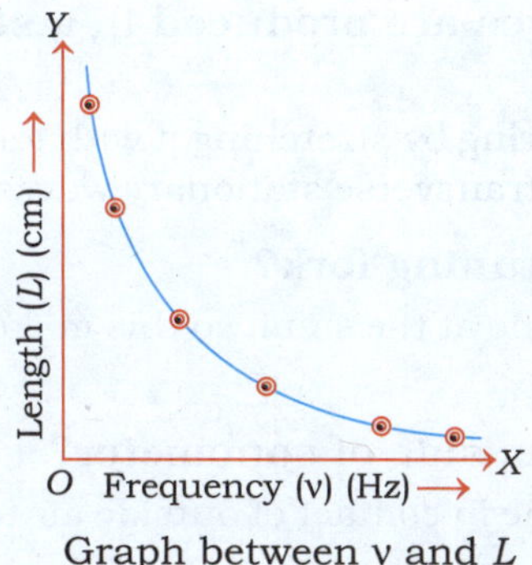

Graph between ν and L

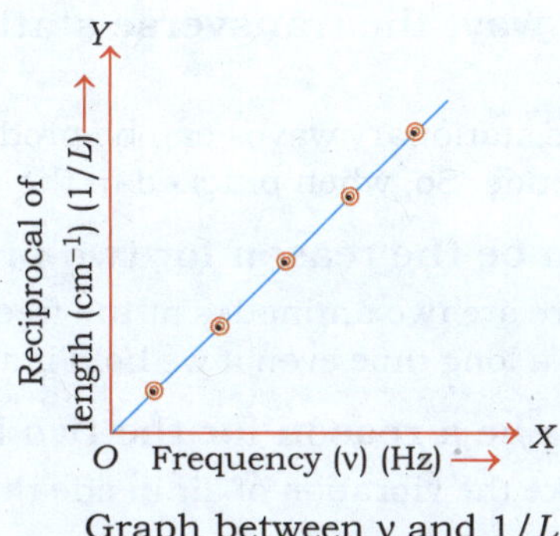

Graph between ν and 1/L

Result

Since, from the graph between the frequency (ν) and the reciprocal of length $\left(\frac{1}{L}\right)$, we conclude that, νL = constant which implies that $\nu \propto \frac{1}{L}$. So, this verifies the law of transverse vibrations of string.

PRECAUTIONS

1. *The wire should be free from kinks. If there are kinks, then the wire should be stretched as far as possible until the kinks get removed.*
2. *The tuning forks which vibrate for one minute should not stuck with any hard surface.*
3. *The paper rider should always be placed exactly in the middle of bridges.*
4. *The tip of the stem of vibrating tuning fork should be gently placed on the top face of sonometer.*
5. *The sonometer wire should be of uniform cross-section.*
6. *Loading of wires should be done within their elastic limits to avoid breaking of wire.*
7. *Pulley used in the experimental set up should be frictionless.*

Sources of Error

1. Load may not get removed after the completion of the experiment.
2. The cross-section of wire may not be uniform.
3. The values marked on the slotted weights and hanger may not be true.
4. Bridges may not be sharp.
5. The resonant length of the string may not be noted accurately. Due to the parallax error, this wrong observation takes place.

Viva-Voce

Q.1 In which way, the transverse stationary waves are produced in a stretched string?

Ans. Transverse stationary waves can be produced in a string by stretching it with tension and fixing it at its two ends. So, when plucked in the middle, the transverse stationary waves are produced it.

Q.2 What can be the reason for two prongs of a tuning fork?

Ans. Since, there are two antinodes at the free ends and one at the stem, so this makes the fork to vibrate for a long time even if we hold it at the stem.

Q.3 What can be a reason for the two holes in the side of sonometer?

Ans. It is to make the vibration of air inside the box to come in contact of outside air to enhance vibrations.

Q.4 What do you mean by free and forced vibrations?

Ans. (i) Vibrations of a vibrating body continued by itself are called **free vibrations.**

(ii) Vibrations of a vibrating body under a periodic force are called **forced vibrations.**

Q.5 In which ways, the resonating length of the string varies?

Ans. If we have the same tuning fork, then the resonating length of the given wire will increase the tension in the string. Also, if we keep the tension constant and along with that, if we change the string, then the resonating length will decrease with increase in higher mass density of wire.

Q.6 Musicians prefer stringed musical instruments. Give the suitable reason.

Ans. Musicians prefer stringed musical instruments because by changing length and point of disturbance, they can create any note and its overtone easily.

Q.7 When does resonance take place?

Ans. If a body is forced to vibrate with a frequency equal to its natural frequency then it executes resonant vibrations.

Experiment 9

AIM

To study the relation between the length of the given wire and tension for constant frequency using a sonometer.

Apparatus and Materials Required

Screw gauge, a meter scale, a sonometer, hanger with 500 g weight, seven 500 g slotted weights, rubber pad, spring balance and a tuning fork of certain frequency.

Theory/Principle

If a string vibrates in resonance with a tuning fork of frequency ν, then the string will also have the same frequency ν.

From Experiment 8, we know that, the frequency ν of the fundamental mode of vibration of string is given by

$$\nu = \frac{1}{2L}\sqrt{\frac{T}{m}} \qquad \ldots(i)$$

$\Rightarrow$ $$T \propto L^2$$

It means that the graph between T and L^2 will be a straight line.

Procedure

Setting up the Sonometer

1. First of all, put the sonometer on the table in such a way that its one end carrying pulley sets on the edge of the table, so that the hanger hangs without touching the table. Then, remove the wire from the pulley.
2. After removing the wire from the pulley, let the hanger to stretch it. Even attach one slotted weight with the hanger, thereby the wire can be stretched completely. Refer to the figure of Experiment (8).
3. Note down the values of slotted weights and hanger with the help of spring balance and then place the wire back on the pulley.

Relation between Length and Tension

4. Now, place the two wooden blocks or bridges to remove the kink and to define the length of resonating wire.
5. It is to be ensured that no any kink in the wire should exist.
6. Besides the checking of kinks in the wire, also confirm whether the wire spreads horizontally along the sonometer or not.
7. Insert a paper rider over the wire just in the middle of the length between the bridges.
8. Now, strike the prong of a tuning fork of a certain frequency (say 256 Hz) with a rubber pad and gently press the tip of its stem on the top of the sonometer. Thereby the wire resonates with the frequency of tuning fork to constitute the phenomenon of **resonance**.

9. Now adjust the length of the resonating wire by adjusting the bridge *F*.
10. Keep on adjusting the separation between the bridges till the paper rider falls down. Ensure that the paper rider should be kept exactly in the middle of the bridges.
11. When the paper rider falls down, this will indicate the condition of resonance. Now, measure the length of the wire between the edge of the bridges with the help of meter scale.
12. Increase the distance between the bridges by 4 to 5 cm by moving them outward. To increase the length of the wire, repeat the step 12 by decreasing the length of the wire till the paper sides falls down. Note the distance between two bridges with the help of meter scale. This gives the resonant length of the wire while decreasing.
13. Now, increase the load on the hanger in the steps of 500 g weight and repeat the above steps (8) to (11).
14. Determine the resonating lengths for different values of tensions with the same tuning fork.
15. Record the readings in the tabular form and plot a graph between L^2 and T.

Observations

Constant frequency of tuning fork, ν = ... Hz

Mass suspended, including mass of the hanger, X = ... g

Table for calculation of resonant length and tension in the wire

S. N.	Load including the mass of the hanger M (kg)	Tension $T = Mg$(N)	Resonant Length of the wire		Mean $l = \frac{l_1 + l_2}{2}$ (cm)	l^2 (cm)	$\frac{T}{l^2}$ (N cm^{-2})
			Length increasing l_1 (cm)	Length decreasing l_2 (cm)			
1.							
2.							
3.							
4.							
5.							

Plotting Graph

Plot a graph between the square of resonating length (L^2) and the tension (T) in the wire by taking (L^2) along the Y-axis and (T) along the X-axis, we get a straight line.

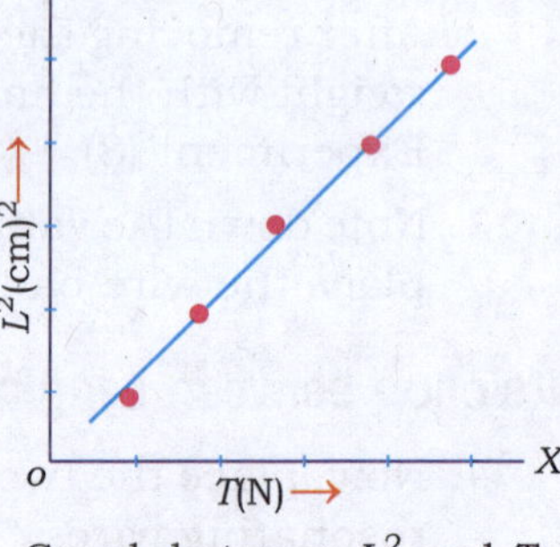

Graph between L^2 and T

Result

From the graph between L^2 and T, we have concluded that

(i) The value of T/L^2 is constant within the experimental limit.

(ii) It is a straight line which shows $T \propto L^2$ for a constant frequency ν.

PRECAUTIONS

Same as Experiment 8.

Sources of Error

Same as Experiment 8.

Viva-Voce

Q. 1 What is the linear mass density of a wire? Also, mention the factors on which it depends.

Ans. Linear mass density of a wire is defined as the mass per unit length of the wire. It depends on the radius and the density of the material of the wire.

Q. 2 Mention about the distance between a node and nearest anti-node.

Ans. The distance between a node and nearest anti-node is equal to the quarter wavelength of the stationary waves. i.e. $\frac{\lambda}{4}$.

Q. 3 State the law of mass and law of diameter.

Ans. According to the law of mass, $\nu \propto \frac{1}{m}$ and according to the law of diameter, $\nu \propto \frac{1}{D}$

Q. 4 A tuning fork completes 1000 vibrations in 4 s, what is time period?

Ans. $T = \frac{4}{1000} = 4 \times 10^{-3}$ s

Q. 5 What are the factors on which the frequency of a tuning fork depends?

Ans. The frequency of a tuning fork depends upon (i) length of the prong, (ii) density of the material of the prong, (iii) elasticity of the material and (iv) thickness of the prong.

The frequency f of the tuning fork is given by

$$f = k\frac{t}{l^2}\sqrt{\frac{E}{\rho}}$$

where E is the elasticity, t is the thickness, l is the length and ρ is the density of the material of the tuning fork.

Q. 6 What is the natural frequency of sonometer wire under tension?

Ans. The expression for natural frequency n of sonometer wire vibrating in one loop is given as

$$n = \frac{1}{2l}\sqrt{\frac{T}{m}}$$

where, T is the tension, m is the mass per unit length and l is the resonant length of the wire.

Q. 7 What are the laws of vibrating strings?

Ans. The frequency of vibrating string is

(i) inversely proportional to the length of the string.

(ii) directly proportional to the square root of the tension in the string.

(iii) inversely proportional to the square root of the mass per unit length of the string.

Q. 8 How are the longitudinal stationary waves produced in a rod?

Ans. Longitudinal stationary waves can be produced in a rod by damping it and then rubbing it along its length by a designed cloth.

Q. 9 Why does the rider placed at the middle point of the wire between two knife edges fly away at resonance?

Ans. When the vibrating wire is set into resonance the amplitude at the middle point of the wire which is anti-node is maximum. Hence, the paper rider placed here flies away.

Q.10 What is the principle of superposition of waves? [NCERT]

Ans. According to the principle of superposition of waves, the resultant displacement of a particle is equal to the vector sum of the individual displacements given to it by superposing waves.

Q.11 What are stationary waves? [NCERT]

Ans. Superposition of two waves of same frequency and same amplitude and travelling with same velocity in opposite direction produce stationary waves.

Q.12 Under which circumstances are stationary waves formed? [NCERT]

Ans. Stationary waves are formed when a reflected wave gets superposed with its incident wave.

Q.13 Identify the nodes and anti-nodes in the string of your sonometer. [NCERT]

Ans. In a stationary wave, the regions of zero displacement and maximum strain are called nodes. While the regions of maximum displacement and zero strain are called anti-nodes.

Q.14 Keeping the material of wire and tension fixed, how will the resonant length change, if the diameter of the wire is increased? [NCERT]

Ans. Keeping the material of wire and tension fixed, if the diameter of the wire is increased, then the resonant length of the wire will decrease. As we know that,

$$\nu = \frac{1}{LD}\sqrt{\frac{T}{\pi\rho}} \Rightarrow \nu \propto \frac{1}{D} \text{ and } L \propto \frac{1}{D}.$$

Q.15 What is the ratio of the first three harmonics produced in a stretched string fixed at the two ends? [NCERT]

Ans. The ratio of the first three harmonics produced in a stretched string fixed at the two ends is $\nu_1 : \nu_2 : \nu_3 = 1:2:3$.

Experiment 10

AIM

To find the speed of sound in air at room temperature using a resonance tube by two resonance positions.

Apparatus and Materials Required

A rubber pad, resonance tube, two tuning forks of known frequencies (preferably of 480 Hz and 512 Hz), water in a beaker, plumbline, a set square, one thermometer.

Description of Apparatus

Resonance Tube Apparatus

The resonance tube apparatus consists of a cylindrical tube *CD* about one metre long and 5 cm in diameter which is made of metal, fixed on a vertical wooden plank. A glass tube of small bore is fixed along the meter scale and is connected to metallic tube near its lower end. The apparatus of the resonance tube is shown below.

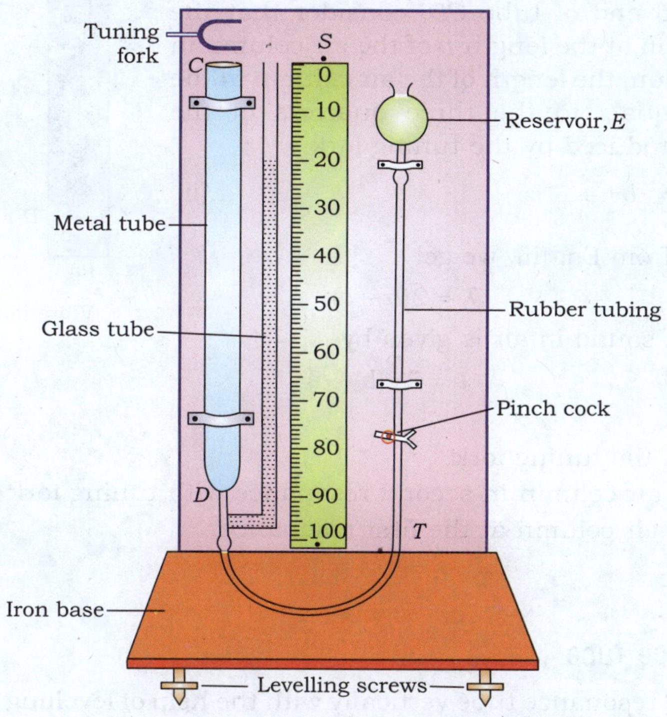

Experimental apparatus of resonance tube

Theory/Principle

If a vibrating tuning fork of known frequency (say ν) is held over the mouth of an air column in the glass tube *CD*, then a standing wave pattern is formed in the tube. Instantaneously, a superposition between a forward moving wave and a reflected wave takes place in the tube to cause the resonance. Thus, it leads to the noticeable increase in the amplitude of the sound.

Therefore, for resonance to occur, a node (i.e. a point having zero amplitude) must be formed at the closed end and an anti-node (i.e. a point having maximum amplitude) must be formed at the open end.

To Determine the Speed of Sound in Air

Consider at length *a* of the air column, the first loud sound is heard that means the air column of length *a* having the natural frequency equals to the natural frequency of the tuning fork, then the vibration of air column with maximum amplitude starts. Since, the length of vibrating air column is little longer than the length of air column in tube *CD*,

$$\therefore \quad \frac{\lambda}{4} = a + e \qquad \ldots\text{(i)}$$

where, $e = 0.6\,r$ (where, r =radius of glass tube) is the end correction for resonance tube and λ is wavelength of sound produced by tuning fork.

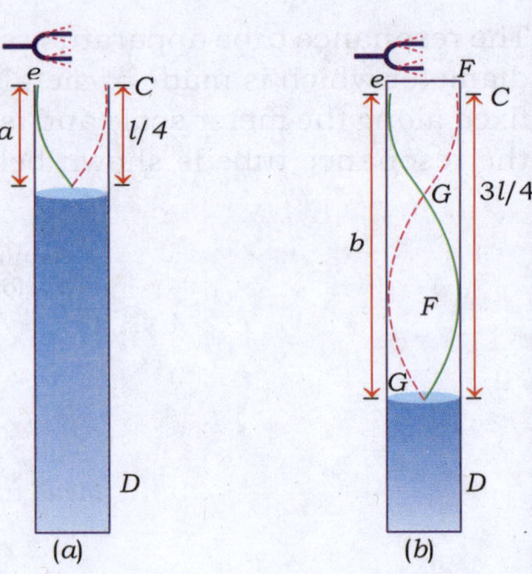

Vibrations in the resonance tube

On lowering the closed end of tube *CD*, consider that the resonance position listen at the length *b* of the air column in the tube. In this condition, the length of the air column in the tube approximately equals to the three quarters of the wavelength of sound produced by the tuning fork.

$$\text{i.e.} \quad \frac{3\lambda}{4} = b + e \qquad \ldots\text{(ii)}$$

On subtracting Eq. (i) from Eq. (ii), we get

$$\lambda = 2(b - a)$$

Therefore, the speed of sound in air is given by

$$v = 2\nu(b - a)$$

where, ν = frequency of the tuning fork,

b = length of air column in second resonance with tuning fork

and *a* = length of air column at the first resonance.

Procedure

Adjustment of Resonance Tube

1. First of all, fix the resonance tube vertically with the help of levelling screws and test it with plumbline.
2. Note the room temperature with the help of thermometer.
3. Note the frequency ν of the tuning fork.
4. Fix the reservoir to the highest point of the vertical rod with the help of clamp.

Determination of First Resonance Position

5. Open the pinch cock and then fill the reservoir with water in such a way that it rises upto the top in the pipe.
6. It is to be confirmed that the water does not spill out even if the reservoir attains the lowest position.
7. For the first resonance position, initiate with the zero length of air column in pipe.
8. Close the pinch cock and lower down the position of reservoir on the vertical rod.
9. Now, set the tuning fork into vibration by striking it on a rubber pad and then take the vibrating tuning fork to just above (about 1 cm above) the mouth of the tube.
10. It should be ensured that the prongs of the tuning fork remain parallel to the ground and lying one above the another thereby the prongs can vibrate vertically.
11. Simultaneously, make the reservoir in lower position which will lead to the lowering of water level in the pipe.
12. Try to listen the sound being produced in the tube. It may not be audible in this position because of dying out of vibration of tuning fork.
13. Now, set the tuning fork into vibration mode again by striking it on the rubber pad and bring the tuning fork near to the free opening of pipe and listen the sound again.
14. By slowly loosen the pinch cock, lower the level of water continuously till the sound of maximum intensity is heard.
15. Now, increase and decrease in the water level by 1 mm to confirm that loudness falls sharply on any side of the resonance position.
16. Fix the position of the tube where the intensity of sound is maximum.
17. Note the length x_1 of the air column in the glass tube from with the help of meter scale and set squares. This corresponds to the **first resonance position** or **fundamental node**.

Determination of Second Resonance Position

18. Now, lower the position of the reservoir R and clamp it to the near position of the tube and opening of the pinch cock till the length of air column in the tube increases about three times of the length x_1.
19. Next find the second resonance position by repeating the steps (9) to (17) and then determine the length of air column x_2 in the glass tube. It is to be ensured that the tuning fork must be of same frequency (ν_1) as used in finding the first resonance position.
20. Take at least four readings (i.e. two for when the level of water is falling and two for when the level of water is rising in the tube) to confirm the lengths x_1 and x_2.
21. Now, repeat the steps (9) to (20) with the second tuning fork of different frequency (ν_2) and determine the respective first and second resonance positions.
22. Calculate the speed of sound by using formula, $v = 2\nu(x_2 - x_1)$ for each frequency.

Observations

1. Temperature of the room, $T =$ ......°C
2. Frequency of the first tuning fork, $\nu_1 =$ ...... Hz
3. Frequency of the second tuning fork, $\nu_2 =$ ...... Hz

Table for the Determination of Resonating Length for Different Frequencies

Frequency of tuning fork used	S. N.	Length x_1 for the first resonance position of the tube			Length x_2 for the second resonance position of the tube		
		Water level is falling (cm)	Water level is rising (cm)	Mean length, x_1 (cm)	Water level is falling (cm)	Water level is rising (cm)	Mean length, x_2 (cm)
ν_1 =........ Hz	1						
	2						
ν_2 =........ Hz	1						
	2						

Calculations

1. Frequency of first tuning fork,

$$\nu_1 = \text{......}\ \text{Hz}.$$

Therefore, speed of sound in air,

$$v_i = 2\nu_1 (x_2 - x_1) \text{ ...... ms}^{-1}$$

2. The frequency of second tuning fork,

$$\nu_2 = \text{......}\ \text{Hz}$$

Therefore, speed of sound in air,

$$v_{ii} = 2\,\nu_2 (x_2 - x_1) = \text{........ ms}^{-1}$$

Therefore, mean speed of sound in air,

$$v = \frac{v_i + v_{ii}}{2} = \text{...... ms}^{-1}.$$

Note **Applying the End Correction** When you will be going to take the observations of second resonance position, then be clear that the loudness of sound in second resonance position must be lower than the loudness in the first resonance. So, in case if you will find the different results, then they have to be corrected at the same time by applying end correction.

Result

The speed of sound in air at room temperature is $\frac{v_i + v_{ii}}{2} = \text{...... ms}^{-1}$.

PRECAUTIONS

1. The vibrating tuning fork should not touch the walls of the resonance tube and should be kept just 1 cm above the top of the resonance tube.
2. The tuning fork must be striked on the rubber pad very gently.
3. Second resonance position must be accurately identified as the loudness of sound is very low.
4. Increasing and decreasing of water level in the resonance tube should be done very slowly.
5. The resonance tube should be kept vertically by using the levelling screws and plumbline.
6. The experiment should be performed in a quiet atmosphere, so that the resonance positions may be identified properly.
7. The choice of frequencies of the tuning forks being used should be such that the two resonance positions may be achieved in the air column of the resonance tube.
8. The prongs of the vibrating tuning fork must be kept parallel to the ground and keeping one over the other, so that the vibrations reaching the air inside the tube are vertical.
9. At the time of experiment, room temperature should be measured continuously, so that its mean value can be taken.

Sources of Error

1. Resonance tube may not have uniform cross-sectional area.
2. The pressure of water vapour in the air column may exhibit a higher value of speed of sound.
3. Rising and lowering of water level in resonance tube may not be slow.
4. The prongs of the vibrating tuning fork may touch the tube.

Viva-Voce

Q. 1 Define the resonance of air column.

Ans. Resonance of air column can be defined as the phenomenon in which the frequency of air column becomes equal to the frequency of the tuning fork.

Q. 2 Mention the principle of the working of the resonance tube.

Ans. The resonance tube works on the principle of the air column with the tuning fork.

Q. 3 Define the term end error.

Ans. End error can be defined as the error in the measurement of resonating length due to the non-rigidity of reflecting surfaces.

Q. 4 What is the reason of lying of anti-node just above the edge of the open end of tube?

Ans. The anti-node lies just above the edge of the open end of tube because the sound wave reflects back in the air column from a region slightly above the edge because the tube medium continues upto that region.

Q. 5 Why do we note the length of resonant air column with water level rising and falling?

Ans. This is done because the resonance is not sharp. It is rather flat in nature, i.e. for a small change in the length of air column intensity of sound practically remains the same. Taking mean of the two readings eliminates this error.

Q. 6 Are the waves produced in the resonance apparatus experiment and the sonometer experiment of the same nature? What is the difference between them?

Ans. No, waves produced in resonance apparatus are longitudinal whereas those produced in the wire in sonometer experiment are transverse.

Q. 7 What is the effect of pressure on the speed of sound in a gaseous medium?

Ans. There is no effect of pressure on the speed of sound in a gaseous medium. As the pressure increases, density also increases proportionally so that $\sqrt{\frac{p}{\rho}}$ is constant. Hence, the speed of sound also remains constant.

Q. 8 Does the length of the resonance column increase or decrease with increase of temperature?

Ans. Since, $v = 4v\ (l + 0.3D)$, as the temperature increases, velocity of sound also increases. Hence, l in the above relation will also increase.

Q. 9 Is the velocity of sound more in dry air on in wet air?

Ans. Sound travels faster in wet air as the density of wet air is less than that of dry air $\left(f \propto \frac{1}{\sqrt{\rho}}\right)$.

Q.10 What is theoretical formula for the velocity of longitudinal waves in gaseous medium?

Ans. Velocity v of a longitudinal wave is given as

$$v = \sqrt{\frac{E}{d}}$$

where, E is the bulk modulus of elasticity of the medium and d is the density of the medium.

Q.11 Name the phenomenon responsible for resonance in this experiment.

Ans. In this experiment, for resonance to occur, a node must be formed at the closed end and an anti-node must be formed at the open end of tube. So, due to this reason, the frequency of the air column becomes equal to the natural frequency of the tuning fork.

Q.12 Can you specify the position of nodes and anti-nodes in the air column?

Ans. The node lies at the surface of the water level while the anti-node lies at the open end of the metallic tube.

Q.13 Is the velocity of sound temperature dependent? If yes, write the relation. [NCERT]

Ans. Yes, the velocity of sound is temperature dependent as $v_0 - v_t = 0.61\,T$

where, v_0 = velocity of sound at 0 °C, v_t = velocity of sound at t° C, T = room temperature

Q.14 Write two other examples of resonance of sound from day-to-day life. [NCERT]

Ans. If we consider the musical instruments, then there can be the examples like strings of violin, length of the tube in a flute. While, in the case of mechanical resonance, example like breaking of the wine glass with sound at precise resonant frequency of the glass.

Q.15 What would happen, if the resonant tube is vertical? [NCERT]

Ans. According to the experimental procedure, the resonant tube should be set vertical firstly because the whole experimental apparatus and its procedure depend upon its position. Moreover, if it is not vertical, then it would lead an error in the result.

Q.16 Does velocity of sound depend upon temperature? [NCERT]

Ans. Yes, it increases with rise in temperature. If t°C is the rise in temperature, then

$$v_t = (v_0 + 0.61\,t)$$

where, v_0 is the velocity of sound at 0° C

and v_t is the velocity of sound at t°C.

Q.17 How can you get the velocity of sound by first resonant length? [NCERT]

Ans.

$$v = 4n(l_1 + x)$$

where, n is the frequency of tuning fork,

l_1 is the first resonant length,

x is the end correction

and v is the velocity of sound.

Q.18 You can also determine the frequency of the given tuning fork by a sonometer. Which of the two methods is better? [NCERT]

Ans. Sonometer method is better because it gives sharp resonance whereas in first resonant length method, we do not get sharp resonance.

Q.19 How does the velocity of sound depend upon pressure? [NCERT]

Ans. It is independent of pressure because the velocity of sound v is given as

$$v = \sqrt{\frac{\gamma p}{d}}$$

As pressure p changes, d (density) also changes accordingly, so that the ratio $\frac{p}{d}$ remains constant. Hence, v is independent of pressure.

Activity 1

AIM

To observe change of state and plot a cooling curve for molten wax.

Apparatus and Materials Required

Beaker of 500 mL, tripod stand, wire gauge, clamp stand, hard glass boiling tube, a half degree celsius thermometer, stirrer, stopwatch/stop clock, burner, paraffin wax, a cork with two holes to fit the thermometer vertically, graph paper.

Theory/Principle

Effect of Temperature on the States of Matter

The three states of matter are solid, liquid and gas. While heating a solid, it changes into liquid state and its temperature increases. The process of conversion of solid into a liquid state is known as **fusion** or **melting**. The temperature at which the melting takes place is called **melting point**. As the supply of heat continues, the temperature of the solid-liquid remains constant till whole of the solid changes into liquid. Then, the temperature of molten mass starts increasing. On cooling a liquid, it freezes to solid state at the same temperature as its melting point. In this case also the temperature of liquid-solid remains constant till all the liquid solidifies.

Procedure

Initial Observations Before Setting up the Apparatus

1. Note the least count and range of the given thermometer.
2. Also note the least count of stopwatch or stop clock whichever is being used.
3. Note the room temperature in the beginning of the experiment.

Setting up the Apparatus

4. Now, take a glass test tube and fill its one third part with the paraffin wax and then close it with the cork having two holes.
5. Through these two holes provided in the cork, put the thermometer and stirrer in the glass test tube. It should be ensured that the bulb of the thermometer gets completely dipped into the wax and it should not touch the walls of the glass test tube.
6. Set up the tripod, burner, heating arrangement and beaker having water as shown in figure. Put the beaker on the wire gauge.
7. Dip the glass test tube in the water and then fix it in the clamp stand.

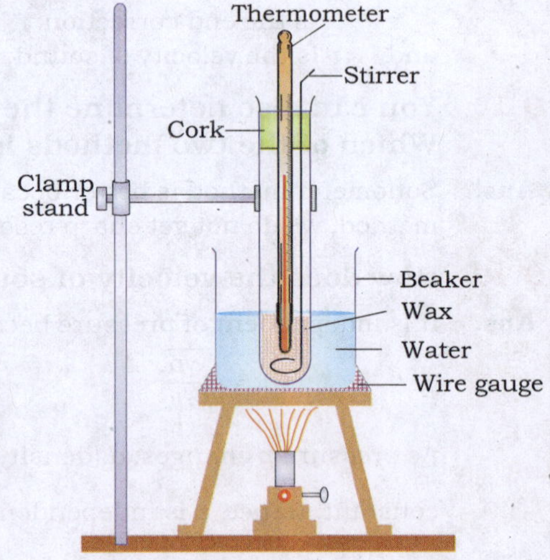

Experimental set up to study the change in state of paraffin wax

Measurement of Melting Point of Wax

8. Heat the water of the beaker with the help of burner and then observe the state of wax. On continuous heating, it starts melting at about 80°C.
9. Continue the heating till all the wax melts and note the approximate melting point.
10. Continue to heat the wax in water till the temperature reaches above 20 °C the melting point as observed in step (9).
11. Turn OFF the burner and stop heating the wax and water and allow them to cool.
12. Raise the clamp to remove the glass test tube from the beaker.
13. Start the stop watch and note the temperature of wax after every time interval of two minutes till the temperature falls to about 35°C.

Note Use the stirrer to cool the molten wax.

14. Note the observations in the tabular form and plot a graph between time and temperature of the wax by taking them along X and Y-axes, respectively.
15. Note the temperature where it gets saturated. This corresponds to the **melting point of the wax.**

Observations and Calculations

1. Least count of thermometer = ... °C
2. Range of thermometer = ... °C to .... °C
3. Room temperature in the beginning of the experiment, θ_1 = ...°C
   Room temperature at the end of the experiment, θ_2 = ... °C
   Mean room temperature, $\theta_0 = \frac{\theta_1 + \theta_2}{2}$ = ...°C
4. Least count of stopwatch = ... s

Table to Study the Variation in Temperature of Wax with Time

Number of observations	Time (s)	Temperature of wax (°C)
1		
2		
3		
4		
5		

Plotting Graph

Graph of falling temperature of wax *versus* time.

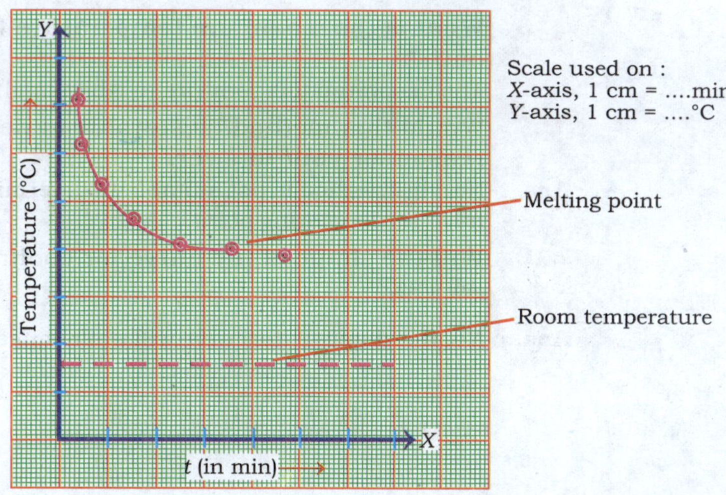

Result

1. On heating, the solid wax melts into the liquid and on cooling, the liquid wax solidifies back into solid state.
2. The melting point of wax is .... °C.
3. During the change of state, the temperature of the wax remains almost constant.
4. Percentage error = ...%.

PRECAUTIONS

1. *The bulb of the thermometer should be completely dipped into the wax and it should not touch the walls of the glass test tube.*
2. *The boiling glass test tube with wax should never be heated directly on a flame.*
3. *The stopwatch should be placed on the right hand side of the apparatus as it may be easy to use.*
4. *Wax should not be heated more than 20 °C above its melting point.*
5. *The temperature and the time reading should be recorded in every two minutes.*

Sources of Error

1. Simultaneous recording of temperature and time may give rise to some errors.
2. Impurities in the wax, change its freezing or melting point.

Viva-Voce

Q. 1 When a tab of spirit is rubbed on the arm before giving injection, it gives cooling effect. Give reason.

Ans. Because the spirit when evaporates absorbing latent heat of vaporisation from the arm and thus, causes cooling effect.

Q. 2 How is melting point of ice affected with increase in pressure?

Ans. On increasing the pressure, the melting point of ice increases and ice melts more easily.

Q. 3 Which causes more severe burns, boiling water or steam?

Ans. Steam causes more severe burns as it contains more energy in the form of latent heat of vaporisation.

Q. 4 A beaker containing ice is heated. No, rise of temperature is recorded by a thermometer put in the beaker unless the whole of ice has melted. Why?

Ans. The heat supplied does not appear on thermometer as it is being used to change the state of ice from solid to liquid.

Q. 5 What happens to the volume, when ice melts?

Ans. The volume decreases as the ice melts.

Q. 6 Why should we never heat the wax directly over a flame? [NCERT]

Ans. We should never heat the wax directly over a flame because solid wax melts into liquid rapidly.

Q. 7 Why is water bath used to melt the wax and heat it further? [NCERT]

Ans. Water bath is used to melt the wax and heat it further because the temperature of wax in the glass tube remains steady till whole of wax melts. After further heating of the wax, temperature starts rising continuously.

Q. 8 What is the maximum temperature to which molten wax can be heated in a water bath? [NCERT]

Ans. The maximum temperature to which molten wax can be heated in a water bath is 20 °C.

Q.9 Would this method be suitable to determine the melting point of plastics? Give reason for your answer. [NCERT]

Ans. No, this method is not suitable to determine the melting point of plastics because plastics do not have sharp melting point.

Q.10 Will the shape of the curve for cooling of hot water be different from that of wax? [NCERT]

Ans. No, the shape of the curve will not change for cooling of hot water.

Activity 2

AIM

To observe and explain the effect of heating on a bimetallic strip.

Apparatus and Materials Required

Iron-brass bimetallic strip with an insulating handle, heater/burner, clamp stand, thermometer.

Description of Bimetallic Strip

Bimetallic strip is made of two bars/strips of different metals or materials having same dimensions.

At room temperature, the bimetallic strip is straight. When the bimetallic strip is heated, both the metallic pieces expand to different extents because they have widely different values of coefficients of linear thermal expansion. This results in the **bending of bimetallic strip**.

Theory/Principle

When there is a change in length of a bar on heating, the **linear thermal expansion** is said to be occurred. Let L_1 and L_2 be the lengths of rod/bar of a metal at temperatures t_1 °C and t_2 °C, such that $t_2 > t_1$. Change in length $(L_2 - L_1)$ is directly proportional to the original length L_1 and the rise in temperature $(t_2 - t_1)$.

$$\Rightarrow \qquad \alpha = \frac{L_2 - L_1}{L_1(t_2 - t_1)}$$

where, α is the **coefficient of linear thermal expansion** of the material.

Thus, the coefficient of linear thermal expansion (α) is the increase in length for unit degree rise in temperature of the bar. Its SI unit is K^{-1}.

Procedure

Heating the Bimetallic Strip

1. Hold the bimetallic strip made up of two strips of different materials (iron and brass) with the help of insulated handle in such a way that it should be kept in horizontal position. Note down the initial temperature of the strip.
2. Mark as *A* and *B* on the two halves of bimetallic strip and turn ON the burner or switch ON the electric heater.
3. Heat the bimetallic strips with the help of burner/heater.

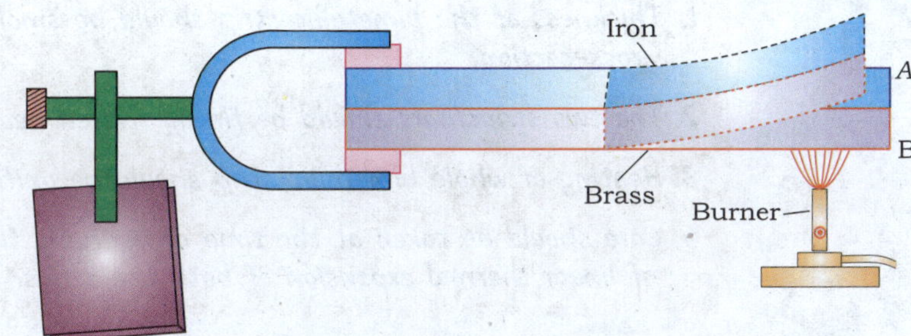

Experimental set up to study the effect of heating on bimetallic strip

4. Note the side of the bimetallic strip which is in direct contact of heat source.

Effect of Heating on the Bimetallic Strip

5. Observe the heating effect of the strip and the direction of the bending of the free end of the strip, i.e. upwards or downwards.
6. Identify which of two metallic strips (*A* or *B*) is on the convex side of the bimetallic strip and which one is on the concave side.
7. Now identify the metallic strip which one has larger linear thermal expansion. The metallic strip which on the convex side of the bimetallic strip will expand more and has larger linear thermal expansion.
8. Note down the values of coefficient of linear thermal expansion of two metals *A* and *B* from the standard table .
9. Now, verify the direction of bending of the metallic strip (whether it is downward or upward) is on the side of that strip which is made up of metal having lower coefficient of linear thermal expansion.
10. Take the bimetallic strip away from the heat source. Allow the strip to cool to room temperature.
11. Repeat steps (1) to (10) to heat the other side of the bimetallic strip.
12. Observe the direction of bending of the bimetallic strip.

Observations

1. Room temperature = ... °C
2. Metallic strip which is on convex side = ...
3. Metallic strip which is on concave side = ...
4. Standard value of coefficient of linear thermal expansion of metallic strip *A* = ... K^{-1}
5. Standard value of coefficient of linear thermal expansion of metallic strip *B* = ... K^{-1}

Result

It has been verified that **on heating, the bending of a bimetallic strip takes place** due to the difference in coefficient of linear expansion of the two metals of the strip.

PRECAUTIONS

1. *Thickness of the bimetallic strip should be small and its length should be large as compared to its cross-section.*
2. *The two strips/bars should be firmly riveted near their ends.*
3. *Heating of whole bimetallic strip should be uniform over its entire length.*
4. *Care should be taken at the time of verifying the expansion with the standard value of coefficient of linear thermal expansion of both the strips.*

Sources of Error

Heating of strip may not be uniform.

Viva-Voce

Q. 1 What is the basic cause of bending of a bimetallic strip?

Ans. The basic cause of bending of a bimetallic strip is the difference between the coefficients of linear expansions of two metals of which strip is made.

Q. 2 What are the different types of thermal expansion?

Ans. The different types of thermal expansion are

(i) Linear expansion

(ii) Superficial expansion

(iii) Cubical expansion

Q. 3 Which pair of metals is used in your activity?

Ans. A pair of brass and iron is used in the activity.

Q. 4 What is the relation between the coefficients of thermal expansion?

Ans. The relation between the coefficients of thermal expansion are

$$\gamma = 3\alpha \text{ and } \beta = 2\alpha \text{ or } \gamma = \frac{3\beta}{2}$$

where, α = linear expansion, β = superficial expansion and γ = cubical expansion.

Q. 5 Name a few devices in which bimetallic strips are generally used as thermostat.

Ans. Bimetallic strips are generally used as thermostat in geysers, air conditioners, automobiles, etc.

Q. 6 You have been given bars of identical dimensions of following metals/materials along with their α values, for making a bimetallic strip

Aluminium ($\alpha = 23 \times 10^{-6}\ K^{-1}$), **Nickel** ($\alpha = 13 \times 10^{-6} K^{-1}$)

Copper ($\alpha = 17 \times 10^{-6} K^{-1}$), **Invar** ($\alpha = 0.9 \times 10^{-6} K^{-1}$)

Iron ($\alpha = 12 \times 10^{-6} K^{-1}$), **Brass** ($\alpha = 18 \times 10^{-6} K^{-1}$)

Which pair of metals/materials would you select as best choice for making a bimetallic strip for pronounced effect of bending? Why? [NCERT]

Ans. The pair of aluminium and invar would be the best choice for making a bimetallic strip because pair of metals with wide difference in their expansivities are selected.

Q. 7 What would be the effect on the bending of the bimetallic strip, if it is heated to a high temperature? [NCERT]

Ans. When a bimetallic strip is heated to a high temperature, then the direction of bending changes.

Activity 3

AIM

To note the change in level of liquid in a container on heating and interpret the observations.

Apparatus and Materials Required

Round bottom flask of 500 mL, narrow tube (or capillary tube) about 20 cm long and of internal diameter 2 mm, rubber cork, glycerine (liquid on which the effect of heating is to be observed), hot water, stand for holding the flask, strip of graph paper and thermometer.

Theory/Principle

For keeping the liquid, we always require a container. When we heat the liquid, the container also gets heated. This results in the expansion of both liquid and container. Thus, they both undergo the cubical thermal expansion. To observe the expansion of liquid only, the following two types of expansions have to be considered

(i) Apparent expansion

(ii) Real expansion

The apparent expansion can be given as

The apparent expansion = The expansion of the liquid – The expansion of the container

The relation between the real and apparent expansions of liquid is

Real expansion = Apparent expansion of the liquid + Expansion of the container

Thus, to find the real expansion of the liquid, the expansion of the container should be taken into consideration.

Procedure

Setting up the Apparatus

1. Clean and dry the round bottom glass flask.
2. Fill the flask with glycerine upto its brim. It is to be ensured that no air bubbles should be present in the glycerine.
3. Fit the cork tightly into the mouth of the flask and put the capillary tube into the flask through the cork in such a way that 6-8 cm of tube remains outside the flask as shown in the figure.
4. Now, the glycerine starts rising in the capillary tube. Mark the level of glycerine in the capillary tube say point *A* as soon as it rises. This will represent the volume of the glycerine at room temperature.

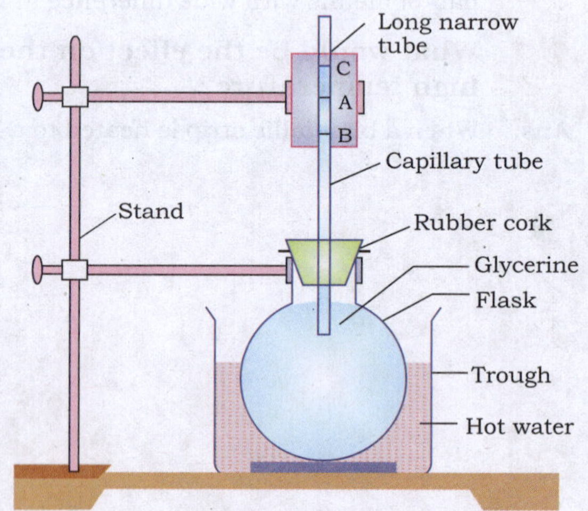

Experimental setup to study the effect of heating on the level of liquid

Note One can use the coloured glycerine, so that there will be no difficulty in marking the level on the transparent glass tube.

Effect of Hot Water on the Liquid Filled in the Flask

5. Place the flask in the trough filled with hot water and hold the flask in position with the help of a stand. Note the initial temperature of liquid with the help of thermometer.
6. Due to the expansion of the flask, the level of liquid in capillary tube falls down upto a point (say *B*) and then it again rises upto a certain level (say *C*) due to the increase in temperature of glycerine. Mark these levels on the capillary tube.
7. Note the corresponding readings of marking of level of glycerine in the capillary tube. These three levels of the glycerine help to determine the cubical expansion of container and real and apparent cubical expansions of liquid (or glycerine).
8. Note the final temperature of the liquid.
9. Repeat the above steps two more times and note the observations in the tabular form.

Observations

1. Least count of thermometer = ... °C 2. Initial temperature of liquid, T_1 = ... °C
3. Final temperature of liquid, T_2 = ... °C

Table to Study the Effect of Heating on the Level of Liquid

S. N	Position of level mark			Cubical expansion of container, AB (mL)	Real cubical expansion of liquid, BC (mL)	Apparent cubical expansion of liquid, AC (mL)
	A	B	C			
1						
2						
3						

Result

When flask is immersed in hot water, the level of glycerine in the tube placed in the flask first falls down to a point *B* and then rises upto a level *C*.

Note When the expansion of flask takes place, the level of liquid in tube falls from *A* to *B*. This fall is equal to the expansion of the container. After sometime, the glycerine also gets heated and expands. This results in the rising of the level of glycerine again and hence it attains a stationary level *C*. *BC* gives the real expansion and *AC* the apparent expansion.

PRECAUTIONS

1. *The capillary tube should be narrow.*
2. *There should not be any air bubble in the liquid filled flask.*
3. *The boiling point of liquid (or glycerine) should be higher than that of water used in the trough.*
4. *There should be sufficient amount of hot water in trough so that flask may get fully immersed into it.*

Sources of Error

1. Heating of the glycerine may not be uniform.
2. Temperature of the hot waterbath may not be steady.

Viva-Voce

Q. 1 Is there a liquid which contracts on heating? If yes, give example.

Ans. Water contracts on heating from 0°C to 4°C.

Q. 2 What is the relation between γ_a and γ_r?

Ans. The relation between γ_a and γ_r is $\gamma_r = \gamma_a + \gamma_g$.

where, γ_r = real cubical expansion of liquid, γ_a = apparent cubical expansion of liquid.

and γ_g = the expansion of the container.

Q. 3 Suggest any two errors in this activity.

Ans. The two errors in this activity are as follows

(i) Flask may not be fully immersed in the liquid.

(ii) There may be air bubbles in the flask.

Q. 4 What do you mean by coefficient of real cubical expansion of a liquid?

Ans. The coefficient of real cubical expansion of a liquid means the actual increase in the volume of a liquid per unit volume per unit degree celsius rise in temperature.

Q. 5 In the activity, what does the level *BC* stand for?

Ans. In the activity, the level *BC* stands for real expansion of liquid.

Q. 6 Water in a flask is heated in one case from 25°C to 45°C and in another case, from 50°C to 70°C. Will the apparent expansion/real expansion be the same in the two cases? [NCERT]

Ans. Real expansion will be same in both the cases.

Q. 7 A liquid of cubical expansivity γ is heated in a vessel having linear expansion $\gamma/3$. What would be the effect on the level of the liquid? [NCERT]

Ans. There will be no change in the level of the liquid.

Activity 4

AIM

To study the effect of detergent on surface tension of water by observing capillary rise.

Apparatus and Materials Required

Capillary tube, beaker of 250 mL, small quantity of solid/liquid detergent, 15/30 cm plastic scale, rubber band, clamp stand and water.

Theory/Principle

As per the theory of Experiment 4 of Section B, it was clear from the relation of surface tension that

$$T \propto h$$

where, T is the surface tenstion and h height of the liquid column.

For pure or distilled water in contact with a clean glass capillary tube, $\theta \approx 8°$ or $\cos\theta \approx 1$.

Thus, $$T = \frac{1}{2} h\rho gr$$

The surface tension of different detergent solutions (colloidal) in water can be compared by using this result. A detergent for which the capillary rise is minimum, is said to have **better cleansing effect**.

Procedure

Setting up the Apparatus

1. Take a capillary tube of uniform bore. Clean and rinse it with distilled water. It should be ensured that the capillary tube is dry and free from grease, oil, etc., and it should be open from both the ends. Also clean and rinse the beaker with water.
2. Pour water to fill the beaker upto half.
3. By using rubber bands, mount the plastic scale with the capillary tube.
4. Now, with the help of clamp stand, hold the scale with capillary in vertical position.
5. The half filled beaker is placed below the lower end of the scale and gradually lower down the scale till its lower end gets immersed below the surface of water in the beaker.

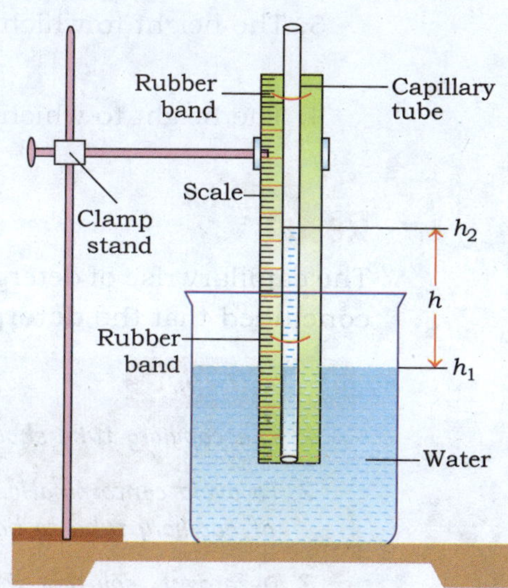

(a) Experimental set up to study the rise of water in the capillary tube

Rise of Water and Mixture of Water and Detergent in the Capillary Tube

6. Note the position of the water level inside h_2 and outside h_1 the capillary tube on the scale.

   The rise of water in the capillary is

$$h = h_2 - h_1$$

7. Rinse the capillary thoroughly in running water and dry it.
8. Take some quantity of detergent and mix it with water in the beaker.
9. Repeat the experiment with detergent solution and find the rise of mixture (water and detergent) in capillary tube again. Let it be h'. You will find that the value of h' will be less than that of h.

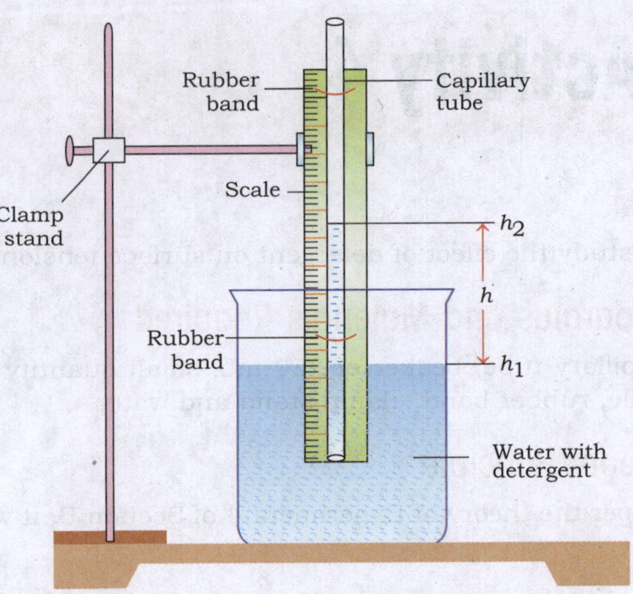

(b) Experimental set up to study the rise of mixture of water and detergent in the capillary tube

Observations and Calculations

1. The position of water level inside that part of the capillary tube which is dipped in the water, h_1 = ... cm.
2. The position of water level inside that the part of the capillary tube which remains outside the surface of water, h_2 = ... cm.
3. The height to which water rises in the capillary tube,

$$h = (h_2 - h_1) \text{ .... cm}$$

4. The height to which the detergent solution rises in the capillary tube,

$$h' = \text{ .... cm}$$

Result

The capillary rise of detergent solution h' is less than the capillary rise of water h. Thus, it can be concluded that the **detergent reduces the surface tension of water**.

PRECAUTIONS

1. *The capillary tube should be kept vertical, otherwise the reading of rising of water may get affected.*
2. *To avoid contamination by hand, we should not touch the inner surface of the beaker and the part of capillary tube to be immersed in water or solution.*
3. *Detergent solution should be prepared by stirring with a glass rod.*
4. *The beaker placed below lower end of tube should not be disturbed.*
5. *The capillary tube should be clean and dry.*
6. *At the time of adding detergent to the water, it should be taken care that the concentration of detergent must not be made high, otherwise the density of solution will change substantially as compared to water. Moreover, two values of angle of contact between the surface of glass and solution may get changed substantially.*

Viva-Voce

Q 1 What is the dimensional formula of surface tension?

Ans. The dimensional formula for surface tension is $[ML^0T^{-2}]$.

Q 2 Do all liquids rise in a capillary tube? Explain.

Ans. No, all liquids do not rise in a capillary tube. Liquids which make a convex meniscus in capillary tube are depressed, e.g. mercury is depressed in glass capillary tube.

Q 3 How is the surface tension of water affected on dissolving a detergent in it?

Ans. The surface tension of water decreases on dissolving a detergent in it.

Q 4 What is the value of surface tension of a liquid at critical temperature?

Ans. The value of surface tension of a liquid is zero at critical temperature.

Q 5 What is the main cause of surface tension?

Ans. The main cause of surface tension is the interatomic force of attraction acting between liquid-liquid molecules.

Q 6 Why is the surface tension a scalar quantity?

Ans. Surface tension is a scalar quantity because it has no specific direction for a given liquid.

Q 7 What is the effect of temperature on surface tension of a liquid?

Ans. The surface tension of a liquid decreases with increase in temperature.

Q 8 Surface tension of liquid is independent of the area of the liquid surface. Give reason.

Ans. According to surface tension, force is independent of the area of liquid surface. Thus, surface tension is also independent of the area of the liquid surface.

Activity 5

AIM

To study the factors affecting the rate of loss of heat of a liquid.

Apparatus and Materials Required

Two copper calorimeters of different sizes (one small and other big), two copper calorimeters of same size (one painted black and other highly polished), two tumblers of same size (one metallic and other plastic), two thermometers, stopwatch/clock, cardboard lids for calorimeters, two laboratory stands, pan to heat water, measuring cylinder and plastic mug.

Theory/Principle

The rate of loss of heat can be given by $\frac{dQ}{dt} = ms\frac{dT}{dt}$

Hence, we can conclude that the rate of loss of heat is directly proportional to rate of change of temperature

i.e. $$\frac{dQ}{dt} \propto \frac{dT}{dt}$$

The rate of loss of heat of a body depends upon

(i) difference in temperature of the hot body and its surroundings.
(ii) area of the surface losing heat.
(iii) nature of the surface losing heat i.e. radiating surface.
(iv) material of the container.

Procedure

Refer to Experiment (6) of Section B to study the difference in temperature of the hot body and its surroundings.

(i) Effect of Area of Surface on Rate of Loss of Heat

1. Find the least count of stopwatch and note it.
2. Note the room temperature in the beginning of the experiment and also note the least count of the two thermometers (T_A and T_B).
3. Consider the big one as (*A*) and small one as (*B*) calorimeters.
4. Heat the water separately in the pan upto 80°C. There is no need to boil the water.
5. Pour 100 mL of hot water in calorimeter *A* and also in calorimeter *B* using plastic mug and measuring cylinder. The water in the calorimeter should be poured with least time loss, so that the temperature of water does not fall down.
6. With the help of clamp stand, suspend a thermometer in both the calorimeters.
7. It is to be ensured that the thermometer bulb should be inside the hot water in the calorimeters and it should not touch the wall of the calorimeter.

8. Note the temperature of water in both the calorimeters initially at an interval of 1 min till the temperature of water in calorimeter is 40-30°C above the room temperature and thereafter at intervals of 2 min when the temperature is 20-10°C above the room temperature.
9. Note the temperatures T_A and T_B in the observation table and plot graphs between T_A *versus* time and T_B *versus* time for both the calorimeters on the same graph paper. It will be observed that the cooling curve for calorimeter of larger surface area is steeper than that for the liquid in the other calorimeter.
10. Determine the slope of T *versus* time graph after 5 min interval.

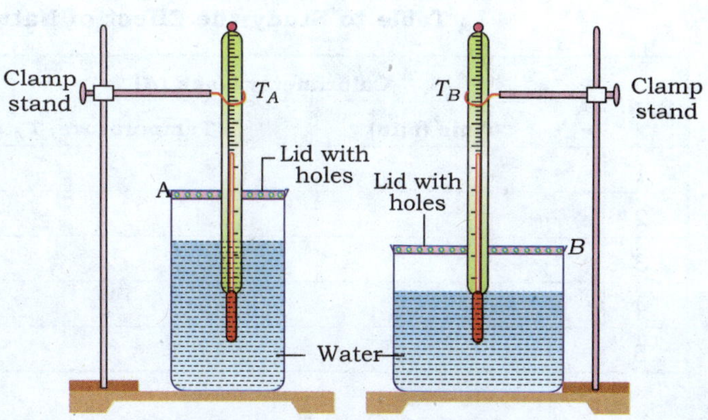

Experimental set up to study the effect of surface area on rate of cooling

(ii) Effect of Nature of Surface of Container on Rate of Cooling of a Liquid

11. Use the two identical small calorimeters one with black (*A*) and the other with highly polished (*B*) surfaces.
12. Repeat the steps (4) to (10).
13. Note the observations and plot a graph by taking time along *X*-axis and temperature *T* along *Y*-axis.

(iii) Effect of Material of Container on Rate of Cooling of a Liquid

14. Use the metallic tumbler (*A*) and the plastic tumbler (*B*) instead of calorimeters.
15. Repeat the steps (4) to (10) as in part (i).
16. Note the observations in the tabular form.

Observations and Calculations

Effect of Area of Surface on Rate of Cooling

1. Least count of thermometer = ... °C
2. Least count of stopwatch = ... °C
3. Room temperature in the beginning of the experiment, θ_1 = ... °C

   Room temperature at the end of the experiment, θ_2 = ... °C

   Mean room temperature, $\theta_0 = \frac{\theta_1 + \theta_2}{2}$ = ... °C

Table to Study the Effect of Area of Surface on Rate of Cooling

S. N.	Calorimeter *A* (Big)		Calorimeter *B* (Small)	
	Time (min)	Temperature, T_A (°C)	Time (min)	Temperature, T_B (°C)
1				
2				
3				
4				
5				

Table to Study the Effect of Nature of Surface of Container on Rate of Cooling

S. N.	Calorimeter black (A)		Calorimeter highly polished (B)	
	Time (min)	Temperature, T_A (°C)	Time (min)	Temperature, T_B (°C)
1				
2				
3				
4				
5				

Table to Study the Effect of Material of Container on Rate of Cooling of a Liquid

S. N.	Metallic tumbler (A)		Plastic tumbler (B)	
	Time (min)	Temperature, T_A (°C)	Time (min)	Temperature, T_B (°C)
1				
2				
3				
4				
5				

Plotting Graph

The graph drawn between time on X-axis and temperature on Y-axis is showing the effect of area of surface on rate of loss of heat.

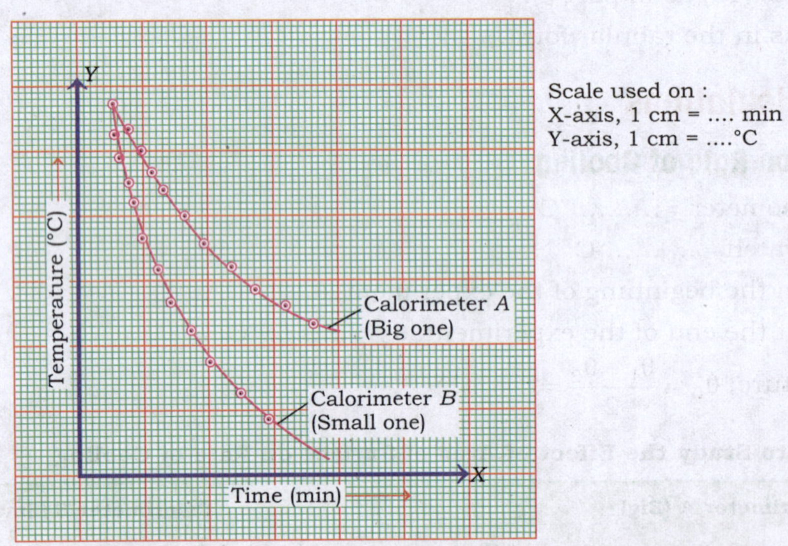

Graph showing the effect of area of surface on rate of cooling

Result

1. The rate of cooling in the larger calorimeter as compared to the smaller calorimeter is .... °C/min.
2. Least rate of cooling observed in calorimeter s .... °C/min.
3. Black surfaces radiate .... heat as compared to white or polished surface in the same time when heated to the same temperature.
4. The rate of cooling of a liquid in the plastic mug is .... °C/min.

PRECAUTIONS

1. *The recording of temperatures (T_A and T_B) and time should be done simultaneously, so the set up should be planned in such a way that the readings can be taken quickly.*
2. *The lid of the calorimeter should be covered with insulating material to make sure that the heat loss is only from the surface of calorimeter.*
3. *Volume of hot water should be taken in equal quantity in each case.*
4. *Do not place two calorimeters very close to each other.*
5. *All the activities should be performed under the similar conditions of wind and temperature of surroundings.*
6. *The bulb of the thermometer should be dipped well inside the water and it should not touch the walls of the calorimeter.*

Sources of Error

1. Surroundings temperature may change.

Viva-Voce

Q. 1 Why should water in calorimeter be constantly stirred?

Ans. Water in calorimeter be constantly stirred because stirring ensures that the temperature of the whole water in the vessel remains uniform.

Q. 2 Why do animals tend to fold their bodies when they feel cold?

Ans. Animals tend to fold their bodies when they feel cold to minimise the surface area which means that heat loss is less.

Q. 3 If the surface of the container is coated with black colour, what will be its effect on the rate of loss of heat?

Ans. If the surface of the container is coated with black colour, then the rate of loss of heat increases.

Q. 4 At what temperature will a body stop radiating?

Ans. The body will stop radiating at temperature 0 K.

Q. 5 A body at higher temperature contains more heat. Comment.

Ans. The statement is not always true. The heat content of a body depends upon its mass, specific heat and temperature.

Q. 6 Why does the rate of cooling decrease when the temperature of liquid is closer to the room temperature?

Ans. The rate of cooling decreases when the temperature of liquid is closer to the room temperature because rate of cooling decreases with decrease in surface area.

Q. 7 Why should a thermometer bulb have a small heat capacity?

Ans. The thermometer bulb having small heat capacity will absorb less heat from the body whose temperature is to be measured. Hence, the temperature of that body will practically remain unchanged.

Q. 8 The rate of cooling in summers is lower than in winters. Give a reason for your answer. [NCERT]

Ans. The temperature difference between a hot object and the surrounding air is smaller in summer. Heat transfers more quickly when the temperature difference is larger.

Q. 9 Surface of metallic kettles are often polished to keep the tea warm for a long time. How? [NCERT]

Ans. Polished surfaces reflect heat, this reduces the amount of heat lost through radiation, keeping the tea warm for a longer period.

Q.10 Why does the rate of cooling decrease when the temperature of liquid is closer to the room temperature? [NCERT]

Ans. It happens because the temperature difference between the liquid and the surrounding is small. According to Newton's law of cooling, the rate of heat loss of a body is directly proportional to the difference in temperature between the body and its surroundings. As this difference diminishes, the rate of cooling slows down.

Activity 6

AIM

To study the effect of load on depression of a suitably clamped meter scale loaded at (i) its end (ii) in the middle

Apparatus and Materials Required

Meter scale, two wedges to rest the ends of the meter scale, thread, slotted weights 200 g each, hanger for slotted weights, graduated scale with a stand to hold the scale vertical, plane mirror, pointer and plasticine.

Theory/Principle

The experimental setup to study the effect of load on depression of a beam load in middle is shown below.

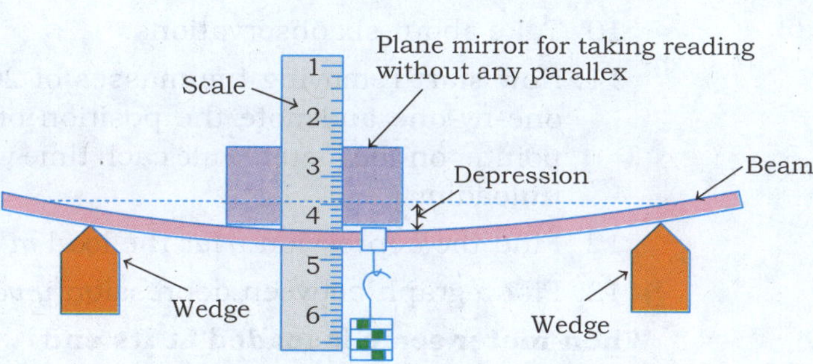

Experimental set-up to study depresion, i.e. sag of a beam with load in the middle

Let a beam be loaded at the centre and supported near its ends with wedges as shown in the figure. Suppose L be the length, b be the breadth and d be the thickness of the bar which is loaded at the centre by a load, $w = mg$.

Then, the depression is given by $y = \dfrac{4wL^3}{bd^3Y}$

where, Y is the Young's modulus of the material of the rod/beam and w is the load (mg).

The depression y is directly proportional to the load (mg). Hence, there is a **linear relationship between depression and load**. On plotting the graph between the load (m) and depression (y) by taking them along X and Y-axes respectively, we get a straight line passing through the origin.

Procedure

When meter scale is loaded at middle.

Set up the Apparatus

1. Find the least count of the vertical scale.
2. Place the meter scale on two wedges with 10 cm length projecting out on either side. Meter scale supported at both ends is like a beam.
3. Now, tie a loop of thread tightly in the middle of the scale placed on two wedges, so that a hanger with slotted weights each of 200 g can be suspended from it. It is to be ensured that the thread does not slip.
4. Place the graduated scale (having least count 0.1 cm) vertically in a stand at the centre of the meter scale used as beam. The vertical scale should be kept on the far side of the meter scale placed on the wedges. This facilitates the reading.
5. Fix a pin to the hanger such that its pointed end is close to the edge of the vertical scale which has graduation marks on it but it should not touch the graduation marks.

6. Hold the mirror strip in a stand at the back of the beam or place the mirror on a stool using plasticine in the middle of the beam.

Note The mirror strip is used to keep away from the parallax error at time of taking the reading.

7. Read the position of the pointer on the vertical scale when no any load is suspended from the beam.

Effect of Load on the Depression of the Beam

8. Suspend the hanger of mass 200 g and note the position of the pointer attached with the hanger when the pointer comes to rest after vibration.
9. Keep on adding 200 g slotted masses gradually to the hanger and note the readings of the position of the pointer on the meter scale each time.
10. Take about six observations.
11. Now start removing the masses of 200 g one-by-one and note the position of the pointer on the meter scale each time while unloading.

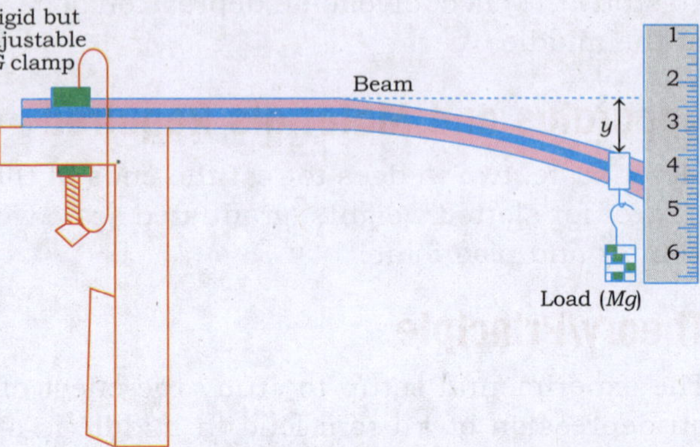

Load attached at the end of the scale

12. Find the depression y for the load m and hence, depression per unit load (or y/m).
13. Plot a graph between depression y *versus* load m and interpret your result.

When meter scale is loaded at its end

14. Clamp the meter scale firmly to the edge of the table, as shown in figure. Ensure that the length and breadth of the scale is projected out. Fix a pin with a tape at the free end of the meter scale along its length to act as a pointer.
15. Fix a graduated scale vertically near the free end of the clamped meter scale and note its least count. Ensure that the pointed end of the pin is just above the graduation marks of the scale but do not touch it.
16. Read the pointer p when meter scale cantilever is without any load.
17. Now, repeat all the observations from (8 to 13) and note the reading.

Observations and Calculations

1. Least count of vertical scale = ... cm
2. Length of the beam between the wedges, L = ... cm
3. Width of the beam between the wedges, b = ... cm
4. Thickness of the beam, d = ... cm

(i) Table to Study the Effect of Load on Depression of a Beam Loaded in the Middle

S. N.	Load, m (g)	Reading of the centre of cantilever			Depression for load, y (cm)	Depression per unit load, $\frac{y}{m}$ (cm/g)
		Load increasing, r_1' (cm)	Load decreasing, r_2' (cm)	Mean reading, $r = \frac{r_1' + r_2'}{2}$ (cm)		
1	0			r_0 =	0	
2	200			r_1 =	$r_1 - r_0$ =	
3	400			r_2 =	$r_2 - r_0$ =	
4	600			r_3 =	$r_3 - r_0$ =	
5	800			r_4 =	$r_4 - r_0$ =	
6	1000			r_5 =	$r_5 - r_0$ =	

From the observation table, it can be seen that the value of y/m remains almost constant for all observations.

(ii) Table to study the effect of load on depression of a Beam loaded of the end.

S. N.	Load, m (g)	Reading of the centre of Cantilever			Depression for load, y (cm)	Depression per unit load, $\frac{y}{m}$ (cm / g)
		Load increasing, r_1' (cm)	Load decreasing, r_2' (cm)	Mean reading, $r = \frac{r_1' + r_2'}{2}$ (cm)		
1.	0			$r_0 =$	0	
2.	200			$r_1 =$	$r_1 - r_0 =$	
3.	400			$r_2 =$	$r_2 - r_0 =$	
4.	600			$r_3 =$	$r_3 - r_0 =$	
5.	800			$r_4 =$	$r_4 - r_0 =$	
6.	1000			$r_5 =$	$r_5 - r_0 =$	

From the observation table, it can be seen that the value of $\frac{y}{m}$ remains almost constant for all observations.

Plotting Graph

On plotting a graph between the values of depression δ on Y-axis and load m on X-axis, we get a straight line.

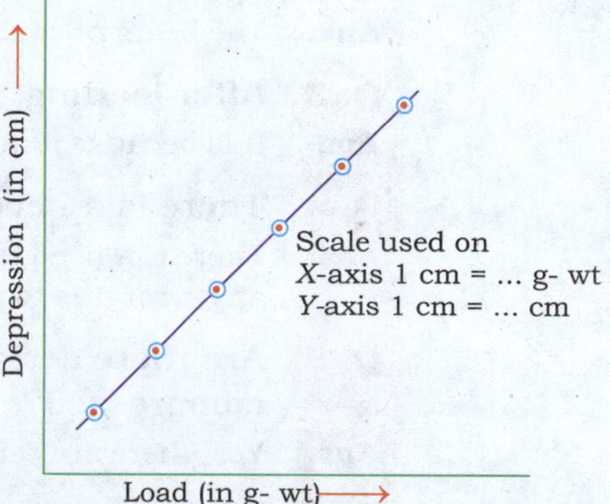

Graph between Load and Depression

Result

The graph between load and depression in both the cases, i.e. when meter rod is loaded (i) at its end (ii) in the middle are straight lines which shows that depression is directly proportional to the load.

PRECAUTIONS

1. The beam should be placed symmetrically on the wedges.
2. The load hanged should not exceed the maximum permissible load within the elastic limit.
3. The weight should be added or removed gently.
4. Mirror strip should be used in order to eliminate any error due to parallax in reading the scale.
5. The thickness of the meter scale placed on the wedges should be uniform and it should be as small as possible.
6. The reading should be taken after sometime when load is applied because the meter scale takes sometime to come in rest position.

Sources of Error

1. The scale should not be loaded beyond its elastic limit.
2. There should be no vibratory motion of the beam when reading is recorded.
3. While noting down the observations, the eye should be normal to the tip of the pin and the graduated scale.

Viva-Voce

Q. 1 Give any two significance of this activity.

Ans. The two significance of this activity are

(i) It helps us to determine Young's modulus of the material of given rod or meter scale.

(ii) We can find that how much load we can put on the given rod or beam.

Q. 2 What is the main source of error in this activity?

Ans. The beam or cantilever may not have uniform thickness and density.

Q. 3 After loading, one should wait for sometime before noting a reading. Why?

Ans. It is because it takes sometime for the oscillations generated at the time of loading to stop.

Q. 4 There is a need to use a plane mirror to take measurements of depression. Why?

Ans. There is a need to use a plane mirror to take measurements of depression because it minimises any error due to parallax.

Q. 5 Are there certain filaments in the bar which are neither extended nor compressed?

Ans. Yes, there are certain filaments which remain unchanged or unstrained.

Q. 6 What is the geometrical shape of the bar that you are using as a cantilever?

Ans. The geometrical shape of the bar used as a cantilever is rectangular bar.

Q. 7 How does the curvature vary along the bent beam?

Ans. The curvature is minimum in the middle and increases towards both ends.

Activity 7

AIM

To observe the decrease in pressure with increase in velocity of a fluid.

Apparatus and Materials Required

Wide tube and narrow tube or venturimeter, two vertical tubes, spirit level, vernier callipers, tap water and meter scale.

Theory/Principle

A venturimeter is a device used to increase the velocity or flow rate of fluid flowing through a pipeline. The velocity of fluid increases by flowing it through the varying cross-sections of the pipe. Experimental set up of a venturimeter is given below.

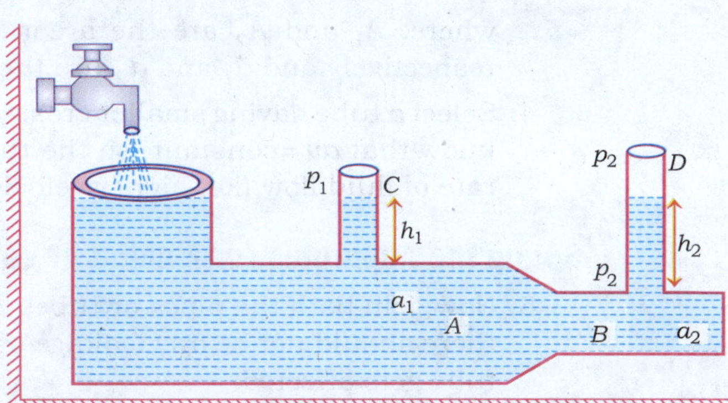

A venturimeter : Experimental set up to observe the decrease in pressure with increase in velocity of a fluid

The principle of the venturimeter is that when a fluid flows through the venturimeter, it accelerates in the **convergent section** and decelerates in the **divergent section**, resulting in a drop in the **static pressure**.

The function of the converging section of the venturimeter is to increase the velocity of the liquid and lower its pressure. The short portion called **throat** has minimum area resulting in the increase in velocity of flow.

In this section, the velocity of flow reaches its maximum value and pressure reaches its minimum value. Subsequently, a decrease in the velocity and an increase in the pressure takes place in course of flow through the diverging section.

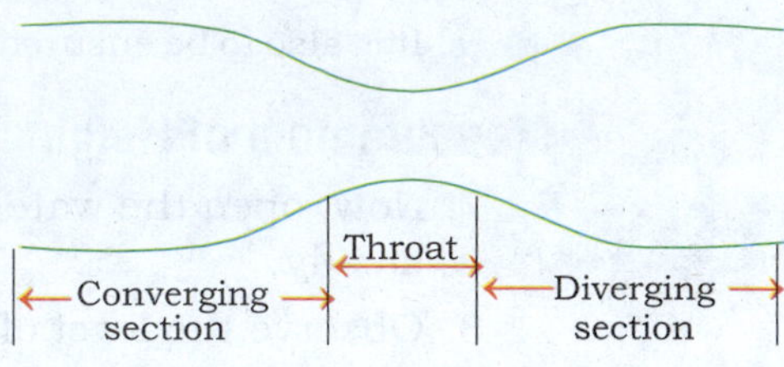

Constructional view showing the principle of venturimeter

Equation of Continuity

According to the equation of continuity,

"The product of area of cross-section (a) of a pipe of varying cross-section and the normal fluid velocity (v) remains constant throughout the flow".

$$\therefore \quad av = \text{constant}$$

Measuring the Pressure Inside the Tubes

We know that the pressure on a horizontal tube having fluid is proportional to the height of level of fluid rising in the vertical tube connected with the horizontal tube.

Let the height h of the fluid rising in the vertical tube and the horizontal tube having fluid pressure p, then

$$p = \rho g h$$

where, ρ = density of the fluid and g = acceleration due to gravity.

Hence, by knowing the height (h) of the fluid rising in the vertical tube, one can determine the fluid pressure inside the horizontal tube (or a tube with which the vertical tube is connected).

Procedure

Determination of Area of Cross-Section of Pipes

1. First of all measure the least count and zero error of the vernier callipers. These both will be taken into account while measuring the corrected diameters of the two pipes.
2. By using the vernier calliper, measure the internal diameters of both the tubes (i.e. wide one and narrrow one).
3. After measuring the internal diameters, calculate the area of cross-section of both the tubes as given below.

$$A_1 = \frac{\pi}{4} d_1^2 \quad \text{and} \quad A_2 = \frac{\pi}{4} d_2^2$$

where, A_1 and A_2 are the areas of cross-section of tube A (wide) and tube B (narrow) respectively and d_1 and d_2 are their respective internal diameters after zero connection.

4. Select a tube having smaller cross-sectional area. Since, from the equation of continuity, we know that av =constant, so the tube having smaller cross-sectional area will have higher rate of fluid flow (i.e. higher velocity of fluid).

Set up the Apparatus (or Making of Venturimeter)

5. Now, join both the pipes or tubes A and B along with the tubes C and D in such a way that there should not be any leakage of water at the junction otherwise the pressure inside the tube gets affected.
6. Place the joined pipes on a horizontal table. It is to be ensured that the table should be horizontal and the vertical tubes C and D connected with the tubes A and B respectively should remain vertical and parallel with each other. The horizontal level of the table should be checked with the help of spirit level to adjust it horizontally (if not).

Note It is also to be ensured that the open free end of the wide tube should be just below the water tap.

Measurement of Heights of Water Rising in Vertical Tubes

7. Now, open the water tap at slow rate thereby the water filled in the pipes A and B remains steady.
8. Observe the level of water in the vertical tubes C and D. It starts rising water in both the tubes. Let the water rise completely in both the tubes.
9. When the water stops rising in the vertical tubes C and D, then measure the heights h_1 and h_2 of the water ascended in both the tubes with the help of meter scale. Note the observations of heights.

Measurement of Pressures Inside the Tubes

10. Now, calculate the pressure by putting the value of heights of water in the formula given below.

$$p_1 = \rho g h_1 \quad \text{and} \quad p_2 = \rho g h_2$$

Hence, with the help of heights h_1 and h_2, the pressures p_1 and p_2 can be measured in both the tubes.

11. Note the observations of pressure.
12. Increase the rate of water by loosening the tap.

13. Repeat the steps (8) to (11) and measure the pressures p_1 and p_2 inside both the tubes again.
14. Take two more readings by repeating the steps (12) and (13) and observe that the pressure is decreased inside the tube having higher rate of flow of fluid.
15. Note the observations in the tabular form.

Observations and Calculations

Measurement of Diameters

1. Least count of vernier callipers = ... cm
2. Zero error of vernier callipers (z) = ... cm
3. Internal diameter of tube A, d_1 = ... cm
4. Corrected internal diameter of tube A, $d_A = d_1 + z$
5. Internal diameter of tube B, d_2 = ... cm
6. Corrected internal diameter of tube B, $d_B = d_2 + z$

Selection of Tube having Higher Flow Rate

1. Area of cross-section of the tube A, $A_1 = \frac{\pi}{4} d_A^2$
2. Area of cross-section of the tube B, $A_2 = \frac{\pi}{4} d_B^2$
3. Equation of continuity, $av = \text{constant}$

   Thus, the tube having smaller cross-sectional area will have higher flow rate.

Measurement of Pressure Inside the Tubes

1. Height upto which the water rises in tube C, h_1 = ... cm
2. Height upto which the water rises in tube D, h_2 = ... cm
3. Density of water, $\rho = 1\ \text{g/cm}^3$
4. Acceleration due to gravity, $g = 980\ \text{cm/s}^2$
5. Pressure inside the tube A, $p_1 = \rho g h_1$ = ... dyne/cm^2
6. Pressure inside the tube B, $p_2 = \rho g h_2$ = ... dyne/cm^2

Table to Measure the Pressure Inside the Horizontal Tubes

S. N.	Area of cross-section of tube A (cm)^2	Area of cross section of tube B (cm)^2	Height of water in the tube C, h_1 (cm)	Height of water in the tube D, h_2 (cm)	Pressure inside the tube A, $p_1 = \rho g h_1$	Pressure inside the tube B, $p_2 = \rho g h_2$
1						
2						
3						

Result

From the above observation table, it is understood that **as soon as the velocity of flow of water increases** (which can be assumed as increases by loosening the water tap), **the pressure inside the tube having smaller cross-sectional area decreases.**

PRECAUTIONS

1. *The zero error of the vernier callipers should be taken into account while measuring the diameters of the tubes.*
2. *The internal diameters should be measured with appropriate significant figures because the square of the internal diameters is used to determine the areas of cross-section of the pipes.*
3. *Selection of the tube having smaller cross-sectional area should be gently done.*
4. *There should not be any leakage and overflow of the water.*
5. *The flow of water in both the pipes i.e. A and B should be steady.*
6. *The joined pipes must be put on the exact horizontal table.*
7. *The vertical tubes C and D should be parallel and vertical to each other.*
8. *Readings of heights should only be taken when the water stops rising in the vertical tubes.*

Viva-Voce

Q. 1 What is a fluid?

Ans. A substance which has the ability to flow is called a fluid. Both gases and liquids are called fluids.

Q. 2 How does fluids differ from solids?

Ans. Solids have a definite shape of their own whereas, fluids do not have a definite shape of their own but acquire the shape of their containers.

Q. 3 If water flowing in a broader pipe enters a narrow pipe, why does the velocity of water increase?

Ans. According to the principle of continuity, the velocity of water in a narrower pipe is greater in comparison to that in a broader.

Q. 4 What happens to the pressure in the narrow tube?

Ans. The pressure in the narrow tube will be smaller than that in the broader tube.

Q. 5 If air is blown below one pan of a physical balance, what will be the effect on the equilibrium of the balance?

Ans. Due to increase in the air velocity below the pan of a physical balance, the pressure falls, hence, the pan goes down.

Q. 6 Give the mathematical relation of Bernoulli's theorem.

Ans. $p + \frac{1}{2}\rho v^2 + \rho gh = \text{constant}$

Q. 7 What is meant by steady flow?

Ans. In a steady fluid flow, the velocity of fluid particles at any point never changes. It remains constant with time.

Project 01

AIM

To study Fortin's barometer and use it to measure the atmospheric pressure.

Apparatus and Materials Required

Fortin's barometer and a thermometer.

Theory /Principle

Atmospheric pressure is the force exerted by the weight of air above us. We measure this pressure using a barometer, which shows how much air is pressing down on a given area. The unit of measurement is newton per square metre (Nm^{-2}).

A Fortin's barometer consists of a narrow glass tube of length about 80 cm. This tube is closed at one end. The tube is completely filled with mercury and kept inverted in a Cistern filled with dry mercury. Usually, the glass tube is protected by enclosing it in a brass tube. The upper part of the brass tube has a slit that enables the level of the mercury in the glass tube to be seen. A scale graduated in millimeters is attached to the brass tube. It functions as the main scale.

For accurate measurements, a vernier scale that can slide over the main scale is also fixed to the barometer. The vernier scale can be moved up and down using a screw.

The bottom of the cistern is like a bag made of flexible leather. The mercury level can be adjusted by means of a screw provided underneath. There is an ivory pointer in the cistern placed at the top. The tip of this pointer coincides with the zero of the main scale. The level of the mercury column in the cistern can be changed with the screw under it. It is so adjusted that the ivory point is exactly at the surface of the mercury in vertical position.

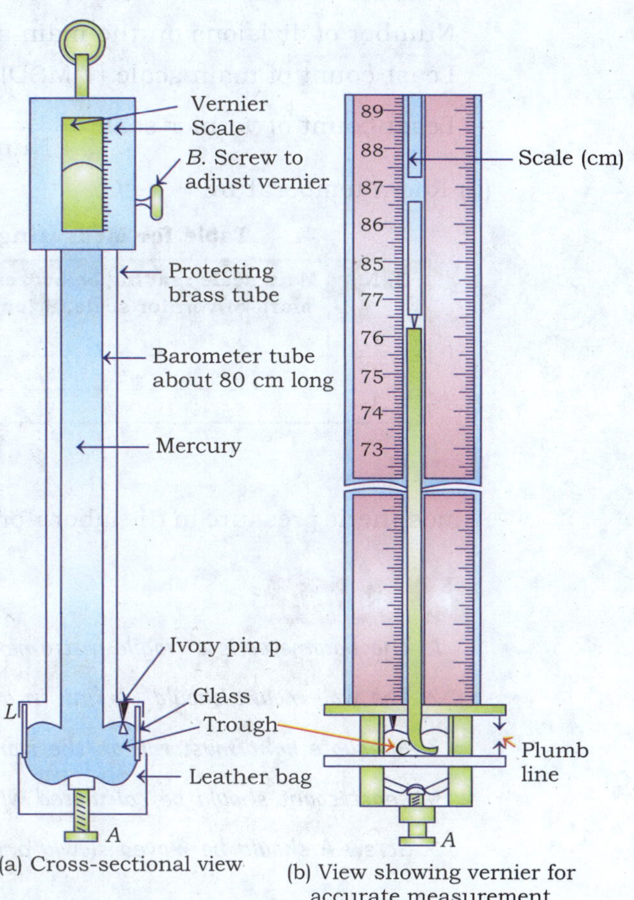

(a) Cross-sectional view

(b) View showing vernier for accurate measurement

Procedure

1. Make the barometer tube vertical using a plumb line.
2. Examine the screw *A*, *B*, pin *P* and vernier *V*.
3. Now, find the least count of the vernier scale.
4. Adjust the level of mercury surface in the through of the barometer with the help of screw *A* and by looking at the ivory pin and its image on the mercury surface in the trough.
5. Adjust the vernier using screw *B* such that the zero of the vernier touches the convex meniscus of mercury in the tube. The eye should be kept at the level of the meniscus.

6. Now, note down the main scale reading and also the reading on the vernier scale.
7. Also, note down the room temperature at the end of the experiment.
8. Repeat the experiment more than two times.

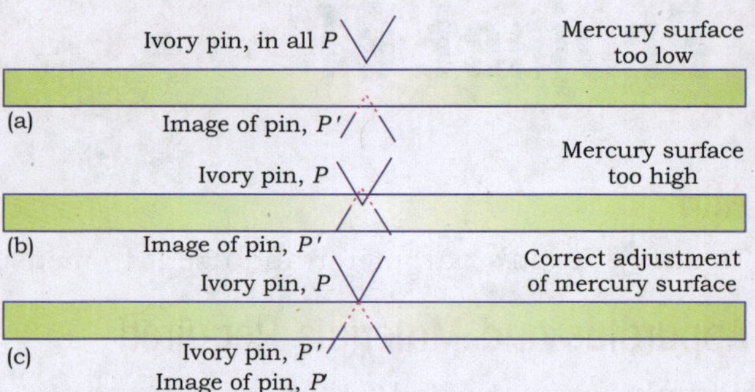

Adjustment of mercury surface in the reservoir

Observations

(i) Vernier constant or least count = ...

Number of divisions on the vernier = ...

Number of divisions on the main scale = ...

Least count of main scale (1 MSD) = ... cm

Least count of vernier scale $= \dfrac{\text{1 MSD}}{\text{Number of divisions on vernier scale}} = \ldots$ cm

(ii) Room temperature = ... °C.

Table for Measuring Height of Mercury Column in a Barometer

S. N.	Main scale reading below zero mark of vernier scale, S (cm)	Vernier scale reading	Height of mercury column $h = (S + n \times \text{least count})$ (cm)
1.			
2.			
3.			

Result

Atmospheric pressure in the laboratory in terms of mercury column = $h \times 13600 \times 9.8$ Nm^{-2} or Pa.

PRECAUTIONS

1. The barometer is a fragile instrument and should be handled carefully.
2. The wall mount should be firm in a room of a laboratory and not in any passage.
3. Adequate light must fall on the ivory pin and the vernier scale.
4. Least count should be calculated with care.
5. Screw A should be moved slowly and gently.

Sources of Error

1. There may be air bubbles in the barometer tube.
2. Ivory pin may not be fixed properly.
3. Room temperature may change, affecting the observations.

Viva-Voce

Q. 1 Is there air in the space above the mercury in the barometer tube?

Ans. No, it is a vacuum known as the torricellian vacuum.

Q. 2 Why is mercury used as the liquid in barometers?

Ans. Mercury is used because it has

(i) High density, which allows for a shorter column length
(ii) Low vapour pressure
(iii) Opacity
(iv) It does not stick to the walls of the glass tube

Q. 3 What would be the height of a water barometer?

Ans. The height of a water barometer would be

$$\frac{13.6}{1} \times 76 \text{ cm} = 1036 \text{ cm}$$

Since, water is 13.6 times less dense than mercury.

Q. 4 What is a torr? How can you express it in terms of Pascals (Pa)?

Ans. A torr is a unit of pressure equivalent to a 1 mm Hg column.

$$1 \text{ torr} = \frac{1}{760} \text{ atm} = \frac{1.013 \times 10^5}{760} \text{ Pa} = 133.3 \text{ Pa}$$

Q. 5 Why does Fortin's barometer need adjustment every time it is used?

Ans. Fortin's barometer requires adjustment because the scale for measuring the height is fixed. As pressure changes, the zero adjustment need to be done, so that the zero point aligns with lower mercury level.

Q. 6 If water is used instead of mercury, what problems would you encounter? [NCERT]

Ans. Using water instead of mercury in instruments like barometers or thermometers would cause problems such as

(i) **Height** Water's lower density means a water barometer would need to be about 13 times taller than mercuryone (around 10.3 m)
(ii) **Temperature Range** Water's freezing point (0°C) and boiling point (100°C) restrict its use in environments outside this range.

Q. 7 What effect would there be of the following
(a) Ivory pin not adjusted as advised?
(b) Barometer is not vertical but titled?
(c) The pin *P* and scale *S* not viewed at eye level? [NCERT]

Ans. (a) **Ivory pin not adjusted as advised** This leads to an incorrect reading of the mercury level, causing inaccurate atmospheric pressure measurements.

(b) **Barometer is not vertical but tilted** A tilted barometer gives a lower mercury column height resulting in an inaccurate, usually lower, atmospheric pressure reading.

(c) **The pin *P* and scale *S* not viewed at eye level** This introduces para-llax error, causing the mercury level to be read inaccurately leading to incorrect pressure readings.

Project 02

AIM

To study the effectiveness of different materials as absorber of sound.

Apparatus and Materials Required

An audio frequency oscillator, two transformers, cathode ray oscilloscope (CRO), microphone, speakers, material like wood, glass, cardboard, mica, connecting wires, Cardboard sheets of different thickness, a meter scale, screw gauge and vernier callipers.

Theory

When sound waves travel through a medium or from one medium to another, their intensity decreases due to the absorption of mechanical energy. This absorption is primarily caused by the viscous forces that resist the relative motion of the medium's particles as the sound wave propagates. When sound transitions from one medium to another, some of the energy is reflected at the boundary between the media and the remaining energy enters the new medium, where it may be absorbed.

In a given medium, if E represents the incident energy and E' is the energy after travelling a distance x, then

$$E' = E \cdot e^{-\mu x}$$

where, μ is the coefficient of linear absorption. The degree of absorption is influenced by

(i) The nature of the absorbing material.

(ii) The distance x, which depends on the thickness of the material through which the sound travels.

The experimental set up includes

1. **An Audio Oscillator** This device generates audio frequency waves, with an adjustable frequency.
2. **Microphone** It receives the sound energy after it comes out of the absorbing material and converts it into electrical energy.

Procedure

(A) To study dependence of absorption of sound on the nature of the material

1. Take sheets of absorbing materials such as glass sheet. Cardboard, plywood, etc.
2. Also, measure thickness of each sheets of different materials using screw gauge/vernier callipers.
3. Make the circuit connecting various components as shown in figure. Connect the high resistance coils of the two transformers to audio oscillator. The low resistance coils are connected to the microphone and the CRO as shown in figure.
4. Switch ON the audio frequency oscillator. Adjust the CRO so that a suitable waveform appears on the CRO. When there is no sheet between the speaker and the microphone, measure the amplitude of the corresponding audio signal on the oscilloscope.

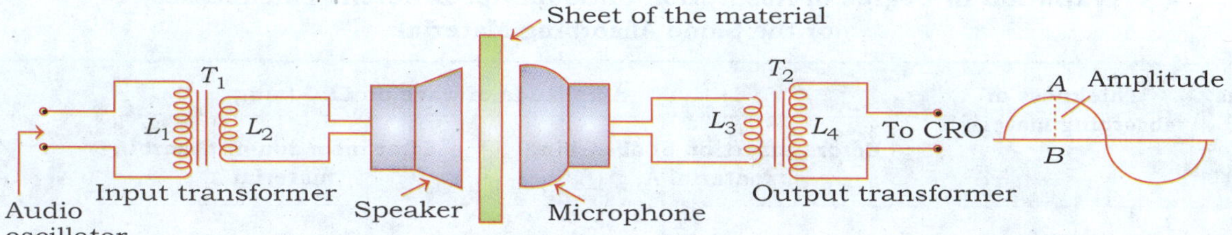

Circuit arrangement of comparing effectiveness of different material as absorbers of sound

5. Now, insert the sheet of the first material in front of the speaker by mounting it on a stand. Due to absorption of sound by the sheet, the amplitude of wave falls. Note the new amplitude on the scale marked on CRO screen.
6. The length *PQ* gives the amplitude of the wave.
7. Insert the remaining sheets of different materials but of the same thickness one by one and note every time the amplitude of the corresponding wave on the CRO as before.
8. Record the observations as shown in table 1.

(B) To study dependence of absorption of sound on the thickness of the sheet

9. We first prepare and select sheet of different thickness but of same material.
10. Measure the thickness of each sheet with vernier callipers or screw gauge at different places to find the mean thickness.
11. Repeat the steps 4 and 5 of the experiment.
12. Record the observations in tabular form to analyse the degree absorption of sound with the thickness of the absorbing material.

Observations

1. Least count of screw gauge/vernier calipers = ... mm
2. Thickness of cardboard = ... mm

   Thickness of glass sheet = ... mm

   Thickness of fibre board = ... mm

   Thickness of plywood = ... mm
3. Frequency of the audio signal used = ... Hz

Absorption of Sound in Different Absorbing Materials of Same Thickness

No. of observations	Name of absorbing material	Amplitude of wave on CRO (mm)		
		Before insertion of absorbing material A_0	After insertion of absorbing material A_1	$\frac{A_1}{A_0}$
1.	Glass			
2.	Card board			
3.	Fibre board			
4.	Plywood			

Variation in Degree of Absorption of Sound for Different Thicknesses of the Same Absorbing Material

No. of bservations	Thickness of absorbing material	Amplitude of wave on *CRO* (mm)		
		Before insertion of absorbing material A_0	After insertion of absorbing material A_1	$\frac{A_1}{A_0}$
1.				
2.				
3.				
4.				

Result

1. Degree of absorption of sound waves is maximum in ...... (material) and minimum in ...... (material).
2. Degree of absorption of sound waves increases/decreases with increase in the thickness of absorbing material (cardboard).

PRECAUTIONS

1. The amplitude of the input audio signal is kept constant while performing the experiment, with different absorbing materials of same thickness.

2. The thickness of absorbing material should not be so high that the corresponding output signal on the screen of CRO is no longer measurable.

3. The respective positions of the speaker, microphone and absorbing material sheets for all sets of experiment should be kept unchanged.

Viva-Voce

Q. 1 What is meant by mechanical energy?

Ans. Mechanical energy of a body is the total of its kinetic and potential energy.

Q. 2 What are the units for measuring the intensity of sound?

Ans. The units are joules per second per square metre (J / sm^{-2}) or watt per square metre (W / m^2).

Q. 3 What factors affect the absorption of sound by a material?

Ans. The absorption of sound depends on

(a) The nature of the material.

(b) The distance of the sound travels through the material.

Q. 4 What is an audio oscillator?

Ans. An audio oscillator converts energy from a direct current (DC). Source into waves of audio frequencies (20 Hz to 20000 Hz).

Q. 5 Assuming $E = E_0 e^{-\mu x}$, how will you define coefficient of linear absorption?

Ans. Now, $E = E_0 e^{-\mu x}$, If $\mu x = 1$, then $E = \frac{E_0}{e}$, If $\mu = \frac{1}{x}$, then $E = \frac{E_0}{e}$

Thus, the coefficient of absorption of sound is the reciprocal of the distance in which the intensity of sound is reduced to $\frac{1}{e}$ of its original density.

Project 03

AIM

To compare the effectiveness of different materials as insulators of heat.

Apparatus and Materials Required

A cylindrical metallic container, a cylindrical plastic container (with height same as that of metal container but having a much higher radius), a thermometer, an insulating lid for plastic container with a hole for inserting a thermometer, different insulating materials in powder of liquid forms.

Theory/Principle

The principle behind comparing the effectiveness of different insulating materials is to evaluate their thermal conductivities. Materials with lower thermal conductivity are more effective insulators.

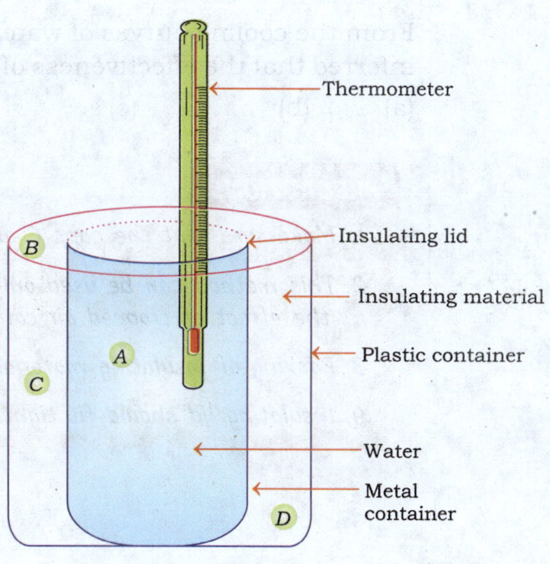

Fig. (A)

Procedure

1. Place the metal container (*A*) inside the plastic container (*B*), ensuring an equal gap all around. Fill this gap with the insulating material you want to study (figure A).
2. Pour hot water (approximately 60°C) in to container *A*.
3. Cover both containers with an insulating lid.
4. Insert a thermometer into container *A* through a hole in the lid, ensuring the bulb is submerged in the water.
5. Record the time taken for every 5°C drop in temperature.
6. Repeat the above procedure using different insulating materials.
7. Plot temperature *versus* time graph for each insulating material on the same graph paper.

Observations

Least count of the thermometer = ...°C

Fall in Temperature with Time for Different Materials as Insulators

S. N.	Name of the Material	Variation of temperature with time								
1.		Temperature								
		Time								
2.		Temperature								
		Time								
3.		Temperature								
		Time								
4.		Temperature								
		Time								

Plotting Graph and Interpretation

Plot a graph between time t and temperature θ for different materials on the same graph paper, taking time on X-axis and temperature on Y-axis.

Steeper the graph, faster the rate of cooling of water thereby implying lower efficiency of the material used as thermal insulator.

Result

From the cooling curves of water drawn for different insulating materials surroundings it can be inferred that the effectiveness of different materials as insulators of heat in decreasing order is

(a) (b) (c) (d)

PRECAUTIONS

1. *Make sure that the gaps C and D are kept the same for all the materials.*
2. *This method can be used only for the insulating materials available in the powdered/liquid form as the effect of trapped air can be minimised for them.*
3. *Packing of insulating material in the gaps C and D should be equally uniform in all the cases.*
4. *Insulating lid should fit tightly to minimise heat loss.*

Viva-Voce

Q. 1 Why is it important to ensure a equal gap around the metal container when placing it inside the plastic container?

Ans. Ensuring a equal gap around the metal container is crucial to maintain uniform insulation and ensure consistent thermal resistance from the insulating material. This helps in obtaining accurate and comparable results for different insulating.

Q. 2 Why do we use hot water at nearly 60°C?

Ans. To ensure a measurable and safe rate of heat loss for accurate data collection.

Q. 3 What is the role of insulating lid?

Ans. To minimize heat loss through the top and ensure heat transfer primarily through the insulating material.

Q. 4 Why does a slower temperature drop indicate about an insulating material?

Ans. It indicates better insulating properties and lower thermal conductivity.

Q. 5 What is the main heat transfer mechanism studied in this experiment?

Ans. Conduction through insulating material.

Project 04

AIM

To compare the Young's modulus of elasticity of different specimen of rubber and compare them by drawing their elastic hysteresis curve.

Apparatus and Materials Required

Two samples of rubber bands of about 10 cm, a rigid support, number of slotted weight (10g) a hanger (10g), a scale and a fine pointer.

Terms and Definitions

- **Elastic hysteresis** When the stress-strain curve does not retrace on reversing the strain, this phenomenon is known as elastic hysteresis.
- **Residual strain** If, upon removing the deforming force, the length of the specimen does not return to its original length, this result is residual strain.

Theory/Principle

1. The stress *versus* strain (or elongation) graph for rubber is not a straight line. Therefore, the Young's modulus of elasticity for rubber cannot be define uniquely. For a given stress, it is defined as the slope of the stress-strain curve at a particular stress-strain point.
2. The area enclosed by the hysteresis curve indicates the energy loss during the loading and unloading cycle.

Procedure

1. Suspend a rubber band from a rigid support and attach a hanger of mass (10 g) along with a fixed point at the lower end.
2. Fix a scale vertically so that the pointer moves freely on the scale and note the reading on the scale.
3. Place a 10g slotted weight in the hanger and wait until the rubber band becomes stationary. Read the position of the pointer.
4. Repeat step 3 by increasing the load in increments of 10g until the total weight is 80-100g.
5. Begin removing the weight in increments of 10g, noting the corresponding pointer reading (allow time for the rubber to stablise before taking each reading).
6. Repeat steps 1 to 5 for different samples of rubber bands.

Observations

(i) Least count of the scale = ... cm

(ii) Original length of unstreched rubber band, L = ...cm

Extension of rubber band on loading

	S. N.	Load suspended = applied force = F (N)	Reading of pointer r (cm)		Extension (cm)	
			Loading	Unloading	Loading	Unloading
	1					
Specimen A	2					
	3					
	1					
Specimen B	2					
	3					

Calculations

1. Plot a graph between the load and extension by taking extension along X-axis and load along Y-axis for loading and unloading.
2. The area of hysteresis loop for specimen A = ...

   The area of hysteresis loop for specimen B = ...

   (This can be done by counting the squares enclosed in the hysteresis loop).

Result

Hysteresis of specimen A is.........(greater/less) than the hysteresis of specimen B.

PRECAUTIONS

1. The weights must be added or removed gently.

2. One should wait for some time after adding or removing the weights before reading is taken.

Viva-Voce

Q. 1 Why can't the Young's modulus of elasticity for rubber be defined uniquely?

Ans. Because the stress-strain curve for rubber is not a straight line, making the Young's modulus variable at different points on the curve.

Q. 2 What does the area enclosed by the hysteresis curve represent?

Ans. It represents the energy loss during the loading and unloading cycle of the material.

Q. 3 How do you ensure the accuracy of the pointer reading when adding weight?

Ans. Allow the rubber band to be stablize before taking the reading of ensure accuracy.

Q. 4 How do you increase the load is increments of 10g during the experiment?

Ans. Incremental loading helps to observe and measure the extension behaviour of the rubber band under controlled conditions.

Q. 5 What should be done after reaching the total weight of 80-100 g in the experiment?

Ans. Start removing the weight in increments of 10g and note the corresponding pointer readings.

Q. 6 What does the area of hysteresis curve depict?

Ans. The area of the hysteresis curve depicts the energy loss during the loading and unloading cycle of the material.

Q. 7 When do the curves obtained while loading and unloading coincide? [NCERT]

Ans. The curves obtained during loading and unloading coincides when there is no energy loss, indicating perfectly elasticity with no hysteresis.

Q. 8 When do the curves obtained while loading and unloading not coincide? [NCERT]

Ans. The curves obtained during loading and unloading do not coincide when there is energy loss in the material, indicating the presence of hysteresis.

Q. 9 For which purpose is the rubber with large hysteresis loop used? [NCERT]

Ans. Rubber with a large hysteresis loop is used in applications where energy absorption and damping are important, such as in vibration dampers, shock absorbers and automotive tyres. The large hysteresis loop indicates significant energy dissipation, which helps in reducing vibrations and absorbing shocks effectively.

Project 05

AIM

To study the effect and nature of surface on emission and absorption of radiation.

Apparatus and Materials Required

Two identical calorimeters with wooden lids having holes for thermometers, two thermometers, clamp stands for holding thermometer, arrangement to coat one calorimeter black and the other shining white, stop-clock, ice.

Theory/Principle

Black surfaces are efficient emitters and absorbers of heat radiation, whereas bright surfaces are inefficient emitters and absorbers of heat radiation.

Procedure

For Emission of Radiation

1. Determine the range and least count of both thermometers.
2. Measure and note the room temperature.
3. Point one calorimeter with black paint or lamp black. Coat the other calorimeter with white paint, aluminium paint or wrap it in shining silver foil.
4. Fill both calorimeters with hot water and place a thermometer in each. Position them 30 cm apart.
5. Start the stop-clock and place it centerally.
6. Record the temperature of both calorimeters every 30 s for the first 10 min, then every minute for the next 10 min.

For Absorption of Radiation

1. Take calorimeters.
2. Fill both with cold water from a refrigerator or by adding ice to tap water.
3. Place thermometers in the calorimeters and position them in front of an electric heater to ensure they receive the same amount of heat.
4. With the help of a stop-clock, take temperature *versus* time data.

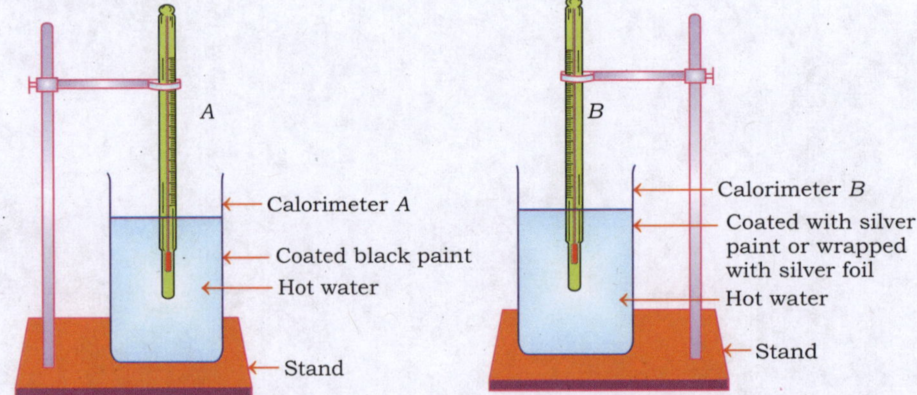

Fig. (a). Experimental setup for studying emission of heat radiation from black surface

Fig. (b). Experimental setup for studying emission of heat radiation from shining surface

Observations and Calculations

Range of thermometer $A = \ldots$ °C

Least count of thermometer $A = \ldots$ °C

Range of thermometer $B = \ldots$ °C

Least count of thermometer $B = \ldots$ °C

Table (a) : For Emission of Radiation

S.N.	Black coated calorimeter			
	Time (t) (min)	Temperature of water (°C)	Time (t) (min)	Temperature of water (°C)
1.				
2.				
3.				

Table (b) For Absorption of Radiation

S.N.	Black coated calorimeter		White painted calorimeter	
	Time (t) (min)	Temperature of water (°C)	Time (t) (min)	Temperature of water (°C)
1.				
2.				
3.				

Graph and Interpretation

Plot a graph between time (on X-axis) and temperature (on Y-axis) for both the calorimeters and for both : emission and absorption, as shown in Fig. (a) and (b).

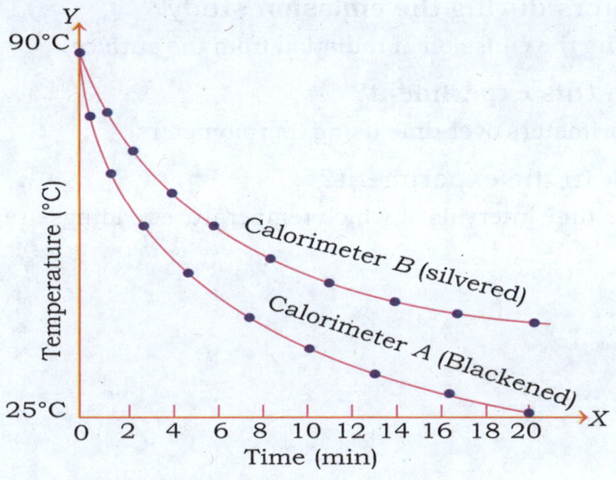

Fig. (a) Temperature *versus* time graph emission of heat radiation

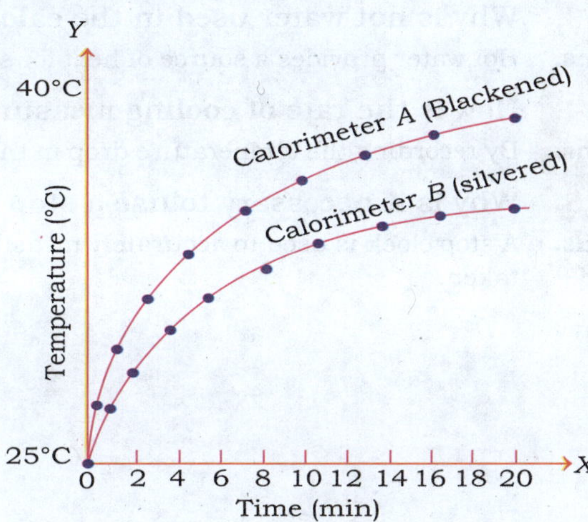

Fig. (b) Temperature *versus* time graph for Time graph for absorption of heat radiation.

Result

1. Compare the rates of cooling in Section (A) in both cases for the same temperature range. It is found that the ....(blackened/silvered) calorimeter is a better emitter of heat.
2. Compare the rise in temperatures of the two calorimeters in Section (B). It is found that the ... calorimeter is a better absorber of radiation.

PRECAUTIONS

1. *Ensure thermometers are properly calibrated before the experiment.*
2. *Avoid touching the surfaces of the calorimeters to prevent heat transfer from your hands.*

Sources of Error

1. Perfectly black and perfectly shining surfaces may not be available.
2. Variations in surrounding temperature during the period of activity may take place.

Viva-Voce

Q 1. Why are two identical calorimeters used in the experiment?

Ans. To ensure that any differences observed in temperature changes are due to the colour of the surfaces and not the properties of the calorimeters themselves.

Q 2. What is the purpose of coating one calorimeter black and the other with a shiny surface?

Ans. The black coating stimulates a surface that efficiently absorbs and emits heats, while the shiny surface stimulates a surface that reflects radiation, thus not absorbing or emitting much heat.

Q 3. Why is hot water used in the calorimeters during the emission study?

Ans. Hot water provides a source of heat for studying the emission of radiation from the surface.

Q 4. How is the rate of cooling measured in this experiment?

Ans. By recording the temperature drop in the calorimeters over time using thermometers.

Q 5. Why is it necessary to use a stop clock in the experiment?

Ans. A stop clock is used to accurately measure the time intervals at which temperature readings are taken.

Project 06

AIM

To study conservation of energy with a simple pendulum.

Apparatus and Materials Required

A heavy spherical bob with a hook, thread, meter scale, a peg (a pencil) or a 15 cm scale), a rigid support and a stand with a clamp.

Theory/Principle

A simple pendulum of length l and mass m oscillates due to the restoring force expressed as $F = -mg \sin\theta$ for small displacements (less than 15°)

Given, $$\sin\theta \approx \theta = \frac{x}{l}$$

The force constant k can be written as $$k = \frac{mg}{l}$$

And the maximum kinetic energy is $$\text{KE} = \frac{1}{2}kx^2$$

Description

When the oscillation of a simple pendulum is restricted into two parts using a peg P at any point on its string, it becomes a two-length pendulum. During one half of the journey, the bob of mass m, has length l_1 and displacement x_1 at position A and for other half it has a length l_2 and displacement x_2. At position B, the bob of mass m has the same kinetic energy. Therefore, energy conservation demands that

$$\frac{1}{2}k_1x_1^2 = \frac{1}{2}k_2x_2^2 \quad \text{or} \quad \frac{l_1}{l_2} = \frac{x_1^2}{x_2^2}$$

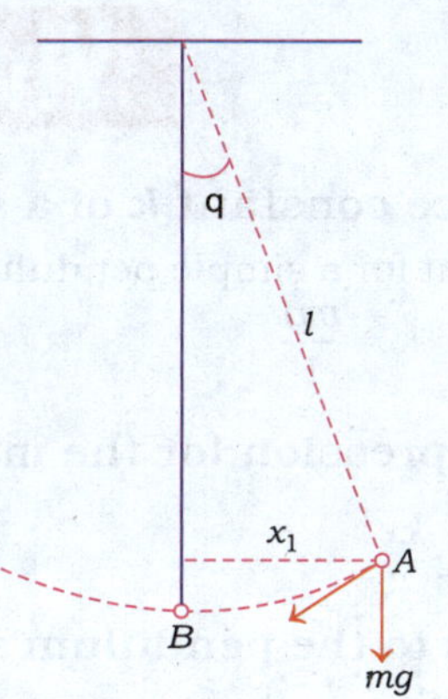

Fig. (a) A simple pendulum

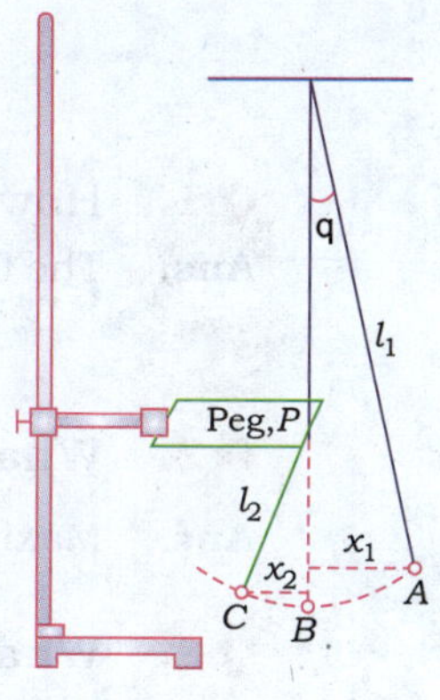

Fig. (b) A two-length pendulum

Procedure

1. Set up a simple pendulum with a heavy bob. Release the bob gently from position A and measure the maximum displacement x_1 using a meter scale.
2. Fix a peg (a pencil or a scale) horizontally to a clamp stand and place it in contact with string of oscillating pendulum.
   Ensure that the peg obstructs the motion of the pendulum when its string is vertical, aligning with its mean position.
3. The effective length of the pendulum is reduced for a portion of its oscillation after being held by the peg.
4. Measure the maximum displacement x_2 using a meter scale when the bob reaches position C.

5. Repeat steps 2 to 4 for different positions of peg P.

6. Record these observations in a table and calculate $\frac{l_1}{l_2}$ and $\frac{x_1^2}{x_2^2}$ for each scenario.

7. Verify the equality, $\frac{l_1}{l_2} = \frac{x_1^2}{x_2^2}$

Observations and Calculations

Length of a simple pendulum $l = \ldots$cm .

S. N.	Displacement of bob		Length of the pendulum		$\frac{l_1}{l_2}$	$\frac{x_1^2}{x_2^2}$
	In position *A* x_1 (cm)	In position *B* x_2 (cm)	In position *A* l_1 (cm)	In position *B* l_2 (cm)		
1.						
2.						
3.						
4.						

Result

Relationship $\frac{l_1}{l_2} = \frac{x_1^2}{x_2^2}$, based on the conservation of energy is verified.

Viva-Voce

Q 1. How is the force constant *k* of a simple pendulum defined?

Ans. The force constant for a simple pendulum is defined as

$$k = \frac{mg}{l}$$

Q 2. What is the expression for the maximum kinetic energy of a pendulum?

Ans. Maximum, KE $= \frac{1}{2}kx^2$

Q 3. What happens to the pendulum's motion when a peg is introduced at some point along its string?

Ans. The pendulum's motion is divided into two parts, making it a two-length pendulum.

Q 4. How do you determine the relationship between the length and displacements in a two-length pendulum?

Ans. The relationship is determined by the equation, $\frac{l_1}{l_2} = \frac{x_1^2}{x_2^2}$

Q 5. What should be observed to verify the energy conservation relationship?

Ans. We should observe the maximum displacement x_1 and x_2 and their respective pendulum length l_1 and l_2.

Appendices

APPENDIX 1

LOGARITHMS

	0′	6′	12′	18′	14′	30′	36′	42′	48′	54′	Mean Differences				
	0°.0	0°.1	0°.2	0°.3	0°.4	0°.5	0°.6	0°.7	0°.8	0°.9	1′	2′	3′	4′	5′
0	.0000	0017	0035	0052	0070	0087	0105	0122	0140	0157	3	6	9	12	15
1	.0175	0192	0209	0227	0244	0262	0279	0297	0314	0332	3	6	9	12	15
2	.0349	0366	0384	0401	0419	0436	0454	0471	0488	0506	3	6	9	12	15
3	.0523	0541	0558	0576	0593	0610	0628	0645	0663	0680	3	6	9	12	15
4	.0698	0715	0732	0750	0767	0785	0802	0819	0837	0854	3	6	9	12	15
5	.0872	0889	0906	0924	0941	0958	0976	0993	1011	1028	3	6	9	12	14
6	.1045	1063	1080	1097	1115	1132	1149	1167	1184	1201	3	6	9	12	14
7	.1219	1236	1253	1271	1288	1305	1323	1340	1357	1374	3	6	9	12	14
8	.1392	1409	1426	1444	1461	1478	1495	1513	1530	1547	3	6	9	12	14
9	.1564	1582	1599	1616	1633	1650	1668	1685	1702	1719	3	6	9	12	14
10	.1736	1654	1771	1788	1805	1822	1840	1857	1874	1891	3	6	9	12	14
11	.1908	1925	1942	1959	1977	1994	2011	2028	2045	2062	3	6	9	11	14
12	.2079	2096	2113	2130	2147	2164	2181	2198	2215	2232	3	6	9	11	14
13	.2250	2267	2284	2300	2317	2334	2351	2368	2385	2402	3	6	8	11	14
14	.2419	2436	2453	2470	2487	2504	2521	2538	2554	2571	3	6	8	11	14
15	.2588	2605	2622	2639	2656	2672	2689	2706	2723	2749	3	6	8	11	14
16	.2756	2773	2790	2807	2823	2840	2857	2874	2890	2907	3	6	8	11	14
17	.2924	2940	2957	2974	2990	3007	3024	3040	3057	3074	3	6	8	11	14
18	.3090	3107	3123	3140	3156	3173	3190	3206	3223	3239	3	6	8	11	14
19	.3256	3272	3289	3305	3322	3338	3355	3371	3387	3404	3	5	8	11	14
20	.3420	3437	3453	3469	3486	3502	3518	3535	3551	4567	3	5	8	11	14
21	.3584	3600	3616	3633	3649	3665	3681	3697	3714	3730	3	5	8	11	14
22	.3746	3762	3778	3795	3811	3827	3843	3859	3875	3891	3	5	8	11	14
23	.3907	3923	3939	3955	3971	3987	4003	4019	4035	4051	3	5	8	11	14
24	.4067	4083	4099	4115	4131	4147	4163	4179	4195	4210	3	5	8	11	13
25	.4226	4242	4258	4274	4289	4305	4321	4337	4352	4368	3	5	8	11	13
26	.4384	4399	4415	4431	4446	4462	4478	4493	4509	4524	3	5	8	10	13
27	.4540	4555	4571	4586	4602	4617	4633	4648	4664	4679	3	5	8	10	13
28	.4695	4710	4726	4741	4756	4772	4787	4802	4818	4833	3	5	8	10	13
29	.4848	4863	4879	4894	4909	4924	4939	4955	4970	4985	3	5	8	10	13
30	.5000	5015	5030	5045	5060	5075	5090	5105	5120	5135	3	5	8	10	13
31	.5150	5165	5180	5195	5210	5225	5240	5255	5270	5284	2	5	7	10	12
32	.5299	5314	5329	5344	5358	5373	5388	5402	5417	5432	2	5	7	10	12
33	.5446	5461	5476	5490	5505	5519	5534	5548	5563	5577	2	5	7	10	12
34	.5592	5606	5621	5635	5650	5664	5678	5693	5707	5721	2	5	7	10	12
35	.5736	5750	5764	5779	5793	5807	5821	5835	5850	5864	2	5	7	10	12
36	.5878	5892	5906	5920	5934	5948	5962	5976	5990	6004	2	5	7	9	12
37	.6018	6032	6046	6060	6074	6088	6101	6115	6129	6143	2	5	7	9	11
38	.6157	6170	6184	6198	6211	6225	6239	6252	6266	6280	2	5	7	9	11
39	.6293	6307	6320	6334	6347	6361	6374	6388	6401	6414	2	4	7	9	11
40	.6428	6441	6455	6468	6481	6494	6508	6521	6534	6547	2	4	7	9	11
41	.6561	6574	6587	6600	6613	6626	6639	6652	6665	6678	2	4	7	9	11
42	.6691	6704	6717	6730	6743	6756	6769	6782	6794	6807	2	4	6	9	11

	0′	6′	12′	18′	14′	30′	36′	42′	48′	54′	Mean Differences				
	0°.0	0°.1	0°.2	0°.3	0°.4	0°.5	0°.6	0°.7	0°.8	0°.9	1′	2′	3′	4′	5′
43	.6820	6833	6845	6858	6871	6884	6896	6909	6921	6934	2	4	6	8	11
44	.6947	6959	6972	6984	6997	7009	7022	7034	7046	7059	2	4	6	8	10
45	.7071	7083	7096	7108	7120	7133	7145	7157	7169	7181	2	4	6	8	10
46	.7193	7206	7218	7230	7242	7254	7266	7278	7290	7302	2	4	6	8	10
47	.7314	7325	7337	7349	7361	7373	7385	7396	7408	7420	2	4	6	8	10
48	.7431	7443	7455	7466	7478	7490	7501	7513	7524	7536	2	4	6	8	10
49	.7547	7558	7570	7581	7593	7694	7615	6727	7638	7649	2	4	6	8	9
50	.7660	7672	7683	7694	7705	7716	7727	7738	7749	7760	2	4	6	7	9
51	.7771	7782	7793	7804	7815	7826	7837	7848	7859	7869	2	4	5	7	9
52	.7880	7891	7902	7912	7923	7934	7944	7955	7965	7976	2	4	5	7	9
53	.7986	7997	8007	8018	8028	8039	8049	8059	8070	8080	2	3	5	7	9
54	.8090	8100	8111	8121	8131	8141	8151	8161	8171	8181	2	3	5	7	8
55	.8192	8202	8211	8221	8231	8241	8251	8261	8271	8281	2	3	5	7	8
56	.8290	8300	8310	8320	8329	8339	8348	8358	8368	8377	2	3	5	6	8
57	.8387	8396	8406	8415	8425	8434	8443	8453	8462	8471	2	3	5	6	8
58	.8480	8490	8499	8508	8517	8526	8536	8545	8554	8563	2	3	5	6	8
59	.8572	8581	8590	8599	8607	8616	8625	8634	8643	8652	1	3	4	6	7
60	.8660	8669	8678	8686	8695	8704	8712	8721	8729	8738	1	3	4	6	7
61	.8746	8755	8763	8771	8780	8788	8796	8805	8813	8821	1	3	4	6	7
62	.8829	8838	8846	8854	8862	8870	8878	8886	8894	8902	1	3	4	5	7
63	.8910	8918	8926	8934	8942	8949	8957	8965	8973	8980	1	3	4	5	6
64	.8988	8996	9003	9011	9018	9026	9033	9041	9048	9056	1	3	4	5	6
65	.9063	9070	9078	9085	9092	9100	9107	9114	9121	9128	1	2	4	5	6
66	.9135	9143	9150	9157	9164	9171	9178	9184	9191	9198	1	2	3	5	6
67	.9205	9212	9219	9225	9232	9239	9245	9252	9259	9265	1	2	3	4	6
68	.9272	9278	9285	9291	9298	9304	9311	9317	9323	9330	1	2	3	4	5
69	.9336	9342	9348	9354	9361	9367	9373	9379	9385	9391	1	2	3	4	5
70	.9397	9403	9409	9415	9421	9426	9432	9438	9444	9449	1	2	3	4	5
71	.9455	9461	9466	9472	9478	9483	9489	9494	9500	9505	1	2	3	4	5
72	.9511	9516	9521	9527	9532	9537	9542	9548	9553	9558	1	2	3	4	5
73	.9563	9568	9573	9578	9583	9588	9593	9558	9603	9608	1	2	3	3	4
74	.9613	9617	9622	9627	9632	9636	9641	9646	9650	9655	1	2	2	3	4
75	.9659	9664	9668	9673	9677	9681	9686	9690	9694	9699	1	1	2	3	4
76	.9703	9707	9711	9715	9720	9724	9728	9732	9736	9740	1	1	2	3	3
77	.9744	9748	9751	9755	9759	9763	9768	9770	9774	9778	1	1	2	2	3
78	.9781	9785	9789	9792	9696	9799	9803	9806	9810	9813	1	1	2	2	3
79	.9816	9820	9823	9826	9829	9833	9836	9839	9842	9845	1	1	2	2	3
80	.9848	9851	9854	9857	9860	9863	9866	9869	9871	9874	0	1	1	2	2
81	.9877	9880	9882	9885	9888	9890	9893	9895	9898	9900	0	1	1	2	2
82	.9903	9905	9907	9910	9912	9914	9917	9919	9921	9923	0	1	1	2	2
83	.9925	9928	9930	9932	9934	9936	9938	9940	9942	9943	0	1	1	1	2
84	.9945	9947	9949	9951	9952	9954	9956	9957	9959	9960	0	1	1	1	2
85	.9962	9963	9965	9966	9968	9969	9971	9972	9973	9974	0	0	1	1	1
86	.9976	9977	9978	9979	9980	9981	9982	9983	9984	9985	0	0	1	1	1
87	.9986	9987	9988	9989	9990	9990	9991	9992	9993	9993	0	0	0	1	1
88	.9994	9995	9995	9996	9996	9997	9997	9997	9998	9998	0	0	0	0	0
89	.9998	9999	9999	9999	9999	1.000	1.000	1.000	1.000	1.000	0	0	0	0	0
90	1.000														

APPENDIX 2

ANTILOGARITHMS

	0	1	2	3	4	5	6	7	8	9	Mean Differences								
											1	2	3	4	5	6	7	8	9
.00	1000	1002	1005	1007	1009	1012	1014	1016	1019	1021	0	0	1	1	1	1	2	2	2
.01	1023	1026	1028	1030	1033	1035	1038	1040	1042	1045	0	0	1	1	1	1	2	2	2
.02	1047	1050	1052	1054	1057	1059	1062	1064	1067	1069	0	0	1	1	1	1	2	2	2
.03	1072	1074	1076	1079	1081	1084	1086	1089	1091	1094	0	0	1	1	1	1	2	2	2
.04	1096	1099	1102	1104	1107	1109	1112	1114	1117	1119	0	1	1	1	1	2	2	2	2
.05	1122	1125	1127	1130	1132	1135	1138	1140	1143	1146	0	1	1	1	1	2	2	2	2
.06	1148	1151	1153	1156	1159	1161	1164	1167	1169	1172	0	1	1	1	1	2	2	2	2
.07	1175	1178	1180	1183	1186	1189	1191	1194	1197	1199	0	1	1	1	1	2	2	2	2
.08	1202	1205	1208	1211	1213	1216	1219	1222	1225	1227	0	1	1	1	1	2	2	2	2
.09	1230	1233	1236	1239	1242	1245	1247	1250	1253	1256	0	1	1	1	1	2	2	2	3
.10	1259	1262	1265	1268	1271	1274	1276	1279	1282	1285	0	1	1	1	1	2	2	2	3
.11	1288	1291	1294	1297	1300	1303	1306	1309	1312	1315	0	1	1	1	2	2	2	2	3
.12	1318	1321	1324	1327	1330	1334	1337	1340	1343	1346	0	1	1	1	2	2	2	2	3
.13	1349	1352	1355	1358	1361	1365	1368	1371	1374	1377	0	1	1	1	2	2	2	3	3
.14	1380	1384	1387	1390	1393	1396	1400	1403	1406	1409	0	1	1	1	2	2	2	3	3
.15	1413	1416	1419	1422	1426	1429	1432	1435	1439	1442	0	1	1	1	2	2	2	3	3
.16	1445	1449	1452	1455	1459	1462	1466	1469	1472	1476	0	1	1	1	2	2	2	3	3
.17	1479	1483	1486	1489	1493	1496	1500	1503	1507	1510	0	1	1	1	2	2	2	3	3
.18	1514	1517	1521	1524	1528	1531	1535	1538	1542	1545	0	1	1	1	2	2	2	3	3
.19	1549	1552	1556	1560	1563	1567	1570	1574	1578	1581	0	1	1	1	2	2	3	3	3
.20	1585	1589	1592	1596	1600	1603	1607	1611	1614	1618	0	1	1	1	2	2	3	3	3
.21	1622	1626	1629	1633	1637	1641	1644	1648	1652	1656	0	1	1	2	2	2	3	3	3
.22	1660	1663	1667	1671	1675	1679	1683	1687	1690	1694	0	1	1	2	2	2	3	3	3
.23	1698	1702	1706	1710	1714	1718	1722	1726	1730	1734	0	1	1	2	2	2	3	3	4
.24	1738	1742	1746	1750	1754	1758	1762	1766	1770	1774	0	1	1	2	2	2	3	3	4
.25	1778	1782	1786	1791	1795	1799	1803	1807	1811	1816	0	1	1	2	2	2	3	3	4
.26	1820	1824	1828	1832	1837	1841	1845	1849	1854	1858	0	1	1	2	2	3	3	3	4
.27	1862	1866	1871	1875	1879	1884	1888	1892	1897	1901	0	1	1	2	2	3	3	3	4
.28	1905	1910	1914	1919	1923	1928	1932	1936	1941	1945	0	1	1	2	2	3	3	4	4
.29	1950	1954	1959	1963	1968	1972	1977	1982	1986	1991	0	1	1	2	2	3	3	4	4
.30	1995	2000	2004	2009	2014	2018	2023	2028	2032	2037	0	1	1	2	2	3	3	4	4
.31	2042	2046	2051	2056	2061	2065	2070	2075	2080	2084	0	1	1	2	2	3	3	4	4
.32	2089	2094	2099	2104	2109	2113	2118	2123	2128	2133	0	1	1	2	2	3	3	4	4
.33	2138	2143	2148	2153	2158	2163	2168	2173	2178	2183	0	1	1	2	2	3	3	4	4
.34	2188	2193	2198	2203	2208	2213	2218	2223	2228	2234	1	1	2	2	3	3	4	4	5
.35	2239	2244	2249	2254	2259	2265	2270	2275	2280	2286	1	1	2	2	3	3	4	4	5
.36	2291	2296	2301	2307	2312	2317	2323	2328	2333	2339	1	1	2	2	3	3	4	4	5
.37	2344	2350	2355	2360	2366	2371	2377	2382	2388	2393	1	1	2	2	3	3	4	4	5
.38	2399	2404	2410	2415	2421	2427	2432	2438	2443	2449	1	1	2	2	3	3	4	4	5
.39	2455	2460	2466	2472	2477	2483	2489	2495	2500	2506	1	1	2	2	3	3	4	5	5
.40	2512	2518	2523	2529	2535	2541	2547	2553	2559	2564	1	1	2	2	3	4	4	5	5
.41	2570	2576	2582	2588	2594	2600	2696	2612	2618	2624	1	1	2	2	3	4	4	5	5
.42	2630	2636	2642	2649	2655	2661	2667	2673	2679	2685	1	1	2	2	3	4	4	5	6
.43	2692	2698	2704	2710	2716	2723	2729	2735	2742	2748	1	1	2	3	3	4	4	5	6
.44	2754	2761	2767	2773	2780	2786	2793	2799	2805	2812	1	1	2	3	3	4	4	5	6
.45	2818	2825	2831	2838	2844	2851	2858	2864	2871	2877	1	1	2	3	3	4	5	5	6
.46	2884	2891	2897	2904	2911	2917	2924	2931	2938	2944	1	1	2	3	3	4	5	5	6
.47	2951	2958	2965	2972	2979	2985	2992	2999	3006	3013	1	1	2	3	3	4	5	5	6
.48	3020	3027	3034	3041	3048	3055	3062	3069	3076	3083	1	1	2	3	4	4	5	6	6
.49	3090	3097	3105	3112	3119	3126	3133	3141	3148	3155	1	1	2	3	4	4	5	6	6

ANTILOGARITHMS (Contd.)

	0	1	2	3	4	5	6	7	8	9	Mean Differences								
											1	2	3	4	5	6	7	8	9
.50	3162	3170	3177	3184	3192	3199	3206	3214	3221	3228	1	1	2	3	4	4	5	6	7
.51	3236	3243	3251	3258	3266	3273	3281	3289	3296	3304	1	2	2	3	4	5	5	6	7
.52	3311	3319	3327	3334	3342	3350	3357	3365	3373	3381	1	2	2	3	4	5	5	6	7
.53	3388	3396	3404	3412	3420	3428	3436	3443	3451	3459	1	2	2	3	4	5	6	6	7
.54	3467	3475	3483	3491	3499	3508	3516	3524	3532	3540	1	2	2	3	4	5	6	6	7
.55	3548	3556	3565	3573	3581	3589	3597	3606	3614	3622	1	2	2	3	4	5	6	7	7
.56	3631	3639	3648	3656	3664	3673	3681	3690	3698	3707	1	2	3	3	4	5	6	7	8
.57	3715	3724	3733	3741	3750	3758	3767	3776	3784	3793	1	2	3	3	4	5	6	7	8
.58	3802	3811	3819	3828	3837	3846	3855	3864	3873	3882	1	2	3	4	4	5	6	7	8
.59	3890	3899	3908	3917	3926	3936	3945	3954	3963	3972	1	2	3	4	5	5	6	7	8
.60	3981	3990	3999	4009	4018	4027	4036	4046	4055	4064	1	2	3	4	5	6	6	7	8
.61	4074	4083	4093	4102	4111	4121	4130	4140	4150	4159	1	2	3	4	5	6	7	8	9
.62	4169	4178	4188	4198	4207	4217	4227	4236	4256	4256	1	2	3	4	5	6	7	8	9
.63	4266	4276	4285	4295	4305	4315	4325	4335	4345	4355	1	2	3	4	5	6	7	8	9
.64	4365	4375	4385	4395	4406	4416	4426	4436	4446	4457	1	2	3	4	5	6	7	8	9
.65	4467	4477	4487	4498	4508	4519	4529	4539	4550	4560	1	2	3	4	5	6	7	8	9
.66	4571	4581	4592	4603	4613	4624	4634	4645	4656	4667	1	2	3	4	5	6	7	9	10
.67	4677	4688	4699	4710	4721	4732	4742	4753	4764	4775	1	2	3	4	5	7	8	9	10
.68	4786	4797	4808	4819	4831	4842	4853	4864	4875	4887	1	2	3	4	6	7	8	9	10
.69	4898	4909	4920	4932	4943	4955	4966	4977	4989	5000	1	2	3	5	6	7	8	9	10
.70	5012	5023	5035	5047	5058	5070	5082	5093	5105	5117	1	2	4	5	6	7	8	9	11
.71	5129	5140	5152	5164	5176	5188	5200	5212	5224	5236	1	2	4	5	6	7	8	10	11
.72	5248	5260	5272	5284	5297	5309	5321	5333	5346	5358	1	2	4	5	6	7	9	10	11
.73	5370	5383	5395	5408	5420	5433	5445	5458	5470	5483	1	3	4	5	6	8	9	10	11
.74	5495	5508	5521	5534	5546	5559	5572	5585	5598	5610	1	3	4	5	6	8	9	10	12
.75	5623	5636	5649	5662	5675	5689	5702	5715	5728	5741	1	3	4	5	7	8	9	10	12
.76	5754	5768	5781	5794	5808	5821	5834	5848	5861	5875	1	3	4	5	7	8	9	11	12
.77	5888	5902	5916	5929	5943	5957	5970	5984	5998	6012	1	3	4	5	7	8	10	11	12
.78	6026	6039	6053	6067	6081	6095	6109	6124	6138	6152	1	3	4	6	7	8	10	11	13
.79	6166	6180	6194	6209	6223	7237	6252	6266	6281	6295	1	3	4	6	7	9	10	11	13
.80	6310	6324	6339	6353	6368	6383	6497	6412	6427	6442	1	3	4	6	7	9	10	12	13
.81	6457	6471	6486	6501	6516	6531	6546	6561	6577	6592	2	3	5	6	8	9	11	12	14
.82	6607	6622	6637	6653	6668	6683	6699	6714	6730	6745	2	3	5	6	8	9	11	12	14
.83	6761	6776	6792	6808	6823	6839	6855	6871	6887	6902	2	3	5	6	8	9	11	13	14
.84	6918	6934	6950	6966	6982	6998	7015	7031	7047	7063	2	3	5	6	8	10	11	13	15
.85	7079	7096	7112	7129	7145	7161	7178	7194	7211	7228	2	3	5	7	8	10	12	13	15
.86	7244	7261	7278	7295	7311	7328	7345	7362	7379	7396	2	3	5	7	8	10	12	13	15
.87	7413	7430	7447	7464	7482	7499	7516	7534	7551	7568	2	3	5	7	9	10	12	14	16
.88	7586	7603	7621	7638	7656	7674	7691	7709	7727	7745	2	4	5	7	9	11	12	14	16
.89	7762	7780	7798	7816	7834	7852	7870	7889	7907	7925	2	4	5	7	9	11	13	14	16
.90	7943	7962	7980	7998	8017	8035	8054	8072	8091	8110	2	4	6	7	9	11	13	15	17
.91	8128	8147	8166	8185	8204	8222	8241	8260	8279	8299	2	4	6	8	9	11	13	15	17
.92	8318	8337	8356	8375	8395	8414	8433	8453	8472	8492	2	4	6	8	10	12	14	15	17
.93	8511	8531	8551	8570	8590	8610	8630	8650	8670	8690	2	4	6	8	10	12	14	16	18
.94	8710	8730	8750	8770	8790	8810	8831	8851	8872	8892	2	4	6	8	10	12	14	16	18
.95	8913	8933	8954	8974	8995	9016	9036	9057	9078	9099	2	4	6	8	10	12	15	17	19
.96	9120	9141	9162	9183	9204	9226	9247	9268	9290	9311	2	4	6	8	11	13	15	17	19
.97	9333	9354	9376	9397	9419	9441	9462	9484	9506	9528	2	4	7	9	11	13	15	17	20
.98	9550	9572	9594	9616	9638	9661	9683	9705	9727	9750	2	4	7	9	11	13	16	18	20
.99	9772	9795	9817	9840	9863	9886	9908	9931	9954	9977	2	5	7	9	11	14	16	18	20

Experiment/Activity No.________ Date ________ Page No. ________

Teacher Signature ________________

Experiment/Activity No.________ Date ________ Page No. ________

Teacher Signature ________

Experiment/Activity No.________ Date ________ Page No. ________

Teacher Signature ________________

Experiment/Activity No.________ Date ________ Page No. ________

Teacher Signature ________________

Experiment/Activity No.________ Date ________ Page No. ________

Teacher Signature ________

Experiment/Activity No.________ Date ________ Page No. ________

Teacher Signature________

Experiment/Activity No.________ Date ________ Page No. ________

Teacher Signature ________

Experiment/Activity No.________ Date ________ Page No. ________

Teacher Signature ________

Experiment/Activity No.________ Date ________ Page No. ________

Teacher Signature ________

Experiment/Activity No.________ Date ________ Page No. ________

Teacher Signature ________

Experiment/Activity No.________ Date ________ Page No. ________

Teacher Signature ________

Experiment/Activity No.________ Date ________ Page No. ________

Teacher Signature ________

Experiment/Activity No.________ Date ________ Page No. ________

Teacher Signature ________________

Experiment/Activity No.________ Date ________ Page No. ________

Teacher Signature ________________

Experiment/Activity No.________ Date ________ Page No. ________

Teacher Signature________________

Experiment/Activity No.________ Date ________ Page No. ________

Teacher Signature ________________

Experiment/Activity No.________ Date ________ Page No. ________

Teacher Signature ________________

Experiment/Activity No.________ Date ________ Page No. ________

Teacher Signature ________________

Experiment/Activity No.________ Date ________ Page No. ________

Teacher Signature ________________

Experiment/Activity No.________ Date ________ Page No. ________

Teacher Signature ________

Experiment/Activity No.________ Date ________ Page No. ________

Teacher Signature ____________

Experiment/Activity No.________ Date ________ Page No. ________

Teacher Signature ________

Experiment/Activity No.________ Date ________ Page No. ________

Teacher Signature ________

Experiment/Activity No.________ Date ________ Page No. ________

Teacher Signature ________

Experiment/Activity No.________ Date ________ Page No. ________

Teacher Signature ________________

Experiment/Activity No.________ Date ________ Page No. ________

Teacher Signature ________________

Experiment/Activity No.________ Date ________ Page No. ________

Teacher Signature ________

Experiment/Activity No.________ Date ________ Page No. ________

Teacher Signature ________

Experiment/Activity No.________ Date ________ Page No. ________

Teacher Signature ________________

Experiment/Activity No.________ Date ________ Page No. ________

Teacher Signature ________________

Experiment/Activity No.________ Date ________ Page No. ________

Teacher Signature ________

Experiment/Activity No.________ Date ________ Page No. ________

Teacher Signature ____________

Experiment/Activity No.________ Date ________ Page No. ________

Teacher Signature ________________

Experiment/Activity No.________ Date ________ Page No. ________

Teacher Signature ________________

Experiment/Activity No.________ Date ________ Page No. ________

Teacher Signature________________

Experiment/Activity No.________ Date ________ Page No. ________

Teacher Signature ____________

Experiment/Activity No.________ Date ________ Page No. ________

Teacher Signature ____________

Experiment/Activity No.________ Date ________ Page No. ________

Teacher Signature________________

Experiment/Activity No.________ Date ________ Page No. ________

Teacher Signature ________

Experiment/Activity No.________ Date ________ Page No. ________

Teacher Signature ________

Experiment/Activity No.________ Date ________ Page No. ________

Teacher Signature ________

Experiment/Activity No.________ Date ________ Page No. ________

Teacher Signature ________

Experiment/Activity No.________ Date ________ Page No. ________

Teacher Signature ________

Experiment/Activity No.________ Date ________ Page No. ________

Teacher Signature ________

Experiment/Activity No.________ Date ________ Page No. ________

Teacher Signature ________________

Experiment/Activity No.________ Date ________ Page No. ________

Teacher Signature ________________

Experiment/Activity No.________ Date ________ Page No. ________

Teacher Signature ________

Experiment/Activity No.________ Date ________ Page No. ________

Teacher Signature ________

Experiment/Activity No.________ Date ________ Page No. ________

Teacher Signature ________________

Experiment/Activity No.________ Date ________ Page No. ________

Teacher Signature ____________________

Experiment/Activity No.________ Date ________ Page No. ________

Teacher Signature ________

Experiment/Activity No.________ Date ________ Page No. ________

Teacher Signature ________

Experiment/Activity No.________ Date ________ Page No. ________

Teacher Signature ________

Experiment/Activity No. ________ Date ________ Page No. ________

Teacher Signature ________

Experiment/Activity No.________ Date ________ Page No. ________

Teacher Signature ________________

Experiment/Activity No.________ Date ________ Page No. ________

Teacher Signature ________

Experiment/Activity No.________ Date ________ Page No. ________

Teacher Signature ________

Experiment/Activity No.________ Date ________ Page No. ________

Teacher Signature ________

Experiment/Activity No.________ Date ________ Page No. ________

Teacher Signature ________

Experiment/Activity No.________ Date ________ Page No. ________

Teacher Signature

Experiment/Activity No.________ Date ________ Page No. ________

Teacher Signature ________________

Experiment/Activity No.________ Date ________ Page No. ________

Teacher Signature ________

Experiment/Activity No.________ Date ________ Page No. ________

Teacher Signature ________

Experiment/Activity No.________ Date ________ Page No. ________

Teacher Signature ________

Experiment/Activity No.________ Date ________ Page No. ________

Teacher Signature ________

Experiment/Activity No.________ Date ________ Page No. ________

Teacher Signature________________

Experiment/Activity No.________ Date ________ Page No. ________

Teacher Signature ________________

Experiment/Activity No.________ Date ________ Page No. ________

Teacher Signature ________________

Experiment/Activity No.________ Date ________ Page No. ________

Teacher Signature ________

Experiment/Activity No.________ Date ________ Page No. ________

Teacher Signature ________________

Experiment/Activity No.________ Date ________ Page No. ________

Teacher Signature ____________

Experiment/Activity No.________ Date ________ Page No. ________

Teacher Signature ________________

Experiment/Activity No.________ Date ________ Page No. ________

Teacher Signature ________________

Experiment/Activity No.________ Date ________ Page No. ________

Teacher Signature ________

Experiment/Activity No.________ Date ________ Page No. ________

Teacher Signature ________

Experiment/Activity No.________ Date ________ Page No. ________

Teacher Signature ________

Experiment/Activity No.________ Date ________ Page No. ________

Teacher Signature ________

Experiment/Activity No.________ Date ________ Page No. ________

Teacher Signature ________

Experiment/Activity No.________ Date ________ Page No. ________

Teacher Signature ________________

Experiment/Activity No.________ Date ________ Page No. ________

Teacher Signature ________